Types of Pentecostal Theology

AAR
AMERICAN ACADEMY OF RELIGION

ACADEMY SERIES

SERIES EDITOR
Aaron W. Hughes, University at Buffalo

A Publication Series of
The American Academy of Religion
and
Oxford University Press

AMERICAN ACADEMY OF RELIGION

Types of Pentecostal Theology

Method, System, Spirit

Christopher A. Stephenson

OXFORD
UNIVERSITY PRESS

OXFORD
UNIVERSITY PRESS

Oxford University Press is a department of the University of Oxford.
It furthers the University's objective of excellence in research,
scholarship, and education by publishing worldwide.

Oxford   New York

Auckland   Cape Town   Dar es Salaam   Hong Kong   Karachi
Kuala Lumpur   Madrid   Melbourne   Mexico City   Nairobi
New Delhi   Shanghai   Taipei   Toronto

With offices in

Argentina   Austria   Brazil   Chile   Czech Republic   France   Greece
Guatemala   Hungary   Italy   Japan   Poland   Portugal   Singapore
South Korea   Switzerland   Thailand   Turkey   Ukraine   Vietnam

Oxford is a registered trade mark of Oxford University Press in
the UK and certain other countries.

Published in the United States of America by
Oxford University Press
198 Madison Avenue, New York, NY 10016

Library of Congress Cataloging-in-Publication Data
Stephenson, Christopher A.
Types of Pentecostal theology : method, system, spirit / Christopher A. Stephenson.
p.   cm.—(Academy series)
Includes bibliographical references (p.) and index.
ISBN 978-0-19-991679-5 (hardcover : alk. paper)—ISBN 978-0-19-991680-1 (ebook)
1. Pentecostal churches—Doctrines. 2. Pentecostalism. 3. Theology, Doctrinal. I. Title.
BX8762.Z5S735   2013
230'.994—dc23   2012003131

The battle's not mine, said little David.

χαρά

CONTENTS

PREFACE

I have often heard and now understand that one never completes a book, but rather gives up on it. During this "giving up" process, I have incurred several debts. Lyle Dabney directed my PhD studies and first encouraged me to expand some of my previous work into a dissertation on pentecostal theology. Ralph Del Colle, Michel Barnes, and Philip J. Rossi, SJ, also gave insightful responses as members of my committee. Amos Yong served as the external reader and commuted to the defense. French Arrington, Simon Chan, Frank Macchia, and Amos Yong supplied detailed responses to my assessments of their theologies, all of which made this a better book. Simon Chan, Frank Macchia, and Amos Yong also graciously provided me with prepublication proofs of their monographs. (Writing about theologians who are still alive and well can be a risky affair!) E-mail exchanges with Grant Wacker, Douglas Jacobsen, and Russell P. Spittler over historical intricacies in chapter 1 were also helpful.

The librarians and staff of both the Raynor Memorial Libraries and the Pentecostal Resource Center assisted with many needs while I was researching and writing. They also proved themselves to be understanding co-workers. In addition, Lynn Anderson of Pearlman Memorial Library assisted with a special collections item that I desperately needed to view for chapter 1.

The Louisville Institute provided generous financial support during the last year of writing. Frederick L. Ware and other group participants in the Institute's colloquium gave critical feedback to an overview of the book.

I am fortunate to work with a press and editors that realize the importance of maintaining the integrity of a PhD dissertation in the published form and devote an entire series to such works. (I am glad that I did not write those content footnotes for nothing!) Cynthia Read and Charlotte Steinhardt of Oxford University Press exhibited great professionalism and patience during the publication process, and Kimberly Rae Connor patiently answered more e-mails than I can count during the initial proposal to the Academy Series. John R. Fitzmier, executive director of the American

Academy of Religion, also approved publication. My anonymous readers gave important suggestions that have been incorporated into the finished product.

In addition to these are a number of friends and family members who have supported me throughout the writing process. My fellow PhD students at Marquette University played a role in sharpening my critical thinking skills. In particular, Bill Oliverio was a uniquely beneficial conversation partner while we, in our respective ways, became more closely acquainted with both the joys and frustrations of examining theological method and hermeneutics among pentecostals. My parents, Richard Stephenson and Kathy Stephenson, have expressed nothing but support during the course of all of my academic studies, which I never would have begun—much less completed—without them. My wife, Lisa, has been both an encouraging spouse and a colleague during this process. While many authors may also be married to their most valued critics, few have the privilege of being married to a critic as informed about their disciplines as she is about mine. We have taught each other that it is impossible simply "to proofread" each other's writing; content always comes up sooner or later! And, finally, I hope that my daughter, Abigail Joy, may one day read with interest the book that far too often kept me away from her.

Portions of chapter 5 are taken with permission from "The Rule of Spirituality and the Rule of Doctrine: A Necessary Relationship in Theological Method," *Journal of Pentecostal Theology* 15, no. 1 (2006): 83–105.

CAS

All Souls' Day, 2011

Types of Pentecostal Theology

Introduction

SETTING THE STAGE

In April 1906, a spiritual revival began at Azusa Street in Los Angeles. While scholars now recognize the pentecostal tradition's multiple points of origin within and without the United States, the events at Azusa are most frequently associated with its birth.[1] In less than a century, pentecostalism has become a global force in Christianity with significant representations on every continent. While sometimes dismissed as *merely* a spiritual movement lacking theology, it was in fact a popular theological tradition from the beginning. Theological interpretations of various pneumatologically centered religious experiences and the biblical texts that became primary in light of those experiences immediately accompanied the spread of the movement. These pentecostals, however, not only *had* religious experiences; they also theologized about them and other theological themes.

Whatever strengths this early theology had, it is marked by at least five detrimental characteristics. First, it was rarely systematic or comprehensive. An abundance of early pentecostal literature was written on any number of issues, such as the Trinity, baptism in the Holy Spirit, glossolalia, divine healing, the *parousia*, sanctification, and so on; however, few attempts were made in this period to give a systematic representation of the whole of the canonical scriptural witness or to develop a comprehensive statement on all of those things that are of concern to Christian theology. Second, most early pentecostal theologians did not have the benefits of formal academic theological training. This has resulted in their being (incorrectly) labeled anti-intellectualist and opposed to learning. Most pentecostals were not opposed to education per se, and many of them were fastidious students of scripture in ways similar to popular American currents at the time. However, their social marginalization, coupled with their desire to proclaim the gospel throughout the world without sparing time for formal academic study, resulted in virtually none of them receiving a thorough theological education. This lack of formal academic theological training necessarily resulted in the following negative characteristics. Third, this theology is informed largely by pre-critical interpretations of biblical texts. This is especially true in regard to Acts 1 and 2, the *locus classicus* of much early pentecostal theology. Fourth, early pentecostal theologians did not have the philosophical training necessary for thorough theological reflection. This is not to say, of course, that they did not have their own philosophical presuppositions, but they were unable to achieve a critical perspective of their presuppositions because they lacked broad exposure to various philosophical problems and approaches. Fifth, the theological developments in the wider Christian tradition did not extensively influence pentecostal theology. While the movement had an ecumenical nature that cut across many denominational boundaries, pentecostal theologians were not adequately aware of other theological communities in the Christian church. Ignorant of many patristic, medieval, and modern theological concerns, pentecostals all too often interpreted biblical texts without the needed influence from the rich interpretive traditions that preceded them.

STATEMENT OF THE PROBLEM

All of these negative characteristics have begun to recede significantly among pentecostal theologians. Pentecostals are now writing systematic theology that gives attention to the whole canonical scriptural witness and that addresses a wide range of doctrinal, ethical, sociopolitical, and philosophical concerns. Further, with their emergence into the middle class (in North America, at least), pentecostals have in increasing numbers pursued higher education in many academic disciplines; theology is no exception. Their formal education has helped correct the inadequacies of the earlier period that were cultivated by their lack of theological training. Pentecostal theologians are now sensitive to the endless complexities of biblical interpretation and are making significant contributions to biblical studies. Pentecostals have also discovered the wider theological tradition and are beginning to draw on its resources in both Eastern and Western theology. Some pentecostals have been involved in formal ecumenical dialogues since the early 1970s, and some are beginning to ask probing questions about a pentecostal perspective of world religions and about the contributions the religions might be able to make to Christian theology.

This book is a study of the major past and present pentecostal systematic theologians responsible for the recession of early pentecostal theology's negative characteristics. Many secondary accounts of pentecostalism focus exclusively on early pentecostals with respect to the history of their growth and expansion,[2] their place within the ethos of American culture,[3] their biblical interpretation,[4] or the theologies of their first leaders.[5] Still other works focus on the diversity of the global movement,[6] the spirituality of grassroots followers,[7] sociological explanations of their origins,[8] or individual theological distinctives.[9] In addition, a number of studies recount the histories of particular pentecostal denominations or figures.[10] Finally, one recent study surveys contemporary pentecostal theology, but treats the material topically rather than assessing major pentecostal theologians individually.[11] The present book takes an important step toward filling the lacuna in the scholarly literature on pentecostalism by offering a person-by-person study of the major systematic theologians within pentecostalism, one of the most globally influential Christian traditions at the beginning of the twenty-first century.

Therefore, to assist the study of pentecostal systematic theology, I offer a typological assessment of the theological methods that pentecostal systematic theologians employ.[12] More specifically, I establish four original types that characterize their different methodological approaches. While the formal and material components of theology cannot be separated altogether, I am interested more in expounding, analyzing, and assessing the broad approaches and basic theological orientations of the pentecostal theologians in question than in giving account of all of the minutiae of their respective theological views. My investigation involves attention to the following concerns: (1) the extent to which the theologians articulate the methods they intend to follow and whether they demonstrate awareness of other methodologies; (2) the relationships among scripture, tradition, and doctrine; (3) the relationship between theology and philosophy; (4) certain metaphysical, epistemological, and hermeneutical presuppositions and approaches; (5) the places given to pneumatology and eschatology, historically two of the most prominent theological themes in the pentecostal tradition; and (6) similarities and differences with contemporary theologians outside pentecostalism.

I follow the discussion of these methodological categories with the proposal that future pentecostal theological method should incorporate a form of *lex orandi, lex credendi* for the benefit of constructive pentecostal theology and spirituality. My proposal incorporates many of the compatible strengths of the four methodologies, while journeying into a territory of the history of Christian theology that pentecostals have only begun to explore.

CRITERIA

Each of the pentecostal systematic theologians that I consider meets all of the following criteria, all of which are necessary to delineate a body of literature manageable for a single monograph. First, each is or was a member of a pentecostal denomination, not a Protestant, Anglican, Roman Catholic, or Eastern Orthodox charismatic. Rather than adopt certain essential characteristics by which to define "pentecostal," I accept each theologian's self-understanding as demonstrated by his denominational affiliation. Second, each is or was engaged in academic theology, that is, each either holds a terminal degree in an area of religious studies or was engaged in teaching theology in academic settings. Five of them hold the PhD or equivalent, while two of them taught at Bible colleges. Third, each has written either (1) a volume that addresses a range of *loci* traditionally associated with systematic theology and that is more than an explanation of a particular denomination's creed or faith statement, or (2) a constructive volume that directly addresses or has implications for theological method.

The third criterion requires additional comment.One of the ironies of the rise of pentecostal systematic theology is that it coincides with an increasing distrust of "system-building" in the academy. Some late modern theologians now prefer to speak of "constructive" theology in explicit contradistinction to "systematic" theology because "systematic" has sometimes described theology as an entirely coherent account of all theological *loci* around a single integrating theme or principle. They fear that any such enterprise inevitably marginalizes or fails to treat certain *loci*. They also resist the notion that there could be a single system of timeless doctrines that does not constantly need to be reevaluated and reformulated in new times and places.[13] Time is yet to tell how pentecostals will negotiate the questions surrounding systematic and constructive theology or whether they will prefer one of these categories over the other. Theological method and hermeneutics is likely to be an area of interest for pentecostal theologians for the foreseeable future.[14] While I am sympathetic to these and other distinctions between systematic and constructive theology, I use the terms more or less interchangeably because the figures I discuss have yet to position themselves explicitly with respect to the distinctions. For the sake of simplicity, I employ the term "systematic theology" in a broad sense that includes constructive, philosophical, fundamental, spiritual, and liturgical theology but excludes works that are only scriptural or historical analyses.

I want to be clear that the theologians I examine are representatives and that I have made no attempt to be exhaustive. As with any typology there may be legitimate cases for including other figures. In light of this, I want to offer a few comments about the ones I include and the ones I do not. First, while it was not a criterion for inclusion, I am pleased that the theologians I discuss in detail represent multiple ethnic and national backgrounds. In addition to Caucasians born in the United States, representatives include a Jew who was born in Scotland and immigrated to the United States, a Singaporean who was educated in the West and returned to Singapore as a theological educator, and an Asian American who was born in Malaysia. I genuinely regret, however, that I am unable to include any women. I diligently searched for women candidates, but was familiar enough with the body of literature in question to know from the outset that the search might be in vain because of the limitation to systematic theologians. While one promising text presented itself early on, I do not include it because its structure is purely catechetical.[15] Women pentecostals in religious studies are to some degree following in the steps of their male pentecostal predecessors by first studying and publishing in the areas of scripture and the history of Christianity (including some of the fine works cited previously). Only recently have women pentecostals begun to turn to constructive theology.[16] I am optimistic that ten years from now a book on pentecostal systematic theology will include the work of a number of bright young women.

Second, a few prominent figures are not included. The most difficult decisions for me were J. Rodman Williams (d. 2008), David K. Bernard, and Veli-Matti Kärkkäinen. Although the significance of Williams's three-volume systematic theology should not be underestimated, he was a charismatic Presbyterian, not a member of a pentecostal denomination.[17] Bernard is probably the premier Oneness pentecostal theologian, but his theological method to date is not significantly different from the figures in chapter 1,[18] whose works are, on the whole, more widely known. This decision makes all of the representatives trinitarians and underscores the fact that my primary concern is with method rather than other theological distinctives per se, even extremely significant ones. That some Oneness and trinitarian theologians can practice essentially the same theological method and reach varying conclusions on fundamental aspects of Christian confession is ripe for further exploration, but I must leave it aside here. Finally, Kärkkäinen may be the most prominent theologian not included. He is a globally recognized pentecostal scholar in the areas of ecumenism and theology of religions. At the same time, his most important works have been primarily descriptive and analytical rather than constructive.[19]

PROCEDURE

Each of the first four chapters contains (1) brief biographical introduction(s), (2) an overview of major works, (3) a statement of the typological category for that methodology, (4) a consideration of continuities with contemporary theologians outside the pentecostal tradition, and (5) an assessment highlighting strengths and weaknesses of the methodology. Since chapter 5 is a constructive proposal rather than a descriptive analysis of another's methodology, it deviates from this form.

Chapter 1 concerns the method of "Bible doctrines," in which systematic theology is little more than the topical arrangement of the biblical texts. The representatives of this approach are Myer Pearlman (d. 1943), E. S. Williams (d. 1981), and French L. Arrington. This methodology is essentially a simplified type of biblical studies presented within the topical structure of traditional systematic theology. The representatives often reduce biblical texts to propositions followed by a list of supporting scripture references. They usually produce flat readings of scripture that tend to give equal weight to all statements in the Bible, inasmuch as they read all statements as the inspired Word of God. In short, they focus theological method on biblical interpretation.

Chapter 2 addresses the method of giving primacy to articulating the relationship between theology and Christian spirituality. The representatives of this approach are Steven J. Land and Simon K. H. Chan. They address the place of elements such as prayer, worship, religious affections, virtues, and spiritual disciplines in systematic theology. Land, with a particular emphasis on eschatology and pneumatology, argues that spirituality is the very mode through which pentecostals express their theology. Chan, with a particular emphasis on ecclesiology, argues that pentecostal theologians should rejuvenate theology and spirituality by incorporating aspects of the wider Christian spiritual tradition and by adopting a normative liturgy built around Word and sacrament. Both Land and Chan see the relationship between pentecostal spirituality and theology as vital to the spiritual formation of believers and to the perpetuation of pentecostal core values to successive generations.

Chapter 3 is devoted to the method of making the kingdom of God the starting point for all other doctrinal *loci*. The representative of this approach is Frank D. Macchia. He articulates a theology of the kingdom of God and ultimately transitions to a thoroughly pneumatological theology, in which the intersection between the kingdom of God and pneumatology serves as the background for the whole of Christian theology. In moving toward a fully pneumatological theology, Macchia argues that an expanded theology of the pentecostal distinctive of baptism in the Holy Spirit should be the principle around which pentecostal systematic theology is organized.

Chapter 4 considers the method of making pneumatology the starting point for philosophical and fundamental theology. The representative of this approach is Amos Yong. Similarly to Macchia, Yong explores traditional doctrinal *loci* from a pneumatological perspective; however, Yong also addresses metaphysical, epistemological, and hermeneutical issues that Macchia does not. By giving a pneumatological account of the God-world relationship ("foundational pneumatology") and of human interpretation and knowing ("pneumatological imagination"), Yong lays the groundwork for a global theology that is characteristically pentecostal.

Chapter 5 is my own contribution to pentecostal theological method, which attempts to incorporate the most important strengths of each of the methodological types. This attempt takes for granted that these four types are not mutually exclusive of each other per se , even if singular aspects of them may be. Neither do they exist on a methodological axis, such that movement from one type to the other is necessarily movement from one pole toward another.[20] My contribution is not a fifth methodological type but rather a proposal for an element of pentecostal theological method that has not yet been sufficiently developed within the four types. Specifically, it is an adaptation of the principle *lex orandi, lex credendi* that I call *regula spiritualitatis, regula doctrinae*, or, "the rule of spirituality and the rule of doctrine." I recommend this principle to pentecostals because it (1) exhibits the traditional pentecostal emphasis on both pneumatology and eschatology; (2) establishes a strong relationship between theology and spirituality, especially in the process of formulating doctrine; (3) is attentive to the hermeneutical matrix constituted by the worshipping communities in which pentecostal theologians are situated; and (4) gives a prominent place to biblical interpretation in systematic theology. I conclude with a brief theology of the Lord's supper that illustrates the salient points of the proposed method. Specifically, I discuss the Lord's supper as a practice that orients participants to the death of Jesus Christ as a pattern for Christian discipleship. After the pattern of *lex orandi, lex credendi*, I allow some of the primary concerns of pentecostal spirituality (eschatology and the universality of the Holy Spirit's works) to raise the theological questions that I address in a doctrine of the Lord's supper. I, in turn, employ a doctrine of the Lord's supper (one that makes pneumatology the entry point into christological emphases and that sees the Lord's supper as an eschatological catalyst) to inform aspects of pentecostal spirituality, in search of some of the ethical and sociopolitical ramifications of celebrating the Lord's supper. By drawing on *lex orandi, lex credendi*, I invigorate pentecostal theology with the help of a methodological principle that enjoys sustained support in both the Christian tradition and contemporary ecumenical discourse. At the same time, because I employ a modified form of *lex orandi, lex credendi* informed primarily by pentecostal concerns, I reach conclusions about the Lord's supper that may be in tension with theologies of the supper within other Christian traditions. My conviction is that before pentecostals can afford to be concerned about the ecumenical reception of their doctrine of the Lord's supper, they need to *formulate* a more adequate one in the first place. After pentecostal theologians have given sufficient consideration to a doctrine of the Lord's supper, they can engage in formal ecumenical dialogue over its details for the benefit of pentecostals and other Christian traditions.

I trust that by establishing this typology and making my own methodological proposal I sufficiently answer in the affirmative the two questions that inquirers have posed to me most frequently during my research: (1) "Do pentecostal systematic theologians actually *have* a theological method?" and (2) "Are there enough pentecostal systematic theologians to support such an investigation?"

CHAPTER 1

⟡

Systematic Theology as "Bible Doctrines"

MYER PEARLMAN, E. S. WILLIAMS,
AND FRENCH L. ARRINGTON

INTRODUCTION AND OVERVIEW

Some pentecostal theologians take the material for their systematic theologies almost exclusively from the Bible. Myer Pearlman, E. S. Williams, and French L. Arrington are representatives of what some call the "Bible doctrines" theological method, according to which systematic theology is little more than a comprehensive, topical organization of the Bible's contents. Proponents of this method primarily summarize scripture and at times simply restate or quote it under theological headings. While the observation that such a genre of theology exists among pentecostals is not new, there is thus far no thorough evaluation of the methodological postures of these works beyond the generally accurate but superficial description "Bible doctrines."[1] However, a number of accompanying methodological tendencies do require attention, such as (1) the primacy and nature of biblical interpretation in systematic theology; (2) the influence of the theology of scripture on systematic theology's structure; and (3) the role of other sources for theology in relation to scripture. The works of Pearlman, Williams, and Arrington are unique among the other works I consider in subsequent chapters because each is a complete systematic theology in itself, not simply a work that has implications for systematic theology as a discipline or that only lays the methodological groundwork for a full-scale systematic theology not yet written. All three works cover a wide spectrum of traditional doctrinal *loci*.

Before proceeding, I first acknowledge that the three systematic theologies considered in this chapter are marketed by denominational publishing houses that do not specialize in literature that meets the criteria of critical scholarship or academic theology—Pearlman's and Williams's by the Assemblies of God and Arrington's by the Church of God (Cleveland, TN)—and that this reality probably produces constraints on their form, style, and contents. My assessments of these works are not intended as representational of these three theologians' other writings, except when explicit similarities are highlighted in the notes. The question of whether the authors would have made their systematic theologies more academically sophisticated in form or content under the auspices of different publishers is purely speculative. Whatever the case, my task is to interpret these texts as they stand rather than to draw conclusions about their authors' potential capabilities in other publishing fora. Second, I realize that it is a delicate venture to describe the method of a theologian who neither demonstrates significant awareness of his own method nor discusses alternative methods that he might consciously avoid. While Arrington is an exception to a degree, this is, on the whole, the case for these three theologians. Because they offer few explicit descriptions of their own intended methodologies, against which I could measure their actual practices, some conclusions must remain tentative. This complexity does not prohibit conclusions completely, since demonstrated self-awareness of their methods is neither necessary nor sufficient for assessing their methods. On the one hand, one could analyze their procedures without any explicit methodological claims, and on the other, one might conclude that they in fact fail to follow any such claims.

Myer Pearlman (d. 1943) was born in Scotland to a Jewish family. He immigrated to the United States in 1915, shortly before his conversion to Christianity at the Glad Tidings Mission in San Francisco, CA. He was one of the first students to attend Central Bible College in Springfield, MO, operated by the Assemblies of God. He joined its faculty immediately after his graduation in 1927, and the institution's Pearlman Memorial Library is named after him. He was an accomplished linguist, whose abilities extended to Greek, Hebrew, French, Italian, and Spanish.[2]

My interest is in Pearlman's most enduring work, *Knowing the Doctrines of the Bible* (1937), which innumerable students attending Assemblies of God educational institutions have read.[3] It is organized under these headings: the scriptures, God, angels, man, sin, the Lord Jesus Christ, the atonement, salvation, the Holy Spirit, the church, and the last things. While this single volume of nearly 400 pages contains no preface or foreword explaining an occasion or reason for its publication, Pearlman wrote it to give basic doctrinal instruction to second-generation pentecostals who desired to be more biblically literate, especially those preparing for ministerial work.[4] The book contains a myriad of references to secondary sources, almost all of which he does not document, even when they are direct quotations. Few of the references involve more than statements such as "according to Dr. Evans . . ." Some of his most frequent citations are of David S. Clarke, A. J. Gordon, and the Westminster Shorter Catechism.[5]

Pearlman feels that his book is important because Christian doctrine has practical consequences. He distinguishes between "theology" and "religion" but claims that the two should exist together. In the Christian life, theology, understood as knowledge of the things of God, should accompany religion, understood as living in relationship with God. Too often one is a theologian without being truly religious or one is religious without having a systematic knowledge of doctrinal truth, but neither of these extremes is desirable. According to Pearlman, one should not reject doctrine due to the misunderstanding that it is not important for day-to-day living; rather, a person's beliefs affect his or her actions. While one could argue that it is more important to live the Christian life than merely to know doctrine, he writes, the Christian life would not exist apart from Christian doctrine. Just as astronomy dispels the false notions of astrology and makes legitimate science of the cosmos possible, "Bible doctrine" exposes false ideas about God and makes Christian living possible.[6]

Ernest Swing Williams (d. 1981) is one of the best-known denominational leaders in the history of the Assemblies of God. He converted to Christianity in 1904, two years before he began to attend meetings at the Azusa Street revival, where he was baptized in the Holy Spirit and first aspired to devote himself to Christian ministry. He conducted evangelistic work and served as pastor of an Apostolic Faith mission in San Francisco, CA before joining the Assemblies of God soon after its original organizational meeting in Hot Springs, AR, in 1914. He eventually served as the denomination's first general superintendent (its highest administrator) from 1929 to 1949, during which time the Assemblies of God enjoyed tremendous numerical growth. Williams also played important roles in the denomination's initial relationships with both the National Association of Evangelicals and the Pentecostal Fellowship of North America. After his tenure as general superintendent, Williams taught theology at Central Bible College for about five years.[7]

My interest is in Williams's three-volume *Systematic Theology* (1953), the only work by a single pentecostal author with the title "systematic theology." It consists of over 800 pages of material first compiled for his use in the classroom.[8] This edited collection of lecture notes[9] is organized under these headings: bibliology, angelology, theology, christology, anthropology, soteriology, pneumatology, ecclesiology, and eschatology.[10] It is more similar than dissimilar to Myer Pearlman's *Knowing the Doctrines of the Bible* and is essentially the same kind of work.[11] One significant distinction between the two, however, is that Williams refers to figures within the history of Christian theology far more frequently than does Pearlman. While Pearlman's *Knowing the Doctrines of the Bible* appears to be primarily a systematic statement of the theology that he thinks his readers should embrace, Williams designed his *Systematic Theology* for broader exposure to the theological tradition. Williams simply assumes that such historical considerations are necessary for a complete theological investigation. Clement of Alexandria, Origen, Ambrose, Augustine, Anselm of Canterbury, Luther, Melanchthon, Calvin, and Arminius are just some of the figures that Williams discusses. His treatments of them are at times little more than caricatures, and they almost never include direct citations of their writings. This, however, does not diminish the fact that he sees engagement with such figures and presentation of their views for his readers as part of the task of systematic theology. While acknowledging that scripture makes no attempt, for example, to explain the many mysteries of the person of Christ, he asserts that God is pleased with human attempts to come to terms with such mysteries; therefore, he discusses various historical accounts of the incarnation and Christ's *kenosis* and encourages his readers to choose the theological perspective that they feel to be most credible.[12] Williams states his intentions for writing *Systematic Theology* as follows:

In so arranging these studies it was my desire that my students might receive, not the theological thought of one school of interpreters only, but a general view; also that they might know the various doctrinal positions, and the reasons why they are believed. While doing this, the desire has been to hold before the students and others who might read this book that form of doctrine which is most surely believed among us, while never attempting to coerce anyone to my personal way of thinking. I have noticed that some attack the beliefs of others, while they know little as to the reasons why others hold to beliefs which differ from their own. . . . Students of Scripture need information. Where there are differences among God's devout children, we do well, as far as we are able, to understand the nature of those differences. . . . Much good has come to me through reading the works of different writers. On some subjects I have seen things differently, but at the same time I have been enabled to understand the position of others better. This enables me to appreciate them more.[13]

Williams presents varying historical views in different ways. Sometimes he merely rehearses perspectives without explicitly approving or disapproving, such as his mentions of original sin and sanctification.[14] Sometimes he chooses individual elements from certain perspectives and adopts a synthesis of those elements as his own view, such as his discussion of atonement.[15] Concerning Christ's second coming, he considers both amillennial and postmillennial views precisely because he wants to expose his readers (whom he assumes to be premillenarians) to them.[16] Occasionally, he just offers the strengths and weaknesses of differing theological views that all seem to have some scriptural support, such as with episcopal, presbyterian, and congregational ecclesiastical governments.[17]

French L. Arrington is an ordained bishop in the Church of God (Cleveland, TN), within which he has significantly influenced theological education. He has served on the denomination's board of education and its commission on doctrine and polity, in addition to devoting himself to pastoral work for over fifteen years. An accomplished scholar and author, he holds a PhD in biblical languages with an emphasis in Pauline studies from St. Louis University, which he received under the direction of Keith F. Nickle (1975).[18] From 1981 to 2002 he was professor of New Testament Greek and Exegesis at Pentecostal Theological Seminary, in Cleveland, TN.

Arrington's *Christian Doctrine* (1992–94) has a more sophisticated writing style than Pearlman's or Williams's systematic theologies and lacks their occasional rhetorical and colloquial tone.[19] It even introduces the reader to basic aspects of historical criticism,[20] while remaining accessible to readers who have no training in academic theology.[21] The entire three volumes contain only two citations of other theological literature and only one reference to a figure in the history of theology.[22] Arrington organizes his material under these headings: doctrine of the scriptures and revelation, doctrine of God, doctrine of creation, doctrine of man, doctrine of Christ, doctrine of sin, doctrine of salvation, doctrine of the Spirit, doctrine of the church, and doctrine of last things.

All in all, Arrington's work is another example of the Bible doctrines genre of pentecostal systematic theology, but one formative characteristic distinguishes it from Pearlman's and Williams's works. As its subtitle indicates, *Christian Doctrine* explores a pentecostal perspective of systematic theology. While Pearlman and Williams certainly consider characteristically pentecostal questions, such as baptism in the Holy Spirit and charismatic gifts of the Spirit, Arrington goes further than they by stating that pentecostals have a distinctive perspective to offer on all doctrine. He writes,

> *Christian Doctrine* . . . is a basic exposition of the Christian faith with an emphasis throughout on the vital role of the Holy Spirit in the life of the Christian and in the worship and ministry of the church. . . . Pentecostal believers have much in common with the faith and practice of other Evangelical Christians. Nevertheless, the Pentecostals' experience and understanding of the Holy Spirit in the life of the individual Christian, and in the life of the church as a body, have prompted them to give a distinctive witness of life in the Spirit, which has helped form their understanding of the Christian faith.[23]

In contrast with Williams, who attempts a systematic theology that is "not the theological thought of one school of interpreters only,"[24] Arrington offers a systematic theology that is "decidedly Pentecostal."[25]

BIBLICAL INTERPRETATION AS THE PRIMARY TASK OF SYSTEMATIC THEOLOGY

Because Pearlman, Williams, and Arrington assume such close relationships between scripture and systematic theology, an investigation of their theological method is largely an inquiry into their specific methods of biblical interpretation. First, they take a common sense approach to interpreting scripture.[26] They exegete statements in straightforward fashion and rarely rely on interpretive tools such as allegory.[27] While Arrington acknowledges that one's pentecostal perspective influences interpretation, he still seems to assume that scripture has a readily accessible plain sense. He writes that although scholarly study can produce special insight into scripture, the average Christian with limited resources and the help of the Holy Spirit is able to understand the Bible.[28]

Second, word study is an integral part of biblical interpretation. All three seem to assume that individual words on their own reflect static meanings that simply need to be uncovered through vocabulary-based study.[29] This is especially true of proper names and titles, which are supposed to reveal the character of the persons and things to which they refer.[30] They base legitimate interpretation of scripture largely on the meanings of individual Hebrew and Greek words, derived from lexical aids.[31] Instead of detailed exegesis based on historical, grammatical, literary, and contextual considerations, one finds extensive word study.

Third, and most important, systematic study requires an interpretive method that works in conjunction with the notion that the Bible is the primary source for doctrine. That is, to learn what to believe about a particular doctrine, one simply gathers information from all parts of scripture relevant to that doctrine and compiles it in theological categories. A statement here or there does not suffice for a proper understanding of a particular doctrine; rather, one consults the entire corpus of scripture to gain a comprehensive view. The Bible is like a field of data, all of the particulars of which one considers and weighs against each other. This investigative approach sometimes leads Pearlman and Williams to offer little more than brief propositions followed by a list of scripture references presented as prooftexts of the propositions.[32] When using such an approach, the interpreter must acknowledge and occasionally harmonize seemingly contradictory data, such as the respective assertions that Moses saw God (Exod 24:9–10) and that no one has ever seen God (John 1:18). Pearlman alleviates this apparent tension by explaining that the former statement refers to a special manifestation of God that allows human apprehension, and that the latter statement means that no one has seen God in himself.[33] Considering the same verses, Williams makes a similar move by distinguishing between God's outward manifestation and his eternal being.[34] While he does not address these two texts, Arrington explicitly acknowledges that it is difficult to reconcile some portions of scripture with other portions and wisely warns against artificial harmonization. He adds that many such interpretive difficulties within scripture are actually results of a failure to interpret correctly.[35]

Also important for the primacy they give to biblical interpretation are some of the conceptual distinctions they make concerning scripture and theology. For example, Pearlman's theological method depends heavily on his descriptions of scripture, doctrine/theology,[36] dogma, and systematic theology. As the verbally inspired and revelatory Word of God,[37] scripture is the source to which one turns for Christian doctrine. Doctrines, however, are not ideas extrapolated from the Bible or further developments of theological trajectories in the Bible; rather, doctrines are contained in the Bible itself. Pearlman states that the doctrine of the Trinity is a revealed doctrine, not the product of human reason. Its content was contained in the Bible before Christians employed the term "Trinity."[38] This illustrates that for Pearlman the Bible does not give rise to Christian doctrines but rather contains them. Dogmas, on the other hand, are creedal (and therefore, later, human) formulations of the doctrines that are revealed in scripture.[39] To preserve the *doctrine* of the Trinity as found in scripture from an overemphasis on either unity or plurality, he says, the early Christian church formulated *dogmas* such as the Athanasian Creed to protect it from error.[40] Dogmas are necessary because people sometimes erroneously interpret the doctrines contained in the New Testament, in spite of the fact that they are clearly revealed.[41]

According to Pearlman, systematic theology is necessary because the biblical texts are not topically arranged. As a science, systematic theology is the logical organization and presentation of "certified facts" concerning God.[42] Summarizing some of the modern branches of theology, Pearlman writes that dogmatic theology is concerned with the Christian faith as contained in creeds; biblical theology, with each writer's presentation of important doctrines; and systematic theology, with the Bible's contents arranged topically and orderly.[43] According to these definitions, Pearlman rightly describes his *Knowing the Doctrines of the Bible* as a combination of biblical and systematic theology that is concerned with both the interpretation of scripture and its systematic presentation.[44] While Williams and Arrington are not as explicit as Pearlman about the relationships among scripture, doctrine, and systematic theology, Pearlman's articulation of these relationships is representative of their approaches. Williams reflects less than Pearlman on the nature of theology and its various types, but he echoes several of Pearlman's sentiments. For example, Williams states that humans are naturally religious and that scripture is fundamental for the scientific arrangement of religious data. Arrington does not give precise definitions of doctrine and theology or how biblical, historical, and systematic theology differ from each other, or specify into which of these categories his work fits. He does, however, describe his book as a biblical and practical presentation of Christian doctrine.[45]

THE FUNCTION OF SCRIPTURE IN SYSTEMATIC THEOLOGY STARTING WITH THEOLOGICAL EPISTEMOLOGY

Scripture not only serves as the primary material for each doctrine but it also plays a fundamental role in the structure of each theologian's systematic theology. Each begins his work by stating the basic tenets of a crude theological epistemology that makes scripture its central component. That is, each discusses scripture as the justification for the claim that one can know anything about God.[46] For example, after his descriptions of the nature of Christian doctrine, Pearlman rhetorically asks how there could be a viable search for truth if there were no authoritative guide to the knowledge of God. After all, human attempts to ascertain God's purposes never produce universal agreement, and philosophy always falls short because humans do not know God by their own wisdom.[47] Although nature reveals God's existence, nature does not provide relief from sin or reveal God's remedy for sin. This knowledge requires a particular kind of revelation. Nature is God's "first book," and the Bible is God's "other book."[48]

Just as it is reasonable to expect such revelation to be written in order to avoid the untrustworthiness of memory and tradition, Pearlman asserts, it is also reasonable to expect that God would inspire the record of this written revelation. While it is conceivable that a religion could be divine without inspired writings, this is not the case with Christianity. Scripture itself (II Tim 3:16 and II Peter 1:21) attests to its own inspiration, which is the Spirit of God's influence on the writer to record the Word of God. Inspiration is different from revelation in that revelation refers to the content of things that God must make known because they are not within the scope of natural human knowledge, whereas inspiration refers to God's act of preserving the writer from error while recording such revelation.[49] Inspiration is also different from illumination, which is the influence of the Holy Spirit that allows one to understand the things of God. Pearlman illustrates the distinction between inspiration and illumination with the example that while the prophets uttered *inspired* speech, they often spoke of that which they were not *illuminated* to understand.[50]

Furthermore, Williams begins his systematic theology with what he calls bibliology. According to him, knowledge of God's existence, in spite of sin, remains universal through the testimony of the natural world, human history, and God's own preservation of it in human consciousness. In addition, all humans have a conception of sin (even if distorted from the Bible's conception) and awareness of the need for both a mediator and sacrificial offering to remedy sin. Knowledge of God's specific plan of salvation, however, is not part of universal consciousness. Only scripture gives such revelation, which is necessary because humans tend naturally to stray from God. Scripture reveals the good news that God has made provision for human salvation. By studying nature, one might theoretically be able to discern as much as God's moral qualities and God's expectations for humans to seek God's favor, but according to Romans 1, no one has actually done this due to the effects of sin. Therefore, revelation in the form of scripture is necessary.[51]

Williams also distinguishes between revelation (the message God gives) and inspiration (the method by which God reveals).[52] While he does not use the term "illumination," Williams essentially operates with this category by insisting that interpreters require help to understand scripture. The Spirit, who inspired the scriptures, also makes them known to the believer.[53]

In addition, the first section of Arrington's systematic theology is devoted to scripture and revelation, which are among those things that he feels one should logically study first.[54] Revelation stands first because without it God would remain hidden, for humans cannot learn about God by searching on their own.[55] Arrington is the only one of the three theologians to use the precise terminology of "general revelation" and "special revelation"[56] (although Pearlman and Williams certainly operate with those concepts as well). One form of general revelation, Arrington states, is human conscience, a result of the image of God that guarantees some degree of awareness of God's moral law in every person. Human conscience is inadequate revelation, however, because sin may influence or even silence it by blinding humans to the significance of God's general revelation; therefore, special revelation, found primarily in scripture, is necessary.[57] While the moral law condemns human sin, it does not offer saving knowledge of God. Scripture provides divine assistance by making humans aware of their spiritual condition. While Arrington indicates elsewhere that special revelation includes more than scripture, he relies primarily on scripture to span the epistemic chasm that general revelation is unable to span.[58]

Arrington defines the inspiration of scripture as that which guarantees the preservation of the truth of revelation. Scripture is the product of the creative work of the Holy Spirit, who gives it a divine quality that distinguishes it from all other literature.[59] The Spirit also illuminates scripture so that interpreters can properly understand it.[60]

Pearlman's, Williams's, and Arrington's respective practices of starting their systematic theologies with theological epistemology contain each of the following tenets: (1) Before one considers various topics in systematic theology one must first give an account of how one claims to have any knowledge of Christian truth or doctrine. (2) God's revelation alone is the source of this knowledge. (3) Some knowledge of God can be attained through general revelation. (4) The inadequacy of general revelation—due in part to the noetic effects of sin[61]—makes special revelation necessary for sufficient knowledge of God. (5) Scripture is the most important form of special revelation. (6) The trustworthiness of scripture depends on the Spirit's inspiration of it. (7) One's ability to interpret scripture correctly depends on the Spirit's illumination of it. And (8) all of these seven characteristics are predicated on the conceptual distinctions among revelation, inspiration, and illumination.

Although none of the three theologians demonstrate any awareness of some of the most basic philosophical questions concerning metaphysics and epistemology—they do not even use this terminology—each frames the starting points for his systematic theology by such questions. Each assumes, even if unconsciously, the context of the epistemological crisis of the late modern world and the ensuing skepticism of some surrounding the possibility of metaphysics. Each also responds to this context by offering scripture as the guarantee that humans can in fact have reliable knowledge of God and, therefore, that systematic theology is a legitimate enterprise. This surfaces in each of their decisions to develop a crude theological epistemology with the categories of revelation, inspiration, and illumination, and in their placements of this theological epistemology before the discussion of all other systematic *loci*. There is nothing peculiar about these pentecostals' claims that scripture is a source of knowledge of God, but what is significant is that this claim stands first and takes the form of a justification of all that follows.[62]

OTHER SOURCES FOR THEOLOGY

Notwithstanding the fundamental role that scripture plays for these theologians, their methods are not strictly *sola scriptura*. In spite of his contention that doctrines are contained in the Bible and his definition of systematic theology as a science that organizes the Bible's contents, Pearlman does not make the Bible the *only* source for his theological reflection. He neither explicitly states that the Bible alone is valid for theology nor confines himself to it in actual practice. For example, he discusses approvingly cosmological, teleological, and anthropological arguments for God's existence.[63] Neither does Williams nor Arrington make the Bible the only source for theology. Williams states that in addition to revelation, knowledge of God comes through intuition, tradition, and reason.[64] Similarly, Arrington observes that while the Bible is a special means of God's communication, truth may also come through song, testimony, or spiritual gifts.[65]

In addition, Pearlman and Arrington intentionally draw on human experience as a source for their theologies.[66] Pearlman rejects metaphysical materialism, the complete eradication of sin through sanctification, and the notion of regenerative punishment resulting in universal salvation because he believes them to be contrary to experience, whereas he affirms the possibility of apostasy because experience demonstrates it.[67] His conception of experience is sometimes naïve, such as when he suggests that early Christian experience of God was self-evidently trinitarian, and therefore, part of the impetus for belief in the Trinity.[68] At the same time, Pearlman shows his awareness that human experience of the divine is not always self-evident when he suggests that the experience some believers interpret as a second definitive work of grace (sanctification) is instead simply an awakening to the position that one already enjoys in Christ.[69]

Arrington makes his reflections on experience more extensive than Pearlman's and focuses them specifically on the unique influence that experience of the Holy Spirit has on one's theology. This means primarily that he considers the relationship among religious experience, interpretation of scripture, and theology. Arrington says that, for pentecostals, biblical interpretation is "pneumatic interpretation." The Spirit deepens their insight into the Bible and makes it come alive for them. The Spirit brings to bear God's revelation for successive generations of believers and helps them understand things that others also understand, but with an added dimension. Because of a common experience of the Spirit, it is possible for pentecostal interpreters to discern an ancient text's meaning.[70] Arrington writes,

> Through the experience of the Holy Spirit, modern readers span the time and cultural differences between them and the ancient author. . . . By the fresh outpouring of the Spirit on the 20th-century church, Pentecostals share in the experience of apostolic believers. The personal experience of Pentecost informs their interpretation of Scripture. Pentecostal believers do not study the Bible in a detached manner. Through the Spirit they have entered into the experience of the first-century Christians. They have received "their Pentecost" and have appropriated into their lives the experiences of Acts 2. . . . Therefore, contemporary Pentecostals now live, through their own experience, the Pentecostal experience of the New Testament believers.[71]

In short, a common experience of the Spirit between ancient authors and modern readers brings the benefit of interpretive insight.

INFLUENCES AND CONTINUITIES

In a number of ways, these pentecostal theologians' ideas about biblical interpretation, the nature of scripture, and the relationship of scripture to theology mirror the theology of the nineteenth-century American Reformed theologian Charles Hodge. Similarities are especially strong in respect to Hodge's articulations of the inductive method of systematic theology and of the notions of revelation, inspiration, and illumination. First, Hodge's theological method is not inductive in the sense of piling up verse after verse of scripture in the hope of achieving the highest possible mathematical probability of a belief, such that more scripture verses suggests higher probability and smaller margin of error in a matter of doctrine. It is inductive because,

Hodge claims, it relies on investigation rather than on a priori speculation.[72] Hodge writes,

> If, therefore, theology be a science, it must include something more than a mere knowledge of facts. It must embrace an exhibition of the internal relation of those facts, one to another, and each to all. . . . The Bible is no more a system of theology, than nature is a system of chemistry or mechanics. We find in nature the facts which the chemist or the mechanical philosopher has to examine, and from them to ascertain the laws by which they are determined. So the Bible contains the truths which the theologian has to collect, authenticate, arrange, and exhibit in their internal relation to each other. This constitutes the difference between biblical and systematic theology. The office of the former is to ascertain and state the facts of Scripture. The office of the latter is to take those facts, determine their relation to each other and to other cognate truths, as well as to vindicate them and show their harmony and consistency.[73]

Again he writes,

> The true method of theology is, therefore, the inductive, which assumes that the Bible contains all the facts or truths which form the contents of theology, just as the facts of nature are the contents of the natural sciences.[74]

These words describe a method of systematic theology that parallels the method of Pearlman, Williams, and Arrington and also shares some of their assumptions and explicit statements about theology as a science, the need to search scripture for all information relevant to a doctrine, and the relationship between biblical and systematic theology. The similarities are most explicit between Hodge and Pearlman, who is the most reflective of the three pentecostals about the specific task of systematic theology. Whether Pearlman read Hodge himself or other sources ultimately dependent on Hodge, it seems clear that Hodge's inductive method influenced Pearlman. At times, even the word choice is so similar that one wonders if Pearlman had Hodge's first volume in front of him and summarized portions of it.[75] Given Pearlman's tendency not to document his sources thoroughly, the lack of any mention of Hodge by name by no means excludes the possibility that his volume served as a template for Pearlman's opening considerations of the nature of theology.[76]

Second, the method of starting systematic theology with a theological epistemology based largely on scripture and especially the distinctions among revelation, inspiration, and illumination constitute additional similarities with Hodge's *Systematic Theology*. Hodge devotes nearly the first

200 pages of his first volume to theological method before describing scripture as the Protestant "rule of faith" and, therefore, the privileged source of theological knowledge.[77] Hodge also defines the inspiration of scripture similarly to Pearlman's, Williams's, and Arrington's definitions and, like they, distinguishes it from revelation with respect to their objects and effects. While revelation's object is to communicate knowledge, inspiration's object is to guarantee infallible teaching. While revelation's effect is the increase of wisdom in recipients, inspiration's effect is the preservation of scripture from error.[78] Hodge further distinguishes inspiration from illumination with respect to their subjects and designs. While inspiration's subjects are only a few people, illumination's subjects are all Christians who read and understand scripture. While inspiration's design is to make certain persons infallible teachers, illumination's design is to make persons holy.[79] These similarities with Hodge in respect to inductive interpretation and the distinctions among revelation, inspiration, and illumination affirm that these pentecostal systematic theologies mirror the patterns of contemporary nonpentecostal works.[80]

ASSESSMENT

At least two strengths commend the Bible doctrines theological method. First, it is utterly committed to the unique place of Christian scripture in theology. While the method itself seems to leave little room for theological development—since doctrines are supposed to be taken straight from a fixed set of texts—its emphasis on scripture could be appropriated into a more critical method that is characterized by constantly engaging and returning to the biblical texts through a process of theological development. Even with the understanding that different readers throughout Christian history will certainly interpret and apply scripture differently, one can still insist that the Bible is the most important body of literature with which the Christian theologian has to do. A second strength is the impetus of each of the Bible doctrines texts to promote a more theologically informed clergy. While pentecostals can and should expect more theological sophistication from their ministers than what these texts provide on their own, pentecostal theologians would be wise to continue to write academic theology suitable for ministerial training.[81] When doing so, they will need to invite more critical thinking and dialogical thinking with their readers than the Bible doctrines texts do.

The Bible doctrines method has several weaknesses. First, it produces systematic theologies that are more frequently assertive than argumentative.

Deductive reasoning is rare,[82] and there is little speculation beyond the bounds of what scripture seems to state plainly.[83] If doctrines are merely statements of the Bible's contents, then there is no need for the theologian to employ a reasoning process that moves from scripture to doctrine or to consider how existing doctrinal opinions shape one's interpretation of scripture. These texts are much more similar to a theology handbook or manual than to what most now consider systematic or constructive theology.

Second, the Bible doctrines method results in theology that neither acknowledges the influence of philosophy in the development of Christian doctrine nor engages contemporary philosophy as a resource for doctrine. This is not to say, of course, that these theologians are not shaped by current philosophical concerns—although they might not even be aware of some of them;[84] rather, it means that their particular arrangements of a doctrine usually remain at the level of simply recognizing various biblical statements on a topic. These statements, therefore, occasionally lack the doctrinal synthesis that comes from a theologian who actively draws on philosophical formulations.[85]

Third, the Bible doctrines method, through its inductive investigation, promotes flat readings of scripture. The representatives give equal weight to all statements in the Bible, inasmuch as they read all statements as the inspired Word of God. One of the most detrimental effects of this is the absence in these systematic theologies of any special significance given to either of the most consistent theological emphases of pentecostalism: pneumatology and eschatology.[86] Even though all three of these authors discuss pneumatology and eschatology in themselves at length, they do not integrate them into the larger fabric of their works in a way that is determinative for the presentation of the content of other doctrines or even the questions that they raise concerning those doctrines.[87] By stressing pentecostals' experience of the Holy Spirit, Arrington comes the closest to making pneumatology an orienting motif, but this has little if any impact beyond affecting interpretation of certain scriptures. He still follows the same general pattern of doctrinal *loci* as Pearlman and Williams.

Fourth, the Bible doctrines method supposes that scripture is the norm for theology and that it is not normed by other factors. For example, Williams and Arrington assume that one can interpret or appropriate scripture independently from one's experiences. That is, they assume that scripture norms experience but is not normed by experience. Williams only hints at this in his comment that scripture must govern experience rather than vice versa,[88] but Arrington is more explicit. In spite of the room that Arrington gives throughout *Christian Doctrine* to the influence of experience of the Spirit on understanding scripture, he still maintains that doctrine should not be derived from personal experience but from proper interpretation of scripture, that the interpreter must "begin with Scripture" rather than experience, and that one's experience cannot be given "the first place" in interpretation. To do so would usurp scripture's authority, which should measure experiences without being measured by them.[89] On the one hand, Arrington attempts to preserve scripture from the normative dimensions of experience while, on the other, he repeatedly states that the normative dimensions of experience give pentecostals insight into interpreting scripture. However, it is impossible to begin with scripture in the strict sense once one concedes that experience influences one's interpretation of scripture. If Arrington bases understanding of scripture in part on experience as he insists, then doctrine is based in part on experience as well. Therefore, one cannot literally begin with scripture in doctrinal pursuits. At best, one can draw on scripture with the realization that it is normed by experience, just as scripture also norms experience by contributing to the hermeneutical frameworks through which we experience and interpret the world.[90]

SUMMARY AND CONCLUSION

I have demonstrated that one of the methodologies employed by pentecostals in systematic theology is to do little more than topically arrange the Bible's contents. I have also shown that understanding Pearlman's, Williams's, and Arrington's strategies for interpreting scripture is the key to understanding their theological method, that their respective theologies of scripture inform the structure of their systematic theologies, and that they give primary place to the Bible without adhering strictly to *sola scriptura*. The Bible doctrines theological method is not limited to a particular historical period of pentecostalism. Arrington employs essentially the same method as Pearlman even though their systematic theologies were published nearly sixty years apart—a time spanning over half of the existence of the pentecostal tradition. As with any theological tradition, there are definitive shifts and trends, but the Bible doctrines method has by no means given way altogether to other approaches.[91]

Pearlman and Williams do not allow pentecostal spirituality to inform their theologies in any meaningful way. While they discuss issues that are usually characteristic of pentecostal concerns, the *shapes* of their theologies hardly vary from evangelical paradigms prominent in America at the times they were writing. Arrington takes steps toward a perspectival hermeneutic by giving more attention than Pearlman and Williams to pentecostal spirituality and experience. However, by attempting to establish the priority of scripture over spirituality and experience, he enters into a logical contradiction. In chapter 5, I attempt to improve on Pearlman and Williams by allowing the pneumatological and eschatological texture of pentecostal spirituality to give shape to doctrinal *loci* and to improve on Arrington by establishing a reciprocal relationship between doctrine and spirituality.

CHAPTER 2

Systematic Theology
and Christian Spirituality

STEVEN J. LAND AND SIMON K. H. CHAN

INTRODUCTION

Some pentecostal theologians make the relationship between theology and spirituality primary for their theological method. Steven J. Land and Simon K. H. Chan are representatives of this approach. Contrary to the occasional descriptions of pentecostalism as a spiritual movement devoid of a theology, these two theologians agree that theology and spirituality are inseparable, although they differ from each other on some of the details of the nature of theology and spirituality and the relationship between them. Whereas Land describes pentecostal theology *as* spirituality, Chan relates spirituality to systematic and liturgical theology. More significantly, eschatology and pneumatology largely shape Land's vision of the relationship between theology and spirituality, whereas ecclesiology largely shapes Chan's. For Land, this takes the form of emphases on the imminent second coming of Jesus and the outpouring of the Holy Spirit, and for Chan this takes the form of emphasis on the ecclesiological dimensions of spiritual formation, liturgy, and the task of theology.

STEVEN J. LAND

Overview

Steven J. Land is president of Pentecostal Theological Seminary in Cleveland, TN (2002–). Land is one of the first pentecostals to hold the PhD or equivalent with emphasis in systematic theology, which he received from Emory University under the direction of Don E. Saliers (1991).[1] An ordained bishop in the Church of God, Land is a recipient of the denomination's Distinguished Educator Leadership award and has served on its commission on doctrine and polity. Land has also been both planter and pastor of multiple churches and is the founder and former director of Mission Possible, Incorporated, an inner-city rehabilitation center in Atlanta, GA, which he directed for twenty-one years.[2]

Land's *Pentecostal Spirituality* (1993) is one of the most widely known and referenced scholarly theology texts by a pentecostal since the appearance of the popular works of Myer Pearlman and E. S. Williams.[3] However, being widely read may be the only similarity among them. Land's work is one of the first pentecostal theologies offered in direct contrast to their kind of works, which Land considers to be no more than outlines of evangelical theology with some minor treatment of pentecostal particulars such as spiritual gifts and baptism in the Holy Spirit.[4] *Pentecostal Spirituality* is instead focused on the relationship between spirituality and theology and the implications of that relationship for each, and it brings to the fore the two theological emphases that are so prominent in pentecostalism's early history but have no formative roles in the works I discussed in chapter 1, namely, eschatology and pneumatology. Its four chapters contain considerations of the following in order: (1) a theoretical introduction to pentecostal spirituality *as* pentecostal theology; (2) the primacy of apocalyptic/eschatology[5] in pentecostal spirituality and theology; (3) the apocalyptic orientation of pentecostal affections and their importance to pentecostal spirituality and theology; and (4) constructive proposals for future pentecostal spirituality and theology under the topics of God, history, salvation, the church, and mission.[6]

As such a groundbreaking work, *Pentecostal Spirituality* is, first, a mild apology for pentecostal theology.[7] This feature surfaces most prominently in Land's responses to claims that pentecostalism's central theological distinctive is baptism in the Holy Spirit and that the movement reduces the Christian life to a series of episodic, emotional experiences. Another form of apology is implicit in Land's contention that pentecostalism is not a revivalistic, spiritual movement lacking and even unconcerned with theology.[8] Land's work is, second, an attempt to situate pentecostalism among other Christian traditions. His primary argument on this front is that pentecostalism is a tradition in its own right, having both similarities and dissimilarities with other Christian traditions, and that incorporating pentecostalism into those traditions would bring fundamental changes to them. He states that the pentecostal tradition traces its roots, through John Wesley, back to both the Eastern and Western sources of early Christianity, and he sketches some of the continuities and discontinuities between pentecostalism and Roman Catholic, Eastern Orthodox, Lutheran, Reformed, and Wesleyan traditions.[9] The text is, third, one of the first attempts to address the question of how to disciple pentecostalism's many converts. Acknowledging this challenge, Land insists that pentecostals teach their followers in ways that do not compromise the fundamental aspects of pentecostal spirituality.[10] It is, fourth, an analysis of the spirituality and theology exhibited during the ten years immediately following the Azusa Street revival in Los Angeles (1906),[11] blended with Land's proposals for how spirituality and theology could operate in the future. He draws heavily on this early period because he sees it as the heart rather than the infancy of pentecostal spirituality and theology.[12]

Spirituality as Theology

The driving force of Land's theological method is the relationship that he posits between spirituality and theology, the question of which, he says, pentecostalism's very existence raises.[13] According to Land, pentecostal spirituality is "the integration of beliefs and practices in the affections which are themselves evoked and expressed by those beliefs and practices," or, the integration of "orthodoxy," "orthopraxy," and "orthopathy."[14] Orthodoxy refers to the worshipping community's right beliefs; orthopraxy, to its right practices; and orthopathy, to its right affections.[15]

Pentecostal spirituality's beliefs and practices shape each other in an enduring, mutually conditioning relationship akin to the relationship between knowledge and lived experience. Among the most important beliefs, for Land, is the "fivefold gospel"—a confession of the five tenets of Jesus Christ as savior, sanctifier, baptizer in the Holy Spirit, healer, and soon coming king. Frequent practices include baptism, the Lord's supper, footwashing, singing, praying, spiritual gifts, and preaching.[16] Concerning such beliefs and practices Land writes,

> The Pentecostal narrative beliefs . . . called forth distinctive practices, which were
> themselves signs, confirmations and celebrations of the power and legitimacy of

the beliefs. And, at times, they became the basis for refining, correcting and supplementing of the beliefs. The worship and witness were the means of expressing and inculcating the narrative beliefs. Beliefs about the Bible, the Second Coming, the Holy Spirit, the Christian life and worship itself are expressed in and shaped by these practices.[17]

One's spirituality consists of the various manifestations of the triadic relationship among one's beliefs, practices, and affections.

Pentecostal theology, according to Land, involves the ongoing process of integrating orthodoxy, orthopraxy, and orthopathy, lest theology fragment into intellectualism, activism, and sentimentalism, respectively. The entire worshipping community carries out the theological process, which involves discerning reflection on lived reality, on a distinctive, apocalyptically oriented praxis governed by the conviction that God is present. Spirituality, which is the fundament and precondition of all theology, calls for theology concerned precisely with this discerning reflection. In turn, both theology's process and its result reflect the distinctively pentecostal spirituality.[18] In short, spirituality is theology's content, medium, and mode of expression, and the theological process effects spirituality by integrating beliefs, practices, and affections. This integration, writes Land, restores theology to its ancient sense of *theologia* and, thus, overcomes a false dichotomy between spirituality and theology.[19] Pentecostal theology, then, has little concern with speculation and rarely finds expression through systematic treatises or academic monographs, a kind of second-order reflection removed from the immediate context of prayer and worship. Rather, it bears the marks of populist folk-religion and more often finds expression through hymns and testimonies, means of communication resultant from the African American and Wesleyan influences on its early ethos.[20] Theology is less a body of material that one masters and more a process one carries out. Describing pentecostal spirituality as primary theology, Land repeatedly draws on hymns and written testimonies in order to establish its early content.[21]

Apocalyptic Affections

The previous examination shows that Land does not reduce theology to beliefs or spirituality to practices, as could be the case within a simplistic coupling of beliefs and practices that refers to theology and spirituality, respectively. Instead, Land defines spirituality as the integration of beliefs, practices, and affections; and theology, as the process of achieving such integration. While there is nothing original about examining the relationship between Christian beliefs and practices,[22] the distinctive of Land's approach is his description that beliefs and practices are rooted in affections that characterize believers.[23] Affections norm beliefs and practices and are also normed by beliefs and practices. Affections give rise to beliefs and practices and are also fueled by beliefs and practices.[24]

As the core into which beliefs and practices are integrated, affections form the heart of pentecostal spirituality; therefore, the nature and role of the affections in Land's triadic spirituality deserve further attention. For Land, pentecostal affections are far more than emotions. They maintain pentecostal spirituality as a way of life aimed at ongoing participation in God's history with the world, not at individual religious experiences. Affections are not merely the intense feelings that someone might have for an object or another person; rather, the biblical narrative shapes them and makes them endure.[25] The affections are specifically Christian in that they are objective, relational, and dispositional. That is, they have their end in God (objective), involve relationships with God and fellow Christians (relational), and characterize the Christian life (dispositional). The dispositional quality is particularly important to Land, for it encourages consistent Christian living by promoting the objective and relational qualities, that is, by giving believers an abiding orientation to God and others.[26]

The primacy of the affections in Land's vision of pentecostal spirituality becomes clear when one sees the correlations that he constructs between three affections and several other triadic structures that are paramount in this spirituality. The affections of gratitude, compassion, and courage have their source in three of God's attributes: righteousness, love/holiness, and power, respectively.[27] These affections are the results of the believer being saved (justified/regenerated),[28] sanctified, and baptized in the Holy Spirit, respectively; therefore, in regard to the fivefold gospel, these affections relate to Jesus Christ as savior, sanctifier, and baptizer in the Holy Spirit, respectively. These affections are opposed by the world, the flesh, and the devil, respectively, which are overcome by faith (I John 5:4), crucifixion (Rom 8:13; Gal 5:24), and resistance (Jas 4:7), respectively. The believer expresses these affections by walking in the light, in love, and in the power of the Holy Spirit, respectively. Finally, these affections are expressed in worship, prayer, and witness, respectively.[29] The integral role of these affections amid elements that are vitally important to pentecostal spirituality and theology—God, Jesus Christ, salvation, and Christian living—is illustrative of the significance of all affections in Land's triadic construal of pentecostal spirituality.

Affections are in reciprocal relationship with prayer. Prayer, as the primary means of pentecostal worship, shapes and is shaped by the affections.

Prayer takes three forms—with intelligible words, without words, and with unintelligible words—each of which evokes and expresses the affections in its own way. Intelligible words are the most common form of prayer and usually communicate gratitude, frequently through attestations in public worship like "Thank you, Lord." Prayer without words refers to sighs and groans, intercessions of the Spirit that cannot be brought to speech (Rom 8:26), which frequently express compassion for the lost. Unintelligible words are glossolalia, the empirical sign most closely connected to courage derived from the Holy Spirit's empowerment. Since affections are central to pentecostal spirituality and since pentecostal theology aims for the production of that spirituality, it follows that pentecostal theology should cultivate the affections. And since prayer evokes the affections, it follows that prayer is indispensable to the theological process. In fact, according to Land, prayer is the pentecostal's primary theological activity. Praying, specifically, praying in the Spirit, both keeps theology from departing from the Spirit and develops the affections, which the Spirit produces in all who believe the gospel.[30]

Apocalyptic vision heightens the intensity of the affections by adding to them a sense of urgency about the church's mission.[31] The Holy Spirit produces a single passion for the kingdom of God, which governs the affections and gives their apocalyptic, and therefore, distinctively pentecostal tenor. The passion for the kingdom governs the three affections of gratitude, compassion, and courage as follows:

> Praying for the kingdom of righteousness and walking in the light are ways of shaping and expressing the affection of gratitude. Giving thanks is a fundamental recognition that one's life and the kingdom are God's gift. . . . Notice that to walk in the light, to be grateful and to long for righteousness in the whole world are what it means to believe in a righteous God. . . . But righteousness will never be perfectly realized in this world. . . . The heart of pentecostal spirituality is love [read: "compassion"]. A passion for the kingdom is a passion for the king; it is a longing . . . to see God and to be at home. . . . The passion for the kingdom means yielding to the Spirit as he searches, fills with love and sighs and groans for the kingdom. When one sighs with the Spirit in longing expectation, then one is disposed rightly. . . . The joy of the Lord is a strength, encouragement and source of hope. This joy is the fruit of the Spirit who gives the believer a "taste" of the power of the age to come. . . . All gifts of the Spirit are eschatological, proleptic signs of a kingdom of joy. . . . Speaking in tongues may express the painful longing of joy or its exultant victory, but true joy always instills courage to press on to the kingdom.[32]

Inasmuch as the single passion for the kingdom gives the apocalyptic orientation to these three (and all) affections, it affirms the significance of apocalyptic for the whole of Land's program.[33]

Apocalyptic/Eschatology and Pneumatology

Land integrates apocalyptic/eschatology and pneumatology into the fabric of *Pentecostal Spirituality* in a way that allows them to give the text its shape. First, concerning the formative role of eschatology, Land's use of the terms "apocalyptic" and "eschatology" require careful consideration. He does not explicitly state precisely what he means by "apocalyptic," which he employs as both a noun and an adjective. In some traditional uses of the term, it is (1) a description of popular beliefs about millenarian expectations and the world's cataclysmic end; (2) a synonym for the descriptive "revelatory"; (3) a genre of Jewish and Christian literature called "apocalypses" in which an otherworldly being mediates revelation to a human recipient; (4) a description of an end-time scenario involving retribution and judgment; and (5) a description of a sociological movement whose ideology bears resemblance to that found in literature called "apocalypses."[34] Land makes only a couple of references similar to the senses of (2), (3), or (5),[35] but whether he uses the term in the senses of (1) or (4) is more difficult to determine. Amid the ambiguity, however, it is clear that Land most frequently associates "apocalyptic" with a specifically Christian notion, namely, belief in the imminent second coming of Jesus Christ.[36] Therefore, Land's observation that early pentecostalism exhibits "apocalyptic eschatology" suggests above all else that the belief in Jesus' imminent second coming (apocalyptic) is integral to a pentecostal theology of the last things (eschatology).[37]

The confession of Jesus as "soon coming king" is the decisive confession that invigorates the other components of the fivefold gospel and all other pentecostal beliefs. Accordingly, Land contends, pentecostal spirituality's eschatological context must receive proper consideration in order for the spirituality to be comprehensible. Apocalyptic, along with the beliefs and practices, is part of the spirituality's distinctive logic. In fact, the eschatological impulse is the driving force of the entire pentecostal tradition. Eschatology, then, is a constitutive part of the whole of theology, not merely an introduction or postscript.[38]

The belief in Jesus' imminent return bespeaks a tension that pentecostals feel constrained to maintain, for it assumes that Jesus has already come once and that he has not yet come again. His coming announced the presence of the kingdom of God, but his outstanding return indicates that the kingdom awaits consummation. The kingdom has both already come and not yet come. Land claims that this "already-not yet" eschatological tension, which is instrumental to understanding pentecostal spirituality, should characterize Christian existence. When the church resolves the tension in favor of either accommodation focused too narrowly on the concerns of the present world (already) or escapism focused too narrowly on the world to come (not yet), movements arise challenging the church to awake and to remember the eschatological tension to which it is called. Pentecostalism is such a movement to the extent that it embodies the already-not yet tension through practices that accentuate each of these two poles. Some already receive physical healing, but not yet is everyone whole. Many already experience the power of the age to come (Heb 6:5), but not yet is God all in all (I Cor 15:28). Future pentecostal theology, he maintains, must keep balanced the already-not yet tension within pentecostalism itself.[39] All of these concerns attest to the prominence of eschatology in Land's vision of pentecostal spirituality and theology.[40]

Land closely relates the formative role that he gives to eschatology to the formative role that he gives to pneumatology. It is precisely the outpouring of the Holy Spirit that fulfills Joel's promise concerning the last days (Joel 2:28–32). Pentecostals understand the dreams and visions referenced there and manifested among them as the workings of the eschatological Spirit. While these and other gifts of the Spirit surfaced in the nineteenth century before the pentecostal movement, Land argues, early pentecostals viewed their own experiences of them through a unique eschatological lens that rendered them signs of the end times. The pentecostal apocalyptic vision depends entirely on the Spirit in two respects. First, the Spirit's promised coming and the Son's promised second coming are part of God's single promise to redeem creation. Second, the believer's longing for Christ and the kingdom is also a longing for the Spirit, who is the kingdom's active presence and who both creates and maintains the already-not yet tension.[41] The following statement summarizes the relationship that Land posits between eschatology and pneumatology:

> The outpouring of the Spirit in the post-Easter community created and sustained the eschatological tension and vision which characterized the early church and the early Pentecostals. Now everything was considered from the standpoint of the imminent parousia. In the transcendent presence of God categories of time and space fused; and, since Jesus was near, so was the end. The Spirit who raised Jesus, made him present in salvation, signs and wonders, and showed things to come. The Spirit who burned as intense hope and energized witness, superintended the ongoing mission. To live in the Spirit was to live in the kingdom. Where the Spirit was present in eschatological power, there was the church of Pentecost.[42]

For Land, there is no eschatology without pneumatology and no pneumatology without eschatology.

Pneumatology is central also to other aspects of pentecostal spirituality and theology. The Holy Spirit makes pentecostal spirituality possible by giving coherence to beliefs, practices, and affections; therefore, pentecostal theology must be gifted by and attuned to the Spirit. Pneumatology also impinges on the fivefold gospel tenet that Jesus baptizes in the Holy Spirit. According to Land, the conceptual distinction between sanctification and baptism in the Holy Spirit is predicated on the distinction between Jesus Christ's and the Holy Spirit's respective missions.[43] While he admits that the fivefold gospel gives priority to Jesus Christ, Land insists that this focus is due to its starting point in the Holy Spirit and that pentecostal spirituality based on the fivefold gospel is "Christocentric precisely because it is pneumatic."[44] In addition to the fivefold gospel, the whole of theology must start with the Spirit inasmuch as theology's concern is God's relationship with the world, for it is the Spirit who is active in the world and among believers. Land also states that the prominence of prayer and worship in pentecostal theology is due to its starting with the Spirit.[45]

Religious Experience

Starting theology with the Holy Spirit, according to Land, raises various hermeneutical and methodological issues, not the least of which is the role and meaning of religious experience for spirituality and theology. Starting with the Spirit amounts to acknowledging the "epistemological priority of the Holy Spirit" in theology, but not to making experience the norm of theology. For example, while experience sometimes gives believers new insights into scripture, all beliefs, practices, and affections have to be tested by scripture. Further, although apocalyptic experience as evidenced in public worship drives pentecostalism, it is in direct contrast to theologies believed to be rooted in human experience or reason that Land defines pentecostal theology as the effort to integrate orthodoxy, orthopraxy, and orthopathy.[46]

Important to Land's notion of pentecostal experience are crises, those times that God intervenes in the Christian life in ways that parallel the coming of the new heaven and earth, the ultimate crisis that pentecostals await. Chief among these crisis experiences are justification/regeneration, sanctification, and baptism in the Holy Spirit, but healings, prophecies, and calls to ministry are also crises that can bring encouragement and new self-understanding.[47] Furthermore, such crisis experiences serve as benchmarks on the way to and necessary preparations for the eschatological goal, which is the kingdom of God in its fullness. The soteriological journey of pentecostals—which Land calls a *via salutis* rather than an *ordo salutis*—is a dialectic between crisis and development in which each experience promotes further growth. As opposed to Christian traditions that rely on sacraments to mark Christian initiation and progression, pentecostals rely on crisis experiences that propel them to the soon approaching end.[48]

In his constructive proposals, Land points to the matter of religious experience as one issue requiring examination beyond his own study. He suggests that future pentecostal treatments of religious experience might have ramifications for questions of pentecostal identity—namely, whether pentecostals are evangelicals and/or fundamentalists[49]—and for pentecostal appropriations of the Wesleyan quadrilateral, the method of incorporating scripture, tradition, reason, and experience into theological method.[50] He admits that new metaphors are needed for crisis experiences and hopes that his articulation of affective transformation might contribute to the development of a soteriology that affirms genuine ontological change in believers.[51]

Trinity and Transformation

In addition, starting theology with the Holy Spirit leads Land to a "re-vision"[52] of pentecostal spirituality. More than simply a revision in the sense of modification, his proposal refers specifically to a restoration of pentecostalism's original apocalyptic vision exhibited in the ten years immediately following the Azusa Street revival. Land believes that this early vision has since waned in intensity, but rather than invigorating it from the perspective of pneumatology per se, he casts his re-vision in light of a social doctrine of the Trinity. He suggests that pentecostals should understand God's unity and identity in respect to the interrelatedness of the three divine persons. Drawing on social trinitarian accounts of *perichoresis* (the idea that divine unity consists in the community of persons) and appropriation (the idea that each divine person plays a unique but cooperative role in creation and redemption), Land offers the social Trinity as a model that might accentuate the church's unity and diversity, crisis and development in soteriological transformation, and God's work in creation from beginning to end.[53] According to Land, the church, as "eschatological trinitarian *fellowship*," mirrors God, who is "eschatological trinitarian *presence*" and who works within history and, thereby, makes it an "eschatological trinitarian *process*," which moves toward a new heaven and earth. Pentecostal spirituality should narrate this process, inasmuch as the church proclaims salvation to be "eschatological trinitarian *passion*" and its mission in the world is "eschatological trinitarian *transformation*." This play on words illustrates and briefly summarizes the trinitarian dimensions of Land's constructive proposals for pentecostal spirituality under the *loci* God, history, salvation, church, and mission.[54] His social trinitarian re-vision of pentecostal spirituality does not contradict but rather stems from theology's starting point in the Holy Spirit, who is the agent of the divine persons' mutual interaction and who enables the integration of beliefs, practices, and affections.[55]

Influences and Continuities

Descriptive Influences

A number of persons influence the descriptive components of *Pentecostal Spirituality*. Land's historical account of early pentecostalism is especially dependent on the works of Walter J. Hollenweger, Donald W. Dayton, and D. William Faupel.[56] The most significant historical claim that Land takes from Hollenweger is that the ten years immediately following the Azusa Street revival exhibit the heart rather than the infancy of pentecostal spirituality and theology. Judging along with Hollenweger that this early spirituality is the norm by which subsequent spirituality should be measured, Land underscores the prominence of pentecostal traits such as (1) an emphasis on oral rather than written liturgy; (2) the narrative shape of pentecostal theology and self-understanding; (3) the importance of prayer, reflection, and discernment in the setting of worshipping communities; (4) the prominence of dreams and visions in public and corporate life; and (5) religious experiences that reflect a view of the correspondence between body and mind. And like Hollenweger, Land expresses concern over the diminishing of these characteristics due to ever-increasing affluence among pentecostals, resulting in social accommodation. Land's adoption of Hollenweger's historical accounts of pentecostal spirituality forms the basis of his conviction that it needs "re-vision." Therefore, since the first ten years of the tradition is the period's age of maturity, Land's claims that pentecostal theology is currently "adolescent" do not refer to pentecostals' initial steps in recent decades to write academic theology, but to a regression from a spirituality and theology that was in fact more mature than those now exhibited at the popular level among many pentecostals. The way forward is in some respect backward, not along the path of an attempted uncritical reduplication of the early spirituality but a reappropriation of it that is essentially faithful to the original vision, especially its apocalyptic tenor.[57]

Land's primary dependence on Dayton's work is his adoption of Dayton's highly influential argument that the four/fivefold gospel most clearly relays the logic of early pentecostal theology. This cluster of beliefs is the wide confessional umbrella under which there was room, according to Dayton, for all the major wings of early pentecostalism. For example, in spite of their internal differences otherwise, both trinitarian and Oneness pentecostals agreed on Jesus' soteriological significance as articulated in the fivefold gospel. Further, pentecostals affirming two distinct works of grace and those affirming three works preached the same "full gospel"—as the four/fivefold gospel was also called—except for respective disagreements about whether to include "Jesus as sanctifier" (hence, both a fourfold and a fivefold pattern).[58]

To Dayton's interpretive grid, Land adds Faupel's work, which is an examination of the prominence of eschatology in early pentecostalism. Faupel, a student of Hollenweger, shares Dayton's emphasis on the fivefold gospel and argues that the emergence of North American pentecostalism in 1906 was due largely to the eschatological significance assigned to experiences of glossolalia: pentecostals saw the gift of the Holy Spirit as empowerment for preaching the gospel to the ends of the earth in the last days.[59] The upshot of Faupel's claim for Land is that the fifth element of the fivefold gospel—"Jesus as soon coming king"—is not merely one element among the others but rather the belief that most thoroughly conditions pentecostal spirituality by making it apocalyptic. Pentecostals believed not only that Jesus was coming, but that he was coming soon.[60]

Constructive Influences

A number of persons influence the constructive components of *Pentecostal Spirituality* as well. Land names Karl Barth, Jürgen Moltmann, and John Wesley as his primary dialogue partners on orthodoxy, orthopraxy, and orthopathy, respectively,[61] although he rarely cites their writings directly. Land states that prayer's prominent place in pentecostal spirituality and theology is similar to its place in Barth's description of the theological task, but he bases this evaluation of Barth almost exclusively on a secondary account.[62] Likewise, Land affirms Barth's notion of the Holy Spirit as the "knowability" of God who makes knowledge of God possible and points the reader to another secondary account.[63] In relation to orthodoxy, Land cites Barth's writings only when describing Barth's sense of human knowledge as "wholistic," but here Land takes his quotation of Barth from another source.[64] Land directly engages Moltmann a little more frequently than Barth.[65] In respect to their basis on a social doctrine of the Trinity, Land's constructive proposals lean heavily on Moltmann, especially the latter's ideas about the trinitarian history of God and its implications for ecclesiology and social praxis.[66] Land refers to Wesley more than Barth and Moltmann combined, yet out of no fewer than nineteen references to Wesley's theology only four contain citations of Wesley's writings. Land documents the remaining references with either secondary sources or nothing at all, including those in connection with orthopathy and with the centrality of religious affections for Wesley's soteriology.[67]

In short, Land takes from the works of Hollenweger, Dayton, and Faupel everything from the time frame of his historical investigation, to his assumptions about the characteristics of mature pentecostal spirituality, to his portrayal of the fivefold gospel as the central pentecostal belief, to his emphasis on the eschatological nature of pentecostal spirituality. Similarly, he rightly describes his indebtedness to other thinkers for his developments of orthodoxy, orthopraxy, and orthopathy, although the influences of Barth, Moltmann, and Wesley seem to be mediated through the secondary accounts of Don E. Saliers, Melvin E. Dieter, Henry H. Knight III, and Theodore H. Runyon.[68]

Finally, *Pentecostal Spirituality* has formal continuities not only with these influences but also with other types of contemporary theology, especially narrative theology and postliberal theology. I choose these two points of comparison because of Land's emphasis on the "narrativity" and "orality" of pentecostal spirituality and theology (categories taken from Hollenweger) and their continuity with Hans W. Frei's descriptions of pre-critical biblical interpretation.[69] Not only did early pentecostals prefer oral means of proclamation over written ones but they frequently couched their oral message in terms of "story." Land states that pentecostals believed their participation in the last days, evangelistic revival to be tantamount to their very inclusion into the story of God's own history with the world. They attested to this inclusion by sharing their own stories, or testimonies, the most frequent mode of expressing the fivefold gospel. Corporate worship was the context that shaped this summary content of pentecostal theology.[70] The formal continuity with Frei's account of pre-critical biblical interpretation lies precisely in the fact that pentecostals believed that the stories in the Gospels and Acts meant exactly what they said. These stories, thus, created a narrative world into which pentecostals entered and in accordance with which pentecostals interpreted reality, especially their own spiritual journeys.[71] Frei writes that

> since the world truly rendered by combining biblical narratives into one was indeed the one and only real world, it must in principle embrace the experience of

any present age and reader. Not only was it possible for him, it was also his duty to fit himself into that world in which he was in any case a member, and he too did so in part by figural interpretation and in part of course by his mode of life. He was to see his disposition, his actions and passions, the shape of his own life as well as that of his era's events as figures of that storied world.[72]

Land's account of the basic tenor of pentecostal spirituality is a veritable historical instantiation of Frei's description of the pre-critical assumption that an overarching story unites the biblical texts and that one should conform one's self-understanding and worldview to that story rather than vice versa.

SIMON K. H. CHAN

Overview

Simon K. H. Chan is Earnest Lau Professor of Systematic Theology at Trinity Theological College (Singapore), where he has taught since 1989. Chan holds the PhD with emphasis in historical theology from Cambridge University, which he received under the direction of Eamon Duffy (1986).[73] As a Singaporean, Chan may be the most widely known Asian theologian writing academic pentecostal theology. He is also an ordained minister in the Assemblies of God, as well as editor of *Trinity Theological Journal*.

My discussion focuses on Chan's *Spiritual Theology*; *Pentecostal Theology and the Christian Spiritual Tradition*; *Liturgical Theology*; and *Pentecostal Ecclesiology*.[74] In *Spiritual Theology* (1998), Chan offers evangelicals an assessment of ascetical and mystical theology in order to expose them to the systematic study of Christian spirituality. Part one develops the implications for spirituality stemming from the systematic *loci* of God, human nature and sin, salvation, and the church. Part two addresses spiritual disciplines such as prayer, spiritual reading, meditation, following a *regula*, discernment of spirits, and spiritual direction as the means through which the Christian life reaches actualization. Decrying the fragmentation of theology into distinct disciplines such as biblical, historical, and practical, Chan grants the existence of spiritual theology as a discipline in its own right partly in hope that an engagement of it as such might encourage further integration of spirituality with all branches of theology.[75]

In *Pentecostal Theology and the Christian Spiritual Tradition* (2000), Chan addresses similar issues as in *Spiritual Theology*, but specifically to a pentecostal audience. His primary argument is that pentecostals must discern the place of their own spirituality within, and thereby view it in light of, the wider Christian spiritual tradition. Only such discernment, Chan argues, can provide the core values of pentecostals with the coherence necessary for them to pass those values on to successive generations, a process he calls "traditioning." Chan claims that this process requires pentecostals to engage in the integrative thinking of systematic theology and to develop a spiritual theology, two activities that they have on the whole neglected to the detriment of discipleship and spiritual formation.[76] As an example of engaging in systematic and spiritual theology, Chan recasts baptism in the Holy Spirit and glossolalia in light of the three ways of the Christian mystical tradition.

In *Liturgical Theology* (2006), Chan returns to a wider evangelical audience that includes pentecostals and offers a theology of worship as the only way for them to fill the deficit of ecclesiology that he believes marks their history. Part one includes discussions of the nature and worship of the church and the shape of Christian liturgy. Part two focuses on the actual practice of liturgy, or, "liturgical spirituality." Chan is intent on developing the "ontological"—as opposed to a purely "sociological" or "functional"—identity of the church as the basis for its practices. For Chan, the church's chief practice and primary reason for existence is worship, and as such, worship is an end in itself.[77] Chan is one of the strongest pentecostal proponents for the need for a traditional, normative liturgy in pentecostal churches.[78]

In *Pentecostal Ecclesiology* (2011), Chan returns to earlier ecclesiological concerns to consider the inevitability of doctrinal development. He argues that pentecostals should acknowledge such development, and that to judge the (il)legitimacy of doctrinal developments they need a more robust ecclesiology. This requires in part acknowledging that the church is closely related to the kingdom of God and that the church defines the rest of creation more than the rest of creation defines the church. The church completes the story of the triune God's economic activity, inasmuch as the Father sends, first, the Son and, second, the Spirit, who then establishes and indwells the church. Drawing especially on Eastern Orthodoxy's strong emphasis on the monarchy of the Father and the ensuing asymmetrical trinitarian relationships, Chan urges pentecostals to follow their occasional impulses toward episcopal ecclesiastical structures by understanding the church as a communion of persons in which hierarchy and reciprocity work together and qualify each other.

Spirituality and the Branches of Theology

According to Chan, spirituality refers to the lived reality of Christian existence expressed primarily through practicing classical spiritual disciplines and corporately celebrating the liturgy. It is a way of life that stems from both nonrational experiences of the transcendent and rational conceptualizations of the transcendent expressed in theological formulations. The systematic study of such spirituality is one of the primary tasks of spiritual theology. While the term "spiritual theology" suggests broadly a manner in which to undertake all theological reflection, it also refers more strictly to a particular branch of theology that seeks to understand the processes of spiritual growth.[79]

Chan's *formal* criteria for spiritual theology are comprehensiveness, coherence, and evocability. Comprehensiveness refers to a conceptual framework that accounts for various polarities such as immanent-transcendent, personal-corporate, and natural-supernatural, all of which should be balanced for adequate spiritual growth.[80] Coherence suggests that spiritual theology should be internally consistent, while leaving room for mystery and paradox. Evocability indicates that spiritual theology should direct attention beyond its rational formulations to the spiritual realities they express. Concerning this last criterion, Chan writes,

> In a normative spirituality the line between dogma and devotion is no longer clearly drawn, and there is freedom of movement between the two. Theological reflection and prayer are no longer discrete activities but exist in a dynamic, ongoing relationship in which one activity enriches the other, stimulating the Christian to new insights and greater fervor.[81]

Chan's *material* criteria for spiritual theology, which he says distinguish his treatment from similar works on spiritual theology, are global-contextual, evangelical, and charismatic. Global-contextual refers to Chan's sensitivity to the plurality of Christian contexts throughout the world and to his determination to represent both Western and Asian perspectives.[82] Evangelical refers not to the spiritual theology of a particular group or affiliation of Christians but to one shaped decisively by the Christian story's emphasis on the life, death, and resurrection of Jesus as well as by the insistence that the believer's conversion involve a personal relationship with Jesus.[83] Charismatic refers to the element of surprise that is possible in spiritual progress because God is not utterly predictable.[84] In short, spiritual theology exists in order to give shape to a particular spirituality that forms the content of the Christian life. Chan grants that there may be a number of legitimate spiritualities shaped by different spiritual theologies, but that in principle there is a single Christian spirituality to the extent that Christians are united by the theology of the ecumenical creeds.[85]

While Chan maintains that all of theology should be attentive to the Christian life and should encourage godly living, he concedes the existence of different branches of theology. He discusses spiritual theology as one such branch in hope that the articulation of its relationship to both systematic and practical theology—all three of which differ in method and content—might encourage greater appreciation of the spiritual nature all theology should have. While systematic theology focuses on rational formulations of Christian experience by addressing a broad range of *loci* in their own right, spiritual theology focuses on the spiritual life by drawing out the implications of those rational formulations. In systematic theology, the spiritual dimensions of Christian faith remain in the background in the pursuit of precise understandings of theological *loci*, and in spiritual theology these detailed explanations remain in the background in the pursuit of a life lived unto God. In addition, whereas practical theology focuses on human action in the world, spiritual theology focuses on human relationship to God. As its name suggests, practical theology seeks the practical application of theology, and spiritual theology seeks the transcendent in every facet of human life. Spiritual theology, Chan claims, necessarily mediates between systematic and practical theology, lest Christian praxis become mere activism.[86]

Elaborating further on the character of systematic theology, Chan states that the fragmentation of theology into several branches changed its very nature and made systematic theology simply one branch among others.[87] Instead of Christian theology being systematic in the sense of its assumption that God has spoken through revelatory scriptures that exhibit conceptual unity,[88] systematics as a branch of theology is now concerned with coalescing revelatory data without finding its practical application. As a result, systematic theology is merely the means to a practical end rather than an end in itself in the pursuit of spiritual knowledge. Systematic theology as a branch of theology, however, can still be of value inasmuch as it continues to assume the unity of the Bible and makes the integration of scripture its chief concern.[89] On the one hand, Chan urges pentecostals to engage in this kind of systematic theology (for example, integrating Lukan and Pauline pneumatology) to better communicate their core values to successive generations, something they have sometimes struggled to do because of their failure to produce systematic theology. On the other hand, pentecostals should not become satisfied with systematic theology alone, thereby reducing Christian faith to the realm of the intellect. They also need to develop a spiritual theology in which reflecting on God's nature and praying to God are indistinguishable acts. Spiritual theology allows systematic theology's truth to come to life.[90]

Chan's discussion of the doctrines of the Trinity and the church (especially in *Spiritual Theology*) illustrates nearly all of his claims about the relationship between spirituality and theology.[91] First, he contends that the doctrine of the Trinity itself is a construal of systematic theology. The doctrine is not the product of creative prooftexting, but rather the result of theologians discovering the larger pattern of scripture and its witness to God's self-revelation.[92]

Second, Chan acknowledges that a Christian spirituality can legitimately cohere around each divine person. For example, a spirituality of the Father might affirm, ecologically, the value of creation and promote stewardship of nature; socially, a common humanity that undermines racial and sexual prejudices; and soteriologically, the continuity between the physical and the spiritual, inasmuch as God is creator of everything. In addition, a spirituality of the Son might accentuate Jesus as a liberator and promote discipleship marked by commitment to social justice; or, it might accentuate Jesus as a suffering servant and promote a Christian life marked by patience in suffering. Further, a spirituality of the Holy Spirit could promote intimacy with the Spirit and encourage a Christian life that is marked by boldness, is open to surprise, and issues forth in mission to the world. However, Chan observes, because spiritualities centered on each divine person have weaknesses, the ultimate goal must be a fully trinitarian spirituality. The implications of the doctrine of the Trinity for spirituality include (1) seeing salvation as essentially personal union with God understood in relational terms, inasmuch as God is a supremely personal being; and (2) maintaining human particularity amid relationality, just as *perichoresis* maintains the distinctions of the divine persons amid their relations. To keep Christian spirituality trinitarian, believers must practice it communally; otherwise, individual personality types might gravitate toward a spirituality focused on one divine person and neglect the others. Therefore, according to Chan, the *locus* of trinitarian spirituality is the church, just as the theological *loci* of God, humanity, sin, and salvation find their logical conclusion in ecclesiology. He summarizes that spirituality is living the Christian life in union with the triune God within the church.[93]

Third, Chan insists that models of the Trinity should be judged by their adequacy for the spiritual life and by their performance in various cultural contexts. Consider, for example, his assessments of both the social doctrine of the Trinity and God's transcendence and immanence. Concerning the former, he states that many Asians may find a model of the Trinity that emphasizes the logical priority of the Father (since the Father alone is without origin) to be a more appropriate one after which to order their societies than a social model of the Trinity that emphasizes egalitarian relationships among the divine persons. A hierarchical model, he adds, has the potential to instill stability and order in the face of chaos, not necessarily promote domination and oppression. Concerning the latter, he states that the doctrine of the Trinity holds together the polarity of transcendence and immanence, among others, by claiming that God is both "wholly other" and "for us." Maintaining this balance is especially important outside the West, for it implies that God is at once distinct from creation and relational, that creation is a free act of God that does not constitute God's being, and that God is not part of the world itself or its processes.[94]

Fourth, Chan opts for a particular form of political theology as a model for ecclesiology. That is, he feels that Asian contexts require a conception of the church as a community that derives its identity by contrasting itself with societal instantiations outside the church and that offers a way of living that is alternative to the world system, rather than one in which the church is a liberating community that seeks social justice by and large through the agency of the liberal-democratic state.[95]

These four aspects of Chan's discussions of Trinity and ecclesiology demonstrate his most basic concerns about the relationship between spirituality and theology by illustrating (1) his notion of the unity of scripture and its use in systematic theology; (2) his articulation of spiritual theology among the other theological disciplines; (3) his description of spiritual theology as the discipline that draws from systematic theology implications for Christian spirituality; and (4) spiritual theology's formal criteria (especially comprehensiveness and evocability) and material criteria (especially global-contextual).

Ascetic Spirituality

Asceticism is the most fundamental marker of Chan's vision of spirituality. He defines asceticism as the shaping of the Christian life through steady, ongoing training, the strict meaning of *askesis*. An ascetical spiritual theology is one in which the disciplined practice of spiritual exercises (a rule of life, or *regula*) constitutes the primary means of spiritual development, and in which corporate liturgical worship is itself a spiritual exercise that the church performs through active participation. A *regula* that includes liturgical worship is the structure of consistent Christian existence marked by regularity. Spiritual exercises such as prayer, meditation, practicing friendship, social action, and *lectio divina* move persons from non-Christian to Christian ways of living, and liturgical worship inculcates worshippers with the gospel over time, largely through the observances of the liturgical calendar throughout the church year.[96]

According to Chan, the most fundamental element of a *regula* is a rule of prayer, which is a rhythm of praying that "help[s] us build a bridge from the simple tasks involving small changes of mental habits, such as learning to acknowledge God in all things, to the higher reaches of prayer in which God becomes all in all." Prayer is the basis of all other practices in Chan's ascetic spirituality, and growth in prayer is the primary measure of growth in the Christian life. Unceasing prayer, or practicing the presence of God, brings God into every arena of one's life and makes possible constant awareness of God's presence. However, he suggests, few are prone to develop such a habit naturally, and the training process of ascetic spirituality is necessary in order to make prayer a way of life. This training process is one of the primary goals of spiritual theology.[97] Such a *regula*, Chan insists, does not preclude the charismatic material criterion of a legitimate spiritual theology; rather, the charismatic dimensions can contribute to a *regula* by keeping it from becoming rote and mundane. Rather than becoming an excuse for a lack of discipline in practicing spiritual exercises, the charismatic dimension should positively influence a *regula* in this way.[98]

These insights about the relationship between the charismatic dimensions and a rule of life within a spiritual theology raise the question of the relationship between the elements of crisis and regulation in pentecostal spirituality. As his notion of *askesis* suggests, Chan contends that pentecostal spirituality must give far more weight to regulation than to crisis experiences, although without excluding them altogether. It is precisely evangelicals' overemphasis on crisis conversion that results in their inability to produce a comprehensive spiritual theology. Chan insists that they must counter this overemphasis by understanding gradual and regulated spiritual disciplines as the normal means of spiritual progress and crisis experiences as the (indispensable) exceptions. Employing a *regula*, he states, provides to persons willing to move slowly and deliberately more opportunity for spiritual development than is available to persons who rely on unpredictable bursts of spiritual fervor.

Against this backdrop and in order to undermine the notion that Christian salvation is a single, isolated event, Chan discusses justification, sanctification (two of pentecostalism's most prized crisis experiences), and glorification, as the soteriological language of steady Christian growth. Here, one of his basic concerns is to demonstrate that a Protestant theology of these three soteriological *loci*, as articulated by certain seventeenth-century Puritans, is compatible with the traditionally but not exclusively Roman Catholic concern for cultivating the moral and theological virtues, the primary means through which Chan develops the ascetical nature of soteriology.[99] For most Christians, spiritual progress comes through small steps such as prayer, practicing the presence of God, acts of reading, service, and obedience.[100] These observations show the close association that Chan makes between the notions of crisis and the charismatic dimensions of spirituality. They also show the strong priority he prescribes for regulation over crisis experiences within a healthy pentecostal spirituality.[101]

The Traditioning Process and Pentecostal Theology

Chan's preference for regulated spirituality is related closely to his idea of "traditioning," the process through which the church passes on its core values. The use of the verbal derivative from *traditio* underscores the active nature of the formation process in which the church must intentionally engage to perpetuate Christian faith to successive generations. Just as a coherent spirituality requires training to shape the Christian person, the traditioning process requires a disciplined effort to develop a coherent set of beliefs for the church to communicate its message clearly. For Chan, then, traditioning is a macrocosm of the individual Christian's spiritual formation.[102] Traditioning requires, first, the integrative thinking of systematic theology, which should be related properly to the art of spiritual theology as described previously. After all, traditioning is the handing on not only of theological beliefs but also of the practices of faith exhibited in a spiritual theology.[103] Chan demonstrates the intersection between spiritual growth and theological traditioning most clearly in his discussion of the ascetic practice of giving and receiving spiritual direction. He writes that the spiritual director should be versed in systematic theology and should use doctrine as a tool for assisting spiritual growth, and that spiritual direction is an integrative process that brings the *loci* of spiritual theology into actual practice. Furthermore, spiritual direction is by nature a traditioning process because the director disciplines the one directed from within the framework provided by the Christian theological tradition.[104]

Traditioning requires, second, situating one's beliefs within the wider Christian theological tradition. According to Chan, pentecostals have been just as slow to do this as to develop systematic theology, preferring frequently to accentuate their own distinctive beliefs and practices rather than to interpret them as existing within a larger theological pattern. Besides unnecessarily separating them from other Christian communions, such a posture also impoverishes the very distinctive beliefs and practices that pentecostals are so intent to affirm. Chan contends that it is precisely pentecostals' failure to develop systematic theology and to interpret their beliefs in light of the larger sphere of Christian theology that leads to their inability to "tradition" their members properly. The result is shallow theological accounts of certain pentecostal beliefs, among the most significant of which are baptism in the Holy Spirit and glossolalia.[105] Chan writes that

> the central doctrine called "baptism in the Spirit" is far richer in Pentecostal *experience* than in Pentecostal *explanation*. . . . This disparity between experience and explanation has serious consequences for Pentecostal traditioning. . . . [W]hen the experience [of baptism in the Holy Spirit] is inadequately conceptualized, what is communicated to the next generation is a constricted concept of the experience, and this concept will in turn evoke an equally narrow experience. . . . If Pentecostals hope to communicate the original reality to subsequent generations, they must come up with an explanation that encapsulates it adequately.[106]

Chan chooses to scrutinize the particular beliefs of baptism in the Holy Spirit and glossolalia for two reasons. First, he hopes to make two of pentecostalism's most fundamental symbols even more significant by subjecting them to systematic reflection (especially on Lukan and Pauline pneumatology). Second, he hopes to demonstrate that even the two most distinctive pentecostal beliefs, which have the least support in the larger Christian tradition, can in fact be successfully situated within it (specifically within Christian mysticism's notion of the three ways). In so doing, he argues for a more convincing theology of glossolalia as the "initial evidence" of baptism in the Holy Spirit as well as for a stronger than usual conceptual relationship between the two.[107]

First, Chan attempts to integrate Lukan pneumatology with other strands of New Testament pneumatology. Observing that pentecostals have relied primarily on Luke-Acts for their doctrine of baptism in the Holy Spirit and glossolalia, Chan states that a truly systematic theology requires them to consider the larger structure of scripture and, therefore, other biblical resources for pneumatology. He refers to this systematic endeavor as a search for "canonical meaning," which the interpretive community (the church) recognizes when it engages the canonical texts, in order to both shape them and to be shaped by them.[108] Just as the church fathers did not simply discover the doctrine of the Trinity within scripture but rather extrapolated it from multiple portions of scripture through an ongoing process of discernment,[109] so pentecostals have to allow the larger canonical witness to inform their pneumatology and acknowledge that their doctrine of baptism in the Holy Spirit and glossolalia is not stated explicitly in any single biblical text. Such an acknowledgment,

Chan insists, need not result in their abandoning the doctrine in the absence of a definitive prooftext, but rather can result in their reclaiming the doctrine in a form that is more convincing than the usual account.[110] Since pentecostals cannot establish the doctrine adequately on the basis of purely biblical or historical arguments, they must engage in the integrative thinking of systematic theology to argue for the unique relationship between baptism in the Holy Spirit and glossolalia.[111] Chan's initiative to integrate various New Testament pneumatologies involves the additional integration of holiness with power and of soteriology with the charismatic dimensions of Christian life. Concerning holiness and power, Chan notes that Matthean pneumatology in particular sets miracles and power demonstrations within the larger context of an ethical community bound to God in covenant relationship. Concerning the soteriological and the charismatic, Chan suggests that Pauline pneumatology (as exhibited in Galatians 3) virtually equates regeneration (the soteriological) with demonstrations of the Spirit (the charismatic).[112]

Second, Chan attempts to situate the pentecostal doctrine of baptism in the Holy Spirit and glossolalia within the larger Christian spiritual tradition by considering it in light of Christian mysticism's three ways of spiritual progress—purgation, illumination, and union.[113] Interpreting the three ways as a recurring pattern of spiritual development, Chan suggests that pentecostals could see their own traditional three-stage soteriological schema including conversion, sanctification, and baptism in the Holy Spirit as a (structurally, if not materially) similar pattern, rather than as a once-for-all chronological progression. The ongoing mystical experience of movement from more active to more passive dimensions of spiritual growth, Chan argues, serves as a more adequate model for the pentecostal claims to "progressive sanctification" and to "many fillings" of the Spirit than does the chronological schema. While pentecostals may experience an initial manifestation of charismatic expressions that they identify as baptism in the Holy Spirit, the three ways provide a model of repetition that encourages them to seek increasingly deeper levels of spiritual growth in which they practice glossolalia as an ascetical act of receptivity.[114] Far from a dismissal of the pentecostal notion of glossolalia as the initial evidence of baptism in the Holy Spirit per se, Chan claims, this integration with the three ways makes that very formulation more convincing by establishing a unique connection between baptism in the Holy Spirit as intense intimacy and glossolalia as the attending sign of spiritual union.[115] Chan rejects the classical formulation of initial evidence in the sense of glossolalia as "empirical proof" in order to reclaim initial evidence in the sense that glossolalia is the most theologically appropriate sign of baptism in the Holy

Spirit. Just as tears might be the most appropriate expression of sadness, glossolalia is the most appropriate expression to signify the paradigm shift that baptism in the Holy Spirit entails. Glossolalia is concomitant with the Spirit's irruptive manifestation.[116]

Ecclesiology
Ontology of the Church

It is no exaggeration to say that the whole of Chan's theology stems from his concerns about some of the inadequacies of evangelical and pentecostal ecclesiology,[117] most particularly their proponents' tendencies to theologize about the church almost exclusively in sociological or functional rather than ontological categories.[118] To the contrary, Chan argues that the church is not merely the result of persons with similar interests gathering to form an organization for pursuing their common goals (the sociological); rather, the church is a body that exists prior to the conversions of individuals (the ontological). Christians do not become an assembly because they convert; instead, they are incorporated into a body that already exists.[119] Chan insists that a theology of the church's ontology is necessary if the church is to be a community that (1) makes possible the spiritual progress of believers; (2) "traditions" its core theological beliefs to successive generations in a coherent and convincing manner; and (3) fulfills its most basic responsibility to worship God. These three characteristics are the most prominent themes in *Spiritual Theology*, *Pentecostal Theology and the Christian Spiritual Tradition*, *Pentecostal Ecclesiology*, and *Liturgical Theology*, respectively.

Chan's theology of the church's ontology emerges within the relationships he articulates between Christian beliefs and practices. Against the background of "new ecclesiologies" in which the identity of the church is described on the basis of its concrete practices rather than in light of idealized heuristic models, Chan acknowledges that formulating a theology of Christian practice is especially complex and must take into account the importance of Christian liturgy.[120] Specifically, he focuses his theology of ecclesial practices on the liturgy by distinguishing between the primary practices that belong to the church's *esse* and secondary practices that belong to its *bene esse*. The primary practices are the very components of the liturgy itself, Word and sacrament.[121] The secondary practices could be any number of ecclesial acts like hospitality or showing mercy, which are no less important than primary practices but do not constitute the church's identity to the same extent as do Word and sacrament. This structure, according to Chan, provides needed criteria for judging the legitimacy of church practices and ensuring that they are genuinely Christian. Secondary practices are judged both by their ability to promote spiritual formation and by whether they are coherently connected to the primary practices of Word and sacrament. Similarly, Word and sacrament are judged by their consonance with the gospel and with Christ's institutions of them, respectively. Chan acknowledges the difficulty of assigning fixed meanings to secondary practices, but states that the meanings of the primary practices of Word and sacrament are officially fixed and accessible to virtually anyone who participates in them regularly. The church's act of teaching these meanings—an ecclesial practice in itself—enables persons to be formed more thoroughly by secondary practices. Because the practices are grounded in Word and sacrament, which are the core of Christian liturgy, they are delineated as Christian practices that transcend actions that might be performed by any number of non-Christian bodies. In short, normative Christian liturgy constitutes the church's ontology in part by grounding its secondary practices in the peculiar Christian practices of Word and sacrament, thus making the church more than a merely sociological entity.[122]

For Chan, the church's primary practices of Word and sacrament culminate in the eucharist, the church's unique affirmation of its ontological bond with Christ. In the eucharist, the many members who have been incorporated into Christ's body become the one body of Christ by eating his body and drinking his blood. Eucharistic communion establishes the church's communal identity.[123] The eucharist constitutes the church as an eschatological community that exists in the already-not yet tension. While Christ is not physically present, the Spirit effects his eucharistic presence and sustains the church as it waits for his return. Eucharist enables the church to maintain the balance of the already-not yet tension through the duality of *anamnesis* and *prolepsis*, both of which are held together by the *epiclesis*. The church both remembers (*anamnesis*) Christ's work and looks forward (*prolepsis*) to new creation when it calls upon the Spirit to descend (*epiclesis*) both as the one who appropriates Christ's work and as the first fruits of the new creation.[124]

Ecclesiology and Pneumatology

Chan's discussions of pneumatology occur most frequently in the context of ecclesiology, as seen readily in his call for an "*ecclesial* pneumatology" and for an "*ecclesiological* pneumatology." Chan believes that *ecclesial* pneumatology is the necessary remedy for a pentecostal ecclesiology developed primarily in sociological terms. In addition to the highly individualized ecclesiology described previously, he states that the sociological model also produces an individualized pneumatology, especially in relation to baptism in the Holy Spirit. On the contrary, an ecclesial pneumatology includes the tenet that the Spirit's work is not primarily in the individual but in the church, which has been baptized in the Spirit before any such actualization manifests in individual Christians. An ecclesial pneumatology is an affirmation that (1) the Spirit repeatedly and dynamically constitutes the church through the *epiclesis* in the Lord's supper, (2) the church is a eucharistic community performing works of reconciliation in the world, and (3) the larger Christian tradition, which is the means through which the Spirit leads the church into truth, must inform theology.[125] Not to be confused with an ecclesial pneumatology, an *ecclesiological* pneumatology is an affirmation that ecclesiology should shape pneumatology, inasmuch as the church is the primary *locus* of the Spirit's work. Concerned by attempted theologies of *Creator Spiritus* and certain affirmations of the Spirit's work outside the church, whether in the form of liberation movements or for the sake of interreligious dialogue, Chan encourages pentecostals to understand the Spirit as "the Spirit of the church and of new creation," thereby resisting the idea that the Spirit effects the new creation apart from the church's proclamation of the gospel. Pentecostals should not base their engagement with the world on the assumption of a common Spirit at work in both the church and the world in an attempt to discern the Spirit in sociopolitical structures that they believe advance the kingdom of God. On the contrary, the church cannot influence the world by manipulating its power structures. It must instead commend the gospel to the world through its proclamation.[126]

Ecclesiology also frames Chan's reflections on how prominent a place pneumatology should receive in theology. On the one hand, he states that baptism in the Holy Spirit, when situated in an ecclesial context and integrated with holiness and sanctification, could become the perspective through which to view spiritual formation in the Christian life. In other words, pentecostals could view all of theology pneumatologically.[127] On the other hand, his suggestion of a pneumatological hermeneutic quickly gives way to a hermeneutic of the Christian spiritual tradition (in this case, the three ways). Chan in fact allows the three ways to inform his reworking of pentecostal soteriology far more than he allows pentecostal soteriology to recast the three ways. It is clear that he incorporates the pentecostal schema of conversion, sanctification, and baptism in the Holy Spirit into the formal structure of the three ways, not vice versa. Elsewhere, Chan seems to deny explicitly the legitimacy of a pneumatological priority in theology by stating that some of the Spirit's work is "functionally subordinated to the Father."[128] He further writes,

> The Christian tradition is quite consistent in affirming the Spirit's hiddenness. The Spirit is not the *direct* focus of our worship. The Nicene Creed identifies the Spirit as one who "together with the Father and the Son is worshipped and glorified." The church has kept to the spirit of [the] Creed by composing few songs in direct praise of or petition to the Spirit. Mostly, the glorification of the Spirit is set within a strictly trinitarian formula such as the Doxology.[129]

The context of these statements is Chan's contention that if pentecostals are to explore Christian experience of God from the perspective of the distinctive role of the Spirit, they must do so within a broader trinitarian framework. He adds that while some contemporary theologians' claims to a pneumatological deficit in the history of theology may be correct, the lack of attention given to the Spirit is due in part to a theologically sound trinitarian framework, within which the Spirit is the hidden bond of love between the Father and the Son. While Chan states that acknowledging the Spirit as hidden does not amount to neglecting the Spirit's work, these statements seriously undermine the pneumatological lens mentioned previously. In any event, whether suggesting a pneumatological hermeneutic or affirming the Spirit's hiddenness, Chan frames pneumatology with ecclesiology. The church is the context of spiritual formation in the form of the pentecostal three-stage soteriology integrated with the three ways, and the church's worship and creedal confession point to the proper place of the Spirit within the Trinity as well as the place of pneumatology within the whole of Christian theology.[130]

Influences and Continuities

As is the case with Land, Chan is influenced by narrative theology and postliberal theology. Here, I refer specifically to Stanley Hauerwas's theology.[131] Integral to Hauerwas's thought is the formative nature of the Christian story on ecclesial communities and the necessarily political identity of ecclesial communities that are decisively shaped by the Christian story. It is within such ecclesial communities that Christians are formed and find their identities.[132] These ideas surface throughout Chan's theology, especially in his accounts of the ontology of the church, the church as the primary *locus* of spiritual formation, and the importance of cultivating virtues through spiritual disciplines. They surface most prominently, however, in Chan's discussions of the kind of political theology required in Asian contexts, namely, one that envisions the church as an alternative community that bears witness to the radical message of the gospel against the state's totalizing claims over its citizens. In fact, Chan frequently accompanies his statements about political theology in Asian contexts by affirming the political theology of Hauerwas and criticizing that of Jürgen Moltmann.[133]

ASSESSMENT

Land and Chan have contributed significantly to pentecostal systematic theology through their respective emphases on Christian spirituality. They not only state that theology and spirituality should be related but also articulate detailed visions of how the two should mutually inform each other. Land and Chan are in fundamental agreement with each other in respect to the constitutive role that spirituality should have in theology, and both argue for a pentecostal spirituality that is centered on prayer and promotes a steady and consistent Christian way of life. Land does so by offering apocalyptic affections as the orienting force of beliefs and practices; Chan, by offering a comprehensive spiritual and liturgical theology that is informed by the wider Christian tradition. Both intentionally combat a pentecostal spirituality that might promote individual religious experiences as the primary means of spiritual growth. While Land stresses more than Chan the positive place of crisis experiences in spirituality, Land also acknowledges that such experiences are parts of an ongoing spiritual journey rather than isolated bursts that are unrelated to what precedes and follows them. The stability that Chan seeks to provide through spiritual disciplines and the cultivation of moral and theological virtues, Land seeks to provide through affections, abiding dispositions that orient the Christian life.

One of the strengths of Land's theology in particular is that it captures the historic importance of eschatology and pneumatology to pentecostalism and critically appropriates certain aspects of them. Concerning eschatology, Land argues for the maintenance of the already-not yet tension of God's kingdom while shunning speculative exercises in the end-time scenarios that sometimes accompanied early pentecostalism's dispensational eschatology. Concerning pneumatology, Land resists its reduction to baptism in the Holy Spirit and glossolalia as traditionally conceived and insists that pneumatology has a decidedly eschatological content that drives pentecostal spirituality.[134]

One of the particular strengths of Chan's theology is his emphasis on liturgical theology and spiritual theology in general. This emphasis has implications for pentecostalism at grassroots levels since Chan makes suggestions that can invigorate their practices in corporate worship and in spiritual formation. The emphasis also has implications for academic theology since pentecostal theologians are only beginning to give attention to liturgical theology and spiritual theology. Indeed, Chan has led the way among pentecostals on these fronts. As proficiency in systematic theology among pentecostals continues to increase, they will need to follow Chan's cues to engage the intersection of systematic theology with liturgy and spirituality. They will also be wise to heed his contention that systematic theology is necessary for spiritual formation and discipleship if pentecostals are to communicate clearly and convincingly their core beliefs and practices to successive generations.

There are, however, some areas of Land's and Chan's theologies that require clarification in future work. First, concerning Land, there is some doubt as to how much of pentecostalism's early spirituality he feels pentecostals should implement today.[135] Especially unclear is whether pentecostals should even write systematic theology, something previously neglected because of the early spirituality's emphasis on oral rather than written theology. While it seems clear that Land wishes pentecostal spirituality to maintain its oral/narrative demeanor, he does not specify whether that demeanor should continue to provide a minimal role for written theology. Land's constructive chapter, itself an outline of a systematic theology predicated on a social doctrine of the Trinity,[136] suggests his support of such large-scale, written works, but *Pentecostal Spirituality* lacks an explicit criticism or rejection of early pentecostalism's avoidance of systematic treatises.[137]

Second, while Land explicitly states that pentecostal spirituality should be correlated to the fivefold gospel, it is unclear how it should relate to the social doctrine of the Trinity, which is more formative of Land's constructive proposals than the fivefold gospel itself. Land maintains the fivefold gospel in part to keep his emphasis on pneumatology from shifting away from christology, and he stresses the social doctrine of the Trinity in part to avoid what he calls the logical conclusion of the fivefold gospel's christocentrism, namely, Oneness pentecostalism. Nonetheless, it is clearly the trinitarian framework that shapes his proposals, without a precise articulation of how the fivefold gospel should function in relation to it. Further, future studies need to consider whether the fivefold gospel, which according to Land makes the Spirit merely instrumental, is compatible with a fully trinitarian or pneumatological starting point for theology.[138] It is not obvious how pneumatology plays any constitutive role in the fivefold gospel. Its soteriological components are clearly oriented to christology, and it speaks of Jesus only as the one who *baptizes* in the Holy Spirit (giver) and not of Jesus as *constituted* by the Spirit (receiver). If a theology that starts with the Holy Spirit is to incorporate the fivefold gospel, it would do well to find space for Spirit-christology, the most logical way of integrating pneumatology into the soteriological components of the fivefold gospel.[139]

Concerning Chan, first, there needs to be a clearer statement of the relationship between spiritual theology and liturgical theology, specifically concerning the practice of spiritual disciplines and the acts of liturgical worship. Chan repeatedly refers to the disciplines as means to an end (spiritual formation), but insists that worship is an end in itself that is offered for no other reason than for the praise of God's glory. This sharp distinction, however, does not maintain, as is seen most clearly in the act of prayer. Prayer is both the primary means through which spiritual progress takes place and a large portion of the liturgy, from the invocation to the Our Father, to the multiple eucharistic prayers, to the benediction. By Chan's own definitions, prayer is both a means to an end *and* an end in itself. In all fairness to Chan, these respective views are expressed on the whole in two different works (*Spiritual Theology* and *Liturgical Theology*, respectively) separated by several years; therefore, the contradiction is not as explicit as it might seem in my account here. Nonetheless, future studies that incorporate Chan's emphases need to consider the ramifications of a closer conceptual relationship between spiritual and liturgical theology as theological disciplines. It is to Chan's credit that his own emphasis on the prominence of prayer in each invites the consideration of such a relationship.

Second, Chan's strong contrast between the sociological and ontological dimensions of the church also suffers from some ambiguities. While his attempt to bolster evangelical and pentecostal ecclesiology with a stronger sense of identity is commendable, his dichotomization, once again, does not maintain. Worship, which he argues constitutes the church's being, is also a socializing act to the extent that a normative liturgy promotes a particular kind of Christian spirituality. Further, Chan's traditioning process is also a process of socialization by which persons are shaped over time through exposure to their faith communities' core values. Chan rightly states that the church is more than a loose association of persons with common interests and goals, but future accounts of pentecostal ecclesiology need to address questions about the church's identity without Chan's bifurcation of being and act.

Third, Chan's attempts to situate pentecostal theology, especially baptism in the Holy Spirit and glossolalia, within elements of the wider Christian tradition are some of the most creative and insightful portions of his constructive theology. At the same time, he goes beyond placing pentecostal theology into conversation with other traditions in order to make pentecostal theology more coherent and seems to assume that if aspects of pentecostal spirituality and theology do not have counterparts in other portions of the Christian spiritual tradition they are, then, illegitimate. While his reshaping of pentecostal *loci* from the perspective of, for example, the three ways is commendable, he seems to have little room for the possibility that pentecostal *loci* should at times reshape the emphases of other traditions. Future work that follows Chan's admirable lead on traditioning needs to give more attention to the possibility that pentecostal perspectives might be able to inform other traditions, in addition to being informed by them.[140]

SUMMARY AND CONCLUSION

I have demonstrated that Land and Chan give such prominence to the relationship between theology and spirituality that they are representative of a major methodological type among pentecostal theologians. For Land, theology *is* spirituality shaped by eschatology and pneumatology. Pentecostals express beliefs through practices governed by affections that have an apocalyptic tenor. Eschatology and pneumatology intersect, inasmuch as the outpouring of the Holy Spirit inaugurates the last days. The promise of Jesus' second coming and the promise of the Spirit's outpouring coincide in the single promise of the fullness of the kingdom of God.

For Chan, pentecostals must define theology in conversation with spiritual, liturgical, practical, and systematic theology. Furthermore, ecclesiology (more so than eschatology or pneumatology) shapes spirituality. Chan's discussions of the ecclesial context of Christian liturgy and spiritual formation, coupled with his notion that one of systematic theology's tasks is the coherent explanation of church tradition, show ecclesiology's prominence. Chan also gives logical priority to ecclesiology over pneumatology in his ideas of ecclesial pneumatology and ecclesiological pneumatology.

Land implies that pentecostal theology is nothing more than pentecostal spirituality and suggests that discursive, doctrinal reflection may betray pentecostal spirituality's commitment to primary theology. Chan is clearer than Land that pentecostals need to engage in systematic theology precisely to preserve their spirituality and to communicate it to successive generations, but he sometimes mutes characteristically pentecostal perspectives by integrating them into the wider Christian spiritual tradition. In chapter 5, I attempt to improve on Land by insisting that spirituality alone is not a sufficient expression of pentecostal theology apart from doctrinal formulation and to improve on Chan by making pneumatology more central and by accentuating rather than muting characteristically pentecostal perspectives.

CHAPTER 3

⚹

Systematic Theology and
The Kingdom of God

FRANK D. MACCHIA

INTRODUCTION AND OVERVIEW

Frank D. Macchia is professor of theology at Vanguard University of South-ern California (Costa Mesa, CA). He holds the DTheol from the University of Basel, which he received under the direction of Jan Milič Lochman (1989), making him one of the first pentecostals to hold the PhD or equiv-alent with emphasis in systematic theology.[1] As an active participant in ecumenical conversations, including participation in the formal dialogues between pentecostals and the World Alliance of Reformed Churches (1997–2003) and in the Faith and Order Commission of the National Council of Churches (2001–),he is one of the first pentecostal systematic theologians to incorporate the gains of ecumenism into his own theology.[2] He has also been the president of the Society for Pentecostal Studies (1999–2000) and the chief editor of its journal, PNEUMA (2001–2009). An ordained minis-ter in the Assemblies of God, he has been the pastor of churches in Illinois and Indiana.[3]

In addition to numerous articles and essays, my interest is in Macchia's published dissertation, Spirituality and Social Liberation; Baptized in the Spirit; and Justified in the Spirit.[4] Spirituality and Social Liberation is a study of Johann (1805–1880) and Christoph (1842–1919) Blumhardt, whose spirituality and theology of the kingdom of God Macchia mines for their relevance to contemporary evangelical theology. Baptized in the Spirit is an articulation of a small-scale pneumatological theology, addressing primarily ecclesiology and soteriology, whose point of orientation is a revised sense of the pentecostal *locus* of baptism in the Holy Spirit. *Justified in the Spirit* is Macchia's detailed pneumatological account of the doctrine of justification in conversation with Roman Catholic, Protestant, and various ecumenical perspectives.

I demonstrate that Macchia sets the whole of his theology against the background of the kingdom of God. Specifically, I trace the place of the kingdom of God in Macchia's theology, with particular attention to three chronological stages of his attention to pneumatology: (1) to an aspect of pneumatology itself (glossolalia), (2) to a pneumatological account of justification, and (3) to pneumatology as an organizing principle for the whole of systematic theology. Along the way, I will demonstrate that the kingdom of God is the most consistent theme in Macchia's theology and that it reaches extensive integration with pneumatology in *Baptized in the Spirit*.

A THEOLOGY OF THE KINGDOM OF GOD

In the concluding chapter of *Spirituality and Social Liberation* (1993), Macchia traces some implications of the Blumhardts' theology of the kingdom of God for evangelical theology.[5] He states that pentecostal eschatology is primarily apocalyptic, that is, marked by the expectation that the kingdom will come from beyond the world and is not present before the eschaton. Such an eschatology, Macchia writes, undermines the kingdom of God's witness to human social existence. The Blumhardts, however, represent a prophetic eschatology, marked by the belief that the kingdom has already dawned—but not been fulfilled—in history and manifested in the healing of the sick and liberation of the poor.[6] He feels that these emphases address the logical contradiction between pentecostals' strong devotion to God's renewal of *individuals* (such as through divine healing) and their frequent neglect of God's interest in the *corporate* realms of human life (such as through social activism). Through their insistence that the kingdom has begun and at the same time is always in the future, the Blumhardts offer pentecostals a model for social liberation that holds together the penultimate and ultimate dimensions of eschatology.[7]

In addition to the tensions between the penultimate and the ultimate, Macchia states, Christoph Blumhardt's balance of the natural and the supernatural could also encourage pentecostals to consider, for example, the cooperative healing activities of things like technological advancements in modern medicine with spiritual practices like prayer. After all, there is more to the miraculous than the merely unexplainable. Also, the balance might encourage evangelicals to broaden their sense of social action beyond prayer and faith only, for there does not have to be a contradiction between prayer for social renewal and concrete involvement in political activity. In short, pentecostals could harness their interest in the miraculous to fight for liberation amid dehumanization and oppression.[8]

A THEOLOGY OF GLOSSOLALIA

In the 1990s, Macchia develops a theology of glossolalia in a series of essays, the chronology of which demonstrates a thematic progression from the relationship between glossolalia and divine presence, to the sacramental quality of glossolalia, to glossolalia and "initial evidence."[9] His accounts constitute the most thorough, coherent, and constructive theology of glossolalia by a pentecostal to date.[10] In "Sighs Too Deep for Words" (1992), Macchia rightly observes that the majority of scholarly treatments of glossolalia, have been offered either from exegetical, historical, psychological, and sociological perspectives, or, from nonpentecostal, theological perspectives.[11] Desiring to fill this void with a *theological* account from *within* the pentecostal tradition, Macchia focuses on the category of theophany in relation to glossolalia, rather than on the abiding concern with glossolalia as initial evidence and its relationship to baptism in the Holy Spirit. Macchia attributes the perennial pentecostal emphasis on initial evidence to factors such as early twentieth-century revivalism's interest in the restoration of signs and wonders coupled with the period's quest for empirical verification of genuine religious experiences, and he argues that the logic of initial evidence has been based all along on the assumption—even if unexpressed—that glossolalia involves an encounter with the divine presence that can be described as "theophanic." That is, glossolalia is characterized by God's spontaneous and dramatic self-disclosure. The pentecostal emphasis, then, has not been on glossolalia per se but on the intensification of divine presence that it represents. Macchia intends to develop a theology of glossolalia that elaborates on the implications of glossolalia's theophanic quality, the dimension most strikingly absent from the few nonpentecostal, theological accounts. He also hopes that a theology of glossolalia will encourage pentecostals to better understanding one of their most distinctive views about religious experience in order to establish a stronger connection between academic theology and charismatic experience.[12]

For Macchia, part of the basis of this theophanic quality is the continuity between Pentecost and Old Testament theophanies, especially Sinai. The theophany of Pentecost is explained by evoking the imagery of fire and smoke from Sinai within the context of the last days outpouring of the Spirit of the Lord (Exod 19:18ff; Joel 2:28–32; Acts 2:17–21). This makes Pentecost, according to Macchia, an explicitly eschatological theophany that inaugurates the final theophany of God that will come in the *parousia*.[13] Glossolalia becomes the sign of this eschatological theophany because at Pentecost God's self-disclosure took up and transformed human language. Pentecost is truly a *"kairos* event" in which God decisively enters the historical process and introduces something new into it. Likewise, glossolalia is a continuing reminder of the Spirit's ability to confront humans in dramatic ways that broaden their horizons and change their outlooks. Interpreting Paul's mention of the Spirit's intercession through sighs too deep for words as a reference to glossolalia (Rom 8:26), Macchia underscores the possibility of Christians finding in glossolalia the encouragement to "sigh" with all of creation for redemption, because glossolalia embodies elements of both transcendence and human frailty. Macchia further establishes glossolalia's association with human limitation on the basis of Paul's comments that glossolalia operates in a period in which humans know only in part and will cease when the perfect comes and humans know as they are known (I Cor 13:12).[14] As an experience of eschatological power and at the same time human limitation, glossolalia affirms transcendence and invites engagement with finite historical particularities.[15]

Macchia's association of glossolalia with theophany and the notion of *kairos* events as well as with both human strength and weakness leads to a discussion of glossolalia in relation to the communion of saints, a theology of the cross, and the new creation. The association also results in an invitation for Christians to seek human liberation along a number of fronts.[16] First, in light of the communion of saints, glossolalia is primarily a corporate experience.[17] While pentecostals tend to associate glossolalia in particular with fullness of the Spirit, Macchia observes Paul's pattern in I Corinthians 12–14 of affirming the significance of glossolalia, while relativizing it in comparison with other spiritual gifts (such as prophecy) and relativizing all spiritual gifts to the perfection of divine love. Macchia contends that if this pattern is taken seriously, fullness of the Spirit should not be connected exclusively to glossolalia but must be broadened to embrace other spiritual gifts as well. This demonstrates the importance of the communion of the saints, for fullness of the Spirit is dependent on spiritual *koinonia*, since no single believer possesses all spiritual gifts.[18] Further, Macchia states that in Acts glossolalia is accompanied by the creation of community through the removal of barriers between rich and poor, Jew and Gentile, and Jesus' followers and John the Baptist's followers (Acts 2, 10, and

19, respectively). He concludes that glossolalia creates Christian community precisely as

> a mystery that cuts through differences of gender, class and culture to reveal a solidarity that is essential to our very being and that is revealed to us in God's own self-disclosure. [Glossolalia] is the lowest common denominator between people who might be very different from one another, revealing a deep sense of equality that cannot be denied and that challenges any discrimination based on gender, class, or race.[19]

Second, glossolalia is inextricably connected to a theology of the cross because it is Jesus' death and resurrection that makes Pentecost an *eschatological* theophany rather than merely one more theophany in a succession. Jesus' death and resurrection are his ultimate expressions of his liberating work "for us." In light of this christological qualification, glossolalia should prompt believers to seek justice "for others." The sighs of glossolalia, when they express self-surrender and abandonment to the redemption of creation, share in Jesus' groaning and suffering on the cross for the whole world.[20]

Third, these acts of liberation for oppressed sisters and brothers take place within the context of the new creation. As the remaking of human language, Pentecost and glossolalia point to the remaking of all things. Glossolalia truly serves as the "initial physical evidence" that the new creation is already under way, at least when it promotes liberating social and ecological action.[21]

In "Tongues as a Sign" (1993), Macchia returns to the idea of glossolalia as theophany and argues that one of the implications of seeing the phenomenon as an intensification of divine presence is acknowledging that glossolalia functions "sacramentally." He says that most pentecostals have tended to resist the category "sacrament" due to their fear of institutionalizing God's Spirit and grace, but they may be able to find common ground with recent Roman Catholic theologies that articulate the efficacy of the sacraments in that they also convey that which they signify. According to Macchia, understanding glossolalia as a sacramental sign that makes present the very empowerment for eschatological mission to which it points gives due respect to the Spirit's freedom, without naively dismissing the Roman Catholic sacramental tradition due to the misunderstanding that it involves a "material causation necessitated by the elements as elements."[22]

Glossolalia's sacramental quality lies in the fact that human utterance realizes God's presence. The upshot for Macchia is that glossolalia—as oral/aural speech frequently accompanied by visible demonstrations and reactions—has more of a sacramental than an evidential relationship to baptism in the Holy Spirit. That is, as an empirical sign, glossolalia is a medium through which believers encounter God's presence analogously to the way they encounter God's presence through the water of baptism or the bread and wine of the Lord's supper. While initial evidence is to be affirmed to the extent that it is based on the insightful discernment of a close relationship between glossolalia and baptism in the Holy Spirit, its emphasis on glossolalia as "proof" of fullness of the Spirit neither exhausts the theological significance of their relationship nor gives accurate account of how glossolalia actually functions for pentecostals, namely, as a means of participating in God's self-disclosure through a medium stemming from the *kairos* event of Pentecost. It must be understood that Macchia is not only offering a constructive argument for how glossolalia *should* function for pentecostals but also a descriptive account of how glossolalia *already* functions for most of them, even if the fundamental logic of the relationship between glossolalia and baptism in the Holy Spirit remains entirely implicit, is glossed as "initial evidence," and is almost always accompanied by an explicit rejection of the category "sacrament."[23] In "Is Footwashing the Neglected Sacrament?" (1997), Macchia contends that glossolalia (along with footwashing and the laying on of hands for healing) constitutes part of a sacramental tradition within pentecostalism because it is an empirical medium through which believers encounter God. While pentecostals frequently *experience* baptism and the Lord's supper as occasions for divine encounter, they *theologize* them as "ordinances" that simply express the participant's repentance and obedience rather than as sacraments that convey the divine presence.[24] In this respect, he notes, pentecostals' theology of the sacraments needs to "catch up" with their experience of them.[25]

In "Groans Too Deep for Words" (1998), Macchia focuses specifically on a theology of initial evidence per se, which so far he had addressed only tangentially to his accounts of theophany and sacrament, and primarily descriptively rather than constructively.[26] He claims that the relative neglect of critical theological reflection on initial evidence, in addition to the predominance of primarily biblical and historical literature, is due also in part to the fact that theological discussions of it within the pentecostal tradition either narrowly defend initial evidence in polemical style or simply admit embarrassment over the doctrine's inadequacies. According to Macchia, the perennial need is for pentecostals to offer a more profound theology of the special relationship between glossolalia and baptism in the Holy Spirit, especially in light of criticisms of initial evidence from outside the pentecostal tradition.[27]

Macchia believes that part of the misguidance of the efforts to establish the initial evidence doctrine lies in the polemical approaches' preoccupation with the number of times Acts mentions glossolalia, instead of sufficient sensitivity to how glossolalia functions and what theological meaning it carries when it is mentioned. Glossolalia functions, he claims, as a sign of crossing boundaries among Diaspora Jews at Pentecost and between Jews and Gentiles later in Acts.[28] Therefore, while initial evidence lies beyond the scope of concern in Acts itself, it is at least based on a legitimate emphasis on the importance of glossolalia in Acts, an importance Macchia points out is acknowledged even by many nonpentecostal scholars who oppose initial evidence as a viable contemporary theological formulation. By emphasizing the connection between glossolalia and baptism in the Holy Spirit, initial evidence points to the heart of baptism in the Holy Spirit, which Macchia defines as encouragement for social engagement.[29] Glossolalia empowers believers to groan with creation in anticipation of ultimate redemption. It also has the potential to move them out of their comfort zones to take up the cause of the powerless and victims of injustice.[30] Thus, Macchia's theology of glossolalia continues his earlier concerns for liberation and social renewal in light of the dawning of the kingdom of God.

PNEUMATOLOGY AND JUSTIFICATION

Beginning with his presidential address to the Society for Pentecostal Studies in 2000, Macchia focuses on one of the mainstays of Protestant soteriology—justification by faith—particularly as it relates to pneumatology.[31] While Macchia's theology of glossolalia is an attempt to broaden the parameters of an aspect of traditional pentecostal *pneumatology itself*, this investigation into the doctrine of justification is his earliest explicit consideration of *pneumatology's potential* for broadening another *locus* of theology. According to Macchia, the benefits of a more thoroughly pneumatological account of justification include implications not only for the doctrine of justification itself but also for the church's mission.

Macchia claims that theological descriptions of justification too often suffer from two basic limitations. First, they contain an anthropocentric restriction of the Spirit's role merely to assisting the human expression of faith in response to God's initiative of declaring the forgiveness of sins, that is, to appropriating subjectively to individuals the objective work of justification accomplished for them by Jesus' death. Second, they reduce justification to God's forensic declaration of the forgiveness of sins, thereby overlooking the need for the redemption of all of creation.[32] Macchia's own conceptual starting point for justification is its intersection with resurrection and pneumatology, based on texts from Romans affirming that Jesus' resurrection was both *for* our justification (4:25) and *by* the Holy Spirit (8:11).[33] These texts, he argues, suggest a fundamental work of the Spirit in justification that goes beyond simply applying Jesus' work on the cross and that involves more than only anthropological-soteriological dimensions, inasmuch as Jesus' resurrection has cosmic effects that supersede human salvation without precluding it.[34]

At the heart of these concerns lies Macchia's attempt to associate justification with God's acts of redemptive justice rather than with punitive justice.[35] Redemptive justice is an expression of God's saving righteousness, not punishment. The Old Testament attests to these redemptive acts as God's acts of deliverance to bring justice to the oppressed. These saving acts provide the context for understanding Jesus' resurrection as God's definitive saving act, which the Spirit accomplishes. Jesus' resurrection by the Spirit brings deliverance from sin and death, reconciliation between God and humans, hope for the oppressed and oppressors, and justice for the entire created order in the form of new creation. Jesus' resurrection is also the template of our own justification by the Spirit, for the same Spirit who raised Jesus will also give life to our mortal bodies (Rom 8:11). Macchia summarizes,

> The Spirit's work in the justified new creation inaugurated in Jesus' life, death, and resurrection will one day be realized in the resurrection of the just and the new heavens and new earth. . . . Jesus was the justified Son of God precisely as the Person of the Spirit, a justification that was fulfilled in his resurrection, and . . . we are justified in him as bearers of the Spirit, an experience that will culminate in our resurrection. The Pauline texts to which I have just referred suggest that the work of the Spirit in Christ is at the very basis of justification.[36]

Rather than simply applying Jesus' objective work of justification, the Spirit will eventually reproduce in us the same work the Spirit performed in Jesus at his resurrection. While ultimate justification—which Macchia envisions *as* resurrection—awaits the eschaton, our reception of the Spirit allows us to experience justification as ours already in faith. The life that the Spirit poured out on creation in Jesus' resurrection, which is the first fruits of the new creation and the basis of righteousness reckoned by faith.

Beyond the immediate scope of justification itself, Macchia states, a pneumatological orientation to the doctrine has implications for Christian ethics. The Spirit's preparation of humans for ultimate justification is, in the end, preparation for resurrection. It is precisely this preparatory work of the Spirit in which the church carries out its mission to the world by resisting forces such as racism and sexism that oppress God's creation.[37] Macchia criticizes the *Joint Declaration on the Doctrine of Justification* (1999) because he feels that it lacks a necessary pneumatological basis and is, therefore, unable to transcend a limited focus on justification as individual renewal, in spite of recent openness in both Roman Catholic and Protestant theological traditions to pneumatology's importance. This pneumatological deficit, he states, leaves doubt about whether one can establish a conceptual basis between justification as declared righteousness and justification as righteousness that renews the individual in a way that points to the transformation of all of creation, not just humans.[38] Macchia feels that, on the whole, the document adequately negotiates the sixteenth-century tensions and disagreements between the two traditions but that the doctrine of justification requires far more constructive theological work that is unbound by such presuppositions if it is to realize its potential influence for establishing justice for creation in preparation for the new creation.[39]

In *Baptized in the Spirit* (2006), Macchia describes a shift in his own thought to associating justification—which he calls "Spirit-baptized justification"— more explicitly with the kingdom of God, an association only implicit in earlier essays. This association stems largely from Macchia's situating the kingdom of God within the context of pneumatology by emphasizing Jesus as the one who both inaugurates the kingdom and baptizes in the Holy Spirit. In this light, Macchia states, justification and sanctification are overlapping metaphors for the Spirit's preparatory work of making creation into God's dwelling place.[40] Justification, then, cannot be distinguished from sanctification by associating the Spirit's work exclusively with the latter. Instead, sanctification, stemming from Jesus' resurrection by the Spirit, is the means by which the Spirit achieves ultimate justification. The righteousness of Christ is truly the life of the Spirit, and we receive the kingdom of God and its righteousness through the Spirit's liberating and renewing presence.[41]

Macchia begins to associate justification more closely and explicitly with the kingdom of God also due to his reading of Jürgen Moltmann's essay describing his own conceptual shift from an emphasis on justification to the kingdom, a shift that parallels Moltmann's shift to giving more attention to the Gospels' soteriology rather than restrictively focusing on Paul's.[42] Macchia clarifies that his own intention is not to shift *from* justification *to* the kingdom per se, as Moltmann suggests, but a shift in justification's meaning in the light of the kingdom of God, which itself is inaugurated by the Spirit in Jesus' life, death, and resurrection, and in Pentecost. Similarly, instead of shifting from Paul to the Gospels, Macchia prefers to read

Paul in light of an apocalyptic understanding of the gospel that is compatible with the Gospels' portrayal of the kingdom of God.[43]

In addition to giving insight into Macchia's notion of justification, this latter point about Paul and the Gospels is part of a larger interpretive method related to canonical criticism. Specifically, he finds the canonical placement of Luke-Acts, John, and Romans significant for understanding justification. John's positioning after Luke nuances Luke's witness to the kingdom by giving it greater depth and breadth by which the reader can understand Luke's fulfillment in Acts and Romans. Macchia acknowledges the use of this interpretive method to develop justification within the context of pneumatology and of the kingdom. The method also informs his construal of baptism in the Holy Spirit in general, which is the background of his discussion of justification in *Baptized in the Spirit*. Seeking to overcome pentecostals' traditional reliance on Luke-Acts alone for their understandings of baptism in the Holy Spirit, Macchia wishes to integrate Luke-Acts with Paul and other canonical voices in order to broaden them.[44] An integrated account of baptism in the Holy Spirit, he says, unites God's sanctifying grace with the inauguration of the kingdom in power, a framework that is implied in Luke and explicit in Matthew, Paul, and John. Indeed, such integration is part of systematic theology's task.[45]

For Macchia, a pneumatological approach to justification ultimately means a trinitarian approach to it.[46] Macchia sees promise in Robert Jenson's proposed trinitarian framework for justification that addresses the Father's self-justification/vindication as creator and God of Israel, the Son's work of justification on our behalf, and the Spirit's work in us to bring about righteousness unto new life. In response, Macchia asks how these three elements converge in the story of Jesus as the man of the Spirit and in the new creation in which righteousness will dwell. To take up this question, he defines the righteousness of justification as "kingdom righteousness," the righteousness that the Spirit inspired through Christ's work of fulfilling the Father's will.[47] Macchia then suggests three dimensions to understanding the righteousness of the kingdom as inaugurated by baptism in the Holy Spirit: first, the Father's bestowal of the Spirit on the Son through conception, baptism, and resurrection; second, the Son's return of devotion to the Father as the man of the Spirit and the incarnate Son who opens the bond of love between Father and Son by dying on the cross and by baptizing in the Holy Spirit; and third, creation's participation in the Spirit through liberating signs of renewal and through the empowerment in daily life attested by love for God and neighbor.[48] This trinitarian structure indicates that baptism in the Holy Spirit is ultimately baptism into divine love, for the Spirit is poured out from the Father who gave the Son and from the Son who gave himself. Seen as participation in the holy love that the Spirit mediates between Father and Son, baptism in the Holy Spirit integrates the Spirit's sanctifying and empowering works.[49] This structure delineates baptism in the Holy Spirit as a trinitarian reality that extends the Father's and Son's reign to all of creation through the Spirit's indwelling. The Spirit is the kingdom that transforms creation, and Christ is its king.[50] Thus, Macchia's theology of justification continues his thematic emphasis on the kingdom of God, specifically within a trinitarian framework.

TOWARD A PNEUMATOLOGICAL THEOLOGY

While in these earlier essays Macchia discusses pneumatology's potential for broadening justification, in *Baptized in the Spirit* (2006) he takes a significant initial step toward developing an entire Christian theology shaped by pneumatology.[51] After broadening the metaphor "baptism in the Holy Spirit" itself, Macchia turns to pneumatology's implications for soteriology, the church, the kingdom, and ethics. He offers all of this in pursuit of a global pentecostal theology.

Baptism in the Holy Spirit as Theology's Organizing Principle

Macchia maintains that although baptism in the Holy Spirit is the "crown jewel" of pentecostal distinctives, it has been widely neglected in recent pentecostal scholarship. He gives four reasons for this recent neglect, including (1) fruits of the late nineteenth- and early twentieth-centuries shift of emphasis from sanctification to baptism in the Holy Spirit, resulting in the conceptual separation of the two, as well as the historical scholarship elucidating this shift; (2) an increased awareness of the diverse social and cultural instantiations of pentecostalism in both its early history and the contemporary global setting, which raises the question of whether the tradition possesses a single central distinctive; (3) a shift of emphasis to eschatology to the neglect of baptism in the Holy Spirit; and (4) a shift among some scholars studying pentecostalism from material theological content per se to theological method.[52] These four reasons are important not only because they justify Macchia's claim that a "return" to baptism in the Holy Spirit is needed in pentecostal systematic theology, but because they frame much of Macchia's account of baptism in the Holy Spirit as the organizing principle of theology. He addresses each of these four reasons, either explicitly or implicitly, by crafting a theology of baptism in the Holy Spirit that (1) resists the separation between sanctification and charismatic empowerment by serving as a soteriological metaphor that includes justification, sanctification, and charismatic gifts; (2) acknowledges the pentecostal tradition's many diversities, while maintaining that there is a single central distinctive; (3) resists a hard shift to eschatology by adopting eschatology as part of its setting and horizon; and (4) serves as systematic theology's operating methodological principle, precisely as the pentecostal tradition's chief doctrinal distinctive.[53]

While Macchia considers his emphasis on baptism in the Holy Spirit a return to pentecostalism's central theological distinctive, he does not return to it without modification. Stated succinctly, he attempts to set baptism in the Holy Spirit within the larger framework of pneumatology itself, something he contends pentecostals have never done, in spite of their perennial concern with the Holy Spirit. Instead, they narrowly associate baptism in the Holy Spirit with empowerment for mission, based almost exclusively on their reading of Acts. While pentecostals may have discerned correctly that the pneumatology of Acts has a primarily missiological and charismatic rather than soteriological thrust, Macchia states, an account of baptism in the Holy Spirit that integrates the missiological and charismatic with the soteriological must be sought by consulting Paul and other canonical voices in addition to Acts. The gain of such integration includes a notion of baptism in the Holy Spirit that is thoroughly eschatological and is broad enough to encompass the entire Christian life in the Spirit, not only its charismatic elements.[54]

The Church and the Kingdom

Macchia articulates a number of baptism in the Holy Spirit's implications for the church and the kingdom, including their nature and relationship to each other. Macchia observes that ecumenical debates over baptism in the Holy Spirit have usually focused on its relationship to Christian initiation.[55] Seen as part of the means by which Jesus inaugurates the kingdom, however, baptism in the Holy Spirit defies exclusive restriction to this ecclesiological realm. While ecclesiology rightly counters the reduction of baptism in the Holy Spirit to the personal renewal of individuals, it frequently limits theological discussion to the perspectives of ecclesiologies that vary in their respective emphases on scripture, sacraments, or charismatic gifts. To move beyond the impasse of ecclesiologically based disputes about Christian initiation, Macchia suggests that the kingdom, which both includes and transcends the church, is a more appropriate context for understanding baptism in the Holy Spirit than the church per se.[56] In Matthew 3, John calls for repentance because of the kingdom's nearness and states that Jesus will baptize in the Holy Spirit. Such close association between these two proclamations, Macchia states, gives baptism in the Holy Spirit a broadly eschatological framework that no single ecclesiology and accompanying account of Christian initiation can exhaust. Baptism in the Holy Spirit inaugurates the kingdom and, therefore, transcends the church.[57]

With this formulation, Macchia attempts to avoid the two extremes of dichotomizing the church and the kingdom and identifying them. While the first is an unwarranted dualism, the second may breed "realized eschatology." This dialectic in the church is an acknowledgment of both the "no" of the church's unfaithfulness to God and the "yes" of God's sustaining grace and the Spirit's presence. Because of this dynamic between "no" and "yes," the church must always look forward to its eschatological fulfillment in the fullness of the kingdom. Although the church points to the kingdom as its unique and irreplaceable sign, it is not the kingdom itself. Macchia argues further that calling the church "Spirit-baptized" implies a logical priority of Christ, Spirit, and kingdom over the church. Baptism in the Holy Spirit gives birth to the church, not vice versa; therefore, it constitutes and transcends the church. Christ, Spirit, and kingdom determine the church's eschatological journey.[58]

Macchia also addresses the classical marks of the church—unity, holiness, catholicity, apostolicity—as he envisions them within a Spirit-baptized ecclesiology. He underscores the fact that they are first marks of the kingdom—and therefore not yet fully realized—in which the church partially participates by the Spirit's presence. As marks of the kingdom, no single church communion can claim them exclusively. And as products of the Spirit's presence, local church bodies bear the marks just as the universal church does.[59] In the case of each mark, Macchia shapes his discussion in light of pneumatology. For example, rather than basing the church's unity on the episcopacy, Macchia grounds it in baptism in the Holy Spirit, through which the church is gathered to the Father who sent both the Son and the Spirit to inaugurate the kingdom. Respect for diversity and desire for visible forms of unity in worship and sacraments characterize the kingdom's unity. Holiness is also a result of the Spirit's work in the church, for those baptized in the Spirit are filled with the presence of a God who is holy love.[60]

Most interesting is Macchia's account of catholicity, especially in light of some of his comments on apostolicity. Reflecting first on the universal church, Macchia writes,

I believe . . . that there is historical validity to the "mother church" idea. The Roman Catholic Church has a certain "parental" role in the family tree of the Christian church in the world. Simply seeking to rediscover the church of Pentecost in the latter rain of the Spirit in a way that ignores this history is unwarranted in my view. We cannot simply live in the biblical narrative as though hundreds of years of church tradition had not transpired. The family of God has a history that cannot be ignored.[61]

Here, Macchia challenges an extreme example of pentecostalism's restorationist impulse, which sometimes dismisses the universal church's history and theological tradition in its attempt to recapture the gifts, practices, and spiritual manifestations found in Acts. While Macchia believes that pentecostals' affirmation of the fullness of charismatic gifts accompanying the Spirit's universal presence captures a certain qualitative dimension of catholicity, he argues that they should develop a greater sense of dependence on and appreciation for the Roman Catholic Church's parental role. At the same time, he clarifies, pentecostals should not uncritically accept its parental role because historical terms alone do not establish catholicity. He writes,

Suffice it to say here that the "mother" Catholic Church belongs herself to a heritage in the outpouring of the Spirit to which she is accountable as any of us and on which she can . . . lay no privileged claim. We as her children and grandchildren respect her role in history in passing on to us a precious heritage in the form of witness. *But our reception of this witness draws us to the same source from which she has received it and must continue to receive it.* . . . From an eschatological perspective, we were born from above, from the Spirit, just as she was and is. . . . In a sense, all Christian communions were born from Pentecost directly and not indirectly, for Pentecost and Spirit baptism are not simply a one-time event now channeled historically through the narrow portals of an apostolic office. . . . Catholicity is consequently polycentric, subsisting within all of the world communions by virtue of the presence of the Spirit.[62]

These statements qualify the degree of pentecostals' dependence on the Roman Catholic Church's witness and proclamation by stressing that all Christian communions stem directly from, and are therefore equally dependent on, baptism in the Holy Spirit. The one catholic church's universality arises from the Spirit's universal presence.

Macchia's comments on apostolicity further qualify his comments on catholicity. He rejects the notions of either a succession or restoration of apostolic ministry as originally commissioned by Jesus and affirms instead certain ministries of oversight given by the Spirit under submission to the original apostolic witness. The critical dialectic between church and kingdom precludes the transference of power from Jesus to any human figure in the church. Rather, baptism in the Holy Spirit makes apostolicity a missionary activity for which all Christians are responsible and grants the ministry of deliverance to all Christians.[63]

Christ and the Kingdom

As mentioned previously, Macchia situates the kingdom of God within the larger context of pneumatology due to Jesus' joint role as inaugurator of the kingdom and as Spirit-baptizer. He suggests that baptism in the Holy Spirit is not only pentecostalism's chief distinctive but is also implicitly foundational for the early church's confession of Jesus' lordship. Contending that the resurrection per se is insufficient for concluding that the Son is preexistent and *homoousios* with the Father, Macchia appeals to the goal of the resurrection, namely, becoming the Spirit-baptizer, as part of the early church's reasoning process for concluding that the Son is God.[64] The Son imparts the Spirit, something only God can do. Macchia suggests that a greater appreciation of baptism in the Holy Spirit in the contemporary global church might encourage further appreciation of this neglected element of the early church's confession of Jesus.[65]

According to Macchia, baptism in the Holy Spirit also attests to the particularity of Jesus, the kingdom he inaugurates, and the church as a sign of the kingdom. It delineates Jesus as the unique Spirit-baptizer and inaugurator of the kingdom. Likewise, the church and the kingdom to which the church points are marked as the unique communities that the Son creates by baptizing in the Holy Spirit. Baptism in the Holy Spirit, then, not only demonstrates the Son's unity with the Father but also resists religious pluralism by affirming the particularity of Jesus, the kingdom, and the church. For Macchia, the understanding of Jesus as the unique Spirit-baptizer is an indispensable part of the gospel, and those who fail to acknowledge him as such may also overlook the continuity between the kingdom and the church, thus diminishing Jesus' and the church's particularity.[66]

INFLUENCES AND CONTINUITIES

Most obvious among the influences on Macchia are Johann and Christoph Blumhardt, from whom Macchia first adopts the theology of the kingdom of God that can be traced throughout his works. The Blumhardts' influence is most explicit, of course, in the final chapter of *Spirituality and Social Liberation*, in which Macchia brings them into conversation with evangelical and pentecostal theology. Nonetheless, Macchia's concern for social justice, as derived in part from the Blumhardts, is present also in his development of glossolalia as an impetus for social engagement, in his close connection between righteousness/justification and justice, and in his notion of baptism in the Holy Spirit as the inauguration of the kingdom that will fill the earth with all righteousness. Also taken in part from the Blumhardts is Macchia's determination not to reduce the kingdom to the church, a theme prominent in the last chapter of *Spirituality and Social Liberation* and also integral to the basic relational structure among baptism in the Holy Spirit, the church, and the kingdom in *Baptized in the Spirit*. Jan Milič Lochman's idea of the Holy Spirit as dialectician between the church and the kingdom is an additional influence on this latter point.[67]

Karl Barth and Jürgen Moltmann, especially with respect to the relationship of their theologies to each other, are also significant influences on Macchia.[68] Macchia's insistence on maintaining divine freedom and sovereignty in part prompts his concern not to conflate the church with the kingdom.[69] He expresses this concern poignantly in a review of Jürgen Moltmann's *The Spirit of Life*, in which Moltmann speaks of God's indwelling all things in terms of God's "immanent transcendence."[70] While praising Moltmann's attempt to affirm both God's immanence and transcendence, Macchia feels that Moltmann underestimates divine transcendence and rejects God's otherness.[71] Macchia responds with Barth's language of God as wholly other, although clarifying that for pentecostals (and for Barth himself) this does not preclude God's ability to confront and apprehend humans in history. Pentecostals need not polarize immanence and transcendence, as Macchia feels Moltmann does.[72]

Barth's influence on Macchia is enduring, surfacing in *Baptized in the Spirit* with respect to issues ranging from scripture to justification, as well as to the implications of God's freedom for the relationship between the church and the kingdom. Indeed, Barth's pondering the possibility of a theology of the third article partially frames Macchia's very idea of a pneumatological pentecostal theology.[73] While Macchia does not turn away from Barth's theology, he seems to grow more sympathetic to Moltmann's theology, including some of the ideas about immanence and transcendence that he criticized in his earlier review of *The Spirit of Life*. While a concern for God's transcendence is certainly still present, Macchia is now able to speak repeatedly of baptism in the Holy Spirit as the means by which creation becomes God's ultimate dwelling place, almost the exact language Moltmann employs to describe God's immanent transcendence in *The*

Spirit of Life.[74] While this does not merit speaking of a shift in Macchia's thought per se—concern for both immanence and transcendence is present throughout—it seems that, at very least, by the publication of *Baptized in the Spirit* (2006) Macchia finds in Moltmann's *The Spirit of Life* certain helpful pneumatological elements that he did not find as helpful in his earlier review of it (1994).[75]

Paul Tillich is a final significant influence on Macchia. His primary interaction with Tillich comes in relation to the idea of the sacramental and glossolalia, which includes Macchia's incorporation of Tillich's notions of the relationship between "structure and ecstasy" and of his "realistic" interpretation of sacramental elements.[76] Discussing the Spiritual Presence in his *Systematic Theology*, Tillich contends that ecstasy does not negate structure, either of the human spirit or of the Spiritual Community. He states that Paul's doctrine of the Spirit, especially as found in I Corinthians, is a classical expression of unity between ecstasy and structure. There, Paul emphasizes the ecstatic dimensions of experiencing the Spiritual Presence, but insists that they be subject to *agape* and *gnosis*. He encourages various *charismata*, especially glossolalia, to the extent that they do not lead to chaos. According to Tillich, the Christian church sometimes fails to replicate such unity between ecstasy and structure, whether in the form of the Roman Catholic tendency to supplant *charismata* with office (what he calls the "profanization of the Spirit") or in the form of the Protestant tendency to replace ecstasy with doctrine or moral structure (what he calls the "profanization of contemporary Protestantism"). For Tillich, the Pauline approach resists both of these tendencies, inasmuch as it provides structure within which ecstasy can operate rather than equating ecstasy with chaos and attempting to smother it.[77]

In an essay entitled "Nature and Sacrament" in *The Protestant Era*, Tillich adopts a "realistic"—as opposed to a "symbolic-metaphoric" or "ritualistic"—interpretation of the nature of sacramental elements. According to the realistic interpretation, there is a *necessary* rather than *arbitrary* relationship between the sacraments and their respective elements. Water, in baptism, and the bread and the wine, in the Lord's supper, have natural powers that suit them to be elements in those sacraments. This realistic interpretation of the elements, Tillich says, assumes an interpretation of nature that he calls "a new realism." To this notion of realism, Tillich adds an insistence that sacraments exist within the context of the concrete history of salvation. Tillich writes,

> Any sacramental reality within the framework of Christianity and of Protestantism must be related to the new being in Christ. No Protestant criticism would be

conceivable in which this foundation was denied. But if the presence of the holy is the presupposition of any religious reality and any church, including the Protestant churches, then it follows that the interpretation of nature in sacramental terms is also a presupposition of Protestantism, for there is no being that does not have its basis in nature.[78]

For Tillich, it is only within the context of salvation history that nature can become sacramental elements, thereby bearing transcendent power.

These theological themes surface, usually with explicit references to Tillich, in Macchia's works on glossolalia. Pentecost is a theophany, a moment of divine self-disclosure. Likewise, the recurring practice of glossolalia among pentecostals has similar theophanic significance. Glossolalia, as frail and broken human speech, becomes a medium through which the intensity of the divine presence, namely the Holy Spirit, is experienced. Glossolalia, then, is a symbol that participates in and conveys the divine presence. Without dismissing the possible benefit of a reformulated variation of initial evidence, Macchia argues that in spite of pentecostals' endless *theologizing* about glossolalia along these lines, it actually *functions* for them as theophany, as a *kairos* event. To use Macchia's terms, glossolalia has a far greater *sacramental* quality, inasmuch as it conveys the divine presence, than *evidential* quality, in the sense of serving as empirical proof.

While Macchia undermines certain aspects of the traditional formulation of initial evidence, he believes that the doctrine, nonetheless, speaks to the integral logical connection between glossolalia and baptism in the Holy Spirit, a connection he affirms and wishes to maintain. Glossolalia is not simply one sign among other spiritual gifts that also function as signs, as some charismatic Protestants and Roman Catholics maintain; rather, glossolalia has the place of primacy because it demonstrates like no other spiritual gift or form of ecstatic speech the inability of *any* human speech to communicate exhaustively the depths of the human encounter with the divine. According to Macchia, glossolalia is an unclassifiable, free speech in response to an unclassifiable, free God. It is the language of the *imago Dei*. The closer one draws to the divine presence, the more urgent and more difficult expression becomes. This is not to say, of course, that the divine presence is identical with the medium itself, but that glossolalia truly is a symbol in the sense that it conveys that in which it participates.[79]

In short, Macchia frames his entire discussion of glossolalia with Tillich's concern that ecstasy and structure remain united. Glossolalia is indeed a free and ecstatic expression in which the divine presence grasps the speaker. At the same time, however, because of its sacramental quality, it is also a structured expression. Glossolalia upholds the concern for the freedom of the Spirit that would resist the objectification of the divine presence in visible forms. At the same time, it also affirms the legitimacy of the divine self-disclosure through natural elements, specifically oral and aural symbols of speech. Because glossolalia is both free and sacramental, it is both ecstatic and structured. Furthermore, by insisting on the *necessary* relationship between glossolalia and baptism in the Holy Spirit, Macchia shifts from the traditional pentecostal account of glossolalia as a *sign* that points away from itself to another more significant reality to glossolalia as a *symbol* that also conveys the divine presence through theophany.[80]

ASSESSMENT

Concerning the strengths of Macchia's theology, first, he assumes that systematic theology involves a constructive element that biblical exegesis, historical study, and social-scientific research do not exhaust, however important each of these may be to systematic theology. This assumption fuels Macchia's early work, which includes the first constructive theology by a pentecostal to address glossolalia in light of a wide number of theological considerations, not simply on the basis of individual texts in Acts and their import for initial evidence.[81] In his work on justification, this assumption surfaces in Macchia's commitment to engage sixteenth-century and following historical debates as well as contemporary theological developments in ecumenism, not only Romans, Galatians, and other relevant New Testament texts.

A second particular strength of Macchia's theology is his mature and critical posture toward ecumenism.[82] First, his description of glossolalia as a symbol of both a visible means of grace and of God's freedom is in part an attempt to transcend the impasse he perceives between Roman Catholic and Reformed theological emphases, respectively. It is still debatable whether pentecostals have historically experienced glossolalia sacramentally as Macchia maintains. Nonetheless, as a constructive formulation of how pentecostals *could* understand it in the future, his account of glossolalia in sacramental terms not only allows pentecostals to enter an ecumenical conversation about tensions between God's grace and freedom but also enables them to challenge both Roman Catholic and Reformed Christians (to keep with Macchia's descriptions) to consider the convergence of divine grace and freedom in glossolalia and other charismatic gifts. This is something those two Christian traditions might not otherwise be required to consider if not in dialogue with pentecostals.[83]

Second, *Baptized in the Spirit* contains several discussions of theological issues within the contexts of their respective formal ecumenical dialogues, such as the relationship between Word and sacrament, Christ's presence in the eucharist, and *koinonia*.[84] Most prominent in the book, however, is, third, Macchia's reformulation of baptism in the Holy Spirit itself, which is motivated in part by a desired ecumenical gain. Surprised that baptism in the Holy Spirit has not received greater ecumenical attention due to the fact that pentecostals and charismatics constitute one of the largest Christian traditions in the world, Macchia feels that it has the greatest potential for shaping an ecumenical pneumatology.[85] He contends that ecumenical progress sometimes requires traditions to accentuate rather than soften their theological distinctives and suggests that pentecostals might have little to offer ecumenical discussions without a distinctive of their own. Therefore, part of the theological task for pentecostals is to develop further their distinctive of baptism in the Holy Spirit in a way that, on the one hand, discourages obsessive preoccupation with distinctives per se to the result of theologically isolating themselves and, on the other, allows them to draw attention to a portion of the biblical witness that other church communions may have neglected. For Macchia, then, pentecostals need to reexamine the crown jewel of their theology for the sake of ecumenism.[86]

Macchia's commitment to ecumenical theology does not render him uncritical of it, however. First, while sympathetic to the need to discuss justification from ecumenical perspectives, he criticizes the *Joint Declaration* for a pneumatological deficiency that renders it incapable of transcending sixteenth-century categories. Second, part of the basic logic of *Baptized in the Spirit* is Macchia's belief that the tendency in ecumenical theology to consider baptism in the Holy Spirit in light of its relationship to Christian initiation has outlived its usefulness.[87] Macchia, therefore, considers it against the background of the kingdom of God rather than against an ecclesiology correlated with a particular view of Christian initiation.

There are, nonetheless, a few areas of Macchia's theology that raise questions and require clarification in future work. I will focus primarily on those associated with *Baptized in the Spirit*. First, Macchia acknowledges the need for pentecostals to resist realized eschatology, and he employs the church-kingdom dialectic in part to assist this effort.[88] Yet, can a soteriology and ecclesiology informed by the metaphor of Christ as the king and the Spirit as the kingdom avoid realized eschatology? It seems that in order to do so, it would need to explain in what sense the Spirit is not yet fully given or to concede that the kingdom has already fully come in the form of the church. Since Macchia rightly rejects the present fullness of the kingdom, the question arises as to whether there is any significant sense in which the gift of the Holy Spirit is outstanding as is the fullness of God's kingdom. While there may be some resources within Macchia's construction of the Spirit's role in our resurrection as ultimate justification that can address an outstanding pneumatological element in soteriology, I am more optimistic about the potential of resisting realized eschatology by orienting the outstanding dimensions of the age to come more closely with christology than with pneumatology. For Paul it is precisely the Spirit who is *already* given to Christians as the guarantee of what they still await (ἀρραβών; II Cor 1:22, 5:5; Eph 1:14). In II Corinthians 5 specifically, Paul calls the Spirit the guarantee "that the mortal will be swallowed up by life" (vv. 4–5). Because of this guarantee, we are confident even while "we are away from the Lord" (v. 6).[89] Just as Jesus' coming inaugurated God's kingdom, his return will usher in its fullness. To wait for the kingdom is to wait for Jesus, for the Spirit is already given as a guarantee of his second coming. While I applaud Macchia's desire to resist realized eschatology, pentecostals should describe the extent to which God's kingdom is outstanding primarily in christological rather than in pneumatological terms.

Second, Macchia will eventually need to give more attention to the significance of Spirit-christology.[90] In *Baptized in the Spirit*, Macchia emphasizes Jesus' impartation of the Spirit more than his reception of it. This decision is consistent with Macchia's desire to set baptism in the Holy Spirit against the background of the kingdom, which Jesus initiates qua Spirit-*baptizer* not qua Spirit-*baptized*, although he is both. However, just as Macchia correctly observes that all four Gospels underscore John's proclamation that Jesus will baptize in the Holy Spirit, all four also note that the Spirit first descends upon him. Matthew's and Luke's birth narratives go even further by attributing Jesus' conception to the Spirit (1:18–20; 1:35). Outside the Gospels, it is through the eternal Spirit that Jesus offers himself unblemished to God (Heb 9:14), and, as Macchia observes in connection with justification, the Spirit raises Jesus from the dead (Rom 8:11). Thus, before Jesus imparts the Spirit, the Spirit conceives and anoints Jesus, is the agency of Jesus' sacrificial offering, and raises Jesus from the dead. While Macchia warns elsewhere that the fivefold gospel is potentially "Christomonistic" on its own,[91] *Baptized in the Spirit* implicitly adopts its christological-pneumatological posture of Jesus *baptizing* in the Holy Spirit only, not *receiving* the Spirit. Like the fivefold gospel, he must address the challenge of incorporating Spirit-christology into a construction that has yet to demonstrate that it can accommodate an emphasis on Jesus' reception of the Spirit.[92] While Macchia's emphasis is understandable within the context of the specific aims of *Baptized in the Spirit*, giving additional attention to *conceptus de Spiritu Sancto* might make more convincing his argument that baptism in the Holy Spirit can be the organizing principle for pentecostal theology.[93]

Third, in *Baptized in the Spirit*, Macchia does not sufficiently engage other pentecostal systematic theologians. For example, Macchia's vision of the relationship between the church and the kingdom contains points of tension with Simon Chan's ecclesiology, in which the kingdom is more the goal toward which the church moves than it is a reality that presently transcends the church.[94] Although Macchia's chapter articulating a "Spirit-baptized ecclesiology" contains limited interaction with Chan, it is replete with citations of Hans Küng.[95] Further, Macchia's lengthy treatment of questions surrounding religious pluralism contains no extensive engagement with Amos Yong's pneumatological theology of religions. I grant that Macchia's preferred dialogue partner, John Hick, serves as an appropriate foil for elucidating his concerns about the peculiarity of Jesus as Spirit-baptizer and of the kingdom he inaugurates. Nonetheless, Macchia might have engaged Yong in relation to the church-kingdom dialectic, which is precisely what raises for Macchia the questions about pluralism. Macchia offers the dialectic to keep church and kingdom from being either conflated or separated, and his dialogue with Hick stands in relation to his attempt to avoid separation. Amid his insistence on holding together the church and the kingdom—both of which exist by virtue of baptism in the Holy Spirit with the result of God filling all things—Macchia would have done well to address Yong's theology of religions, especially pertaining to the Spirit's work outside the church.[96] I am not chiding Macchia for engaging figures such as Küng and Hick—I have already praised his theology's ecumenical posture. The wide array of theologians consulted, of which these two are only representatives, is one of the strengths of *Baptized in the Spirit*. I offer this criticism not to question the presence of theologians like Küng and Hick but rather to question the virtual absence of figures like Chan and Yong, a noteworthy feature of a global pentecostal theology.[97]

SUMMARY AND CONCLUSION

I have demonstrated that Macchia sets the whole of his theology against the background of the kingdom, a theme that is present throughout his works. First, Macchia explicitly adopts the kingdom as a point of concern from the Blumhardts as a way to (1) encourage social engagement, (2) frame justification's cosmic dimensions, and (3) provide the background for broadening baptism in the Holy Spirit. Second, Macchia employs pneumatology to expand (1) glossolalia beyond the boundaries of its narrow association with initial evidence, (2) justification beyond a merely forensic account, and (3) baptism in the Holy Spirit itself and, in turn, additional *loci* such as ecclesiology and soteriology.[98] While both the kingdom of God and pneumatology are two consistent elements in Macchia's theology, they do not fully converge with each other until *Baptized in the Spirit*, in which he adopts the kingdom—rather than the church—as the background for articulating a theology of baptism in the Holy Spirit. This full convergence between the kingdom and pneumatology marks an important step from a theology that *addresses* pneumatology to the formulation of an organizing principle for a *pneumatological theology*.[99]

Macchia establishes the logical priority of the kingdom of God over the church in order to avoid "realized eschatology." However, his choice to associate the kingdom's outstanding dimensions more closely with pneumatology than with christology undermines his effort. If "Christ is the king and the Spirit is the kingdom," as he states, then the extent to which the kingdom of God is still outstanding is blurred, since it is not clear to what extent the gift of the Spirit is still outstanding. In chapter 5, I attempt to improve on Macchia by aligning the kingdom's outstanding dimensions more closely with christology than with pneumatology. The Lord's supper, then, becomes a sacred rite that deters "realized eschatology" by reminding believers that the kingdom has not yet come in fullness.

CHAPTER 4

⌘

Systematic Theology as Philosophical and Fundamental Theology in Pneumatological Perspective

AMOS YONG

INTRODUCTION AND OVERVIEW

Amos Yong is J. Rodman Williams Professor of Theology at Regent University School of Divinity in Virginia Beach, VA, as well as the director of the institution's doctor of philosophy program. He holds the PhD in religion and theology from Boston University, which he received under the direction of Robert Cummings Neville (1998). Having proposed an extensive theology of religions, he is a leading advocate for pentecostals' participation in interreligious dialogue.[1] A past president of the Society for Pentecostal Studies (2008–2009), he is co-editor of its journal, *PNEUMA*. Born in Malaysia, Yong immigrated to the United States and has distinguished himself as one of the most prolific writers in pentecostal theology. He is also a licensed minister in the Assemblies of God.[2]

In addition to numerous articles and essays, my primary interest is in the following monographs: *Discerning the Spirit(s)*; *Beyond the Impasse*; *Spirit-Word-Community*; *The Spirit Poured Out on All Flesh*; *Theology and Down Syndrome*; *The Bible, Disability, and the Church*; *Hospitality and the Other*; *In the Days of Caesar*; *The Spirit of Creation*; *Pneumatology and the Christian-Buddhist Dialogue*; *The Cosmic Breath*; and *Spirit of Love*.[3] In *Discerning the Spirit(s)* (2000), his published doctoral dissertation, Yong develops a pneumatological theology of religions, with a particular call for pentecostals and charismatics to become more interested in interreligious dialogue and comparative theology. Yong contends that allowing pneumatology to take the lead on this front carries potential for bypassing, or at least suspending, certain christological roadblocks that tend to emerge in discourse between Christianity and other religious traditions. By developing a "foundational pneumatology," Yong claims that the Holy Spirit may be at work within other religions in spite of the lack of an explicit confession of the lordship of Jesus Christ. It is incumbent on Christians, therefore, to discern the presence, activity, or absence of the Spirit (or spirits) operative in world religions. Pentecostals' perennial openness to the ways of the Spirit in the world, he says, makes them especially capable of developing such a pneumatological theology of religions. In *Beyond the Impasse* (2003), Yong distills the basic ideas of *Discerning the Spirit(s)* for certain evangelicals who sometimes lack a pneumatology sufficient for overcoming their propensity to associate world religions exclusively with demonic activity.[4]

In *Spirit-Word-Community* (2002), Yong develops a theological method and hermeneutic, the internal logic that drives the whole of his theology. His basic contention is that theological method and theological hermeneutics are inherently related and that a trinitarian perspective should guide each of them. Theological reflection and interpretation involve the constant and inescapable interplay of Spirit-Word-Community, in which each one conditions the other without taking priority over the other. In the process of developing a metaphysic, ontology, and epistemology, Yong expounds on the notion of foundational pneumatology first articulated in *Discerning the Spirit(s)* and *Beyond the Impasse* and articulates his most detailed account of what he calls the "pneumatological imagination." This book is the most elaborate constructive exercise in theological method and hermeneutics by a pentecostal to date.[5]

In *The Spirit Poured Out on All Flesh* (2005), Yong offers a small-scale systematic theology from a pentecostal perspective. It advances on three fronts—the ecumenical, the interreligious, and the convergence between religion and science—and covers such *loci* as soteriology, ecclesiology, public theology, and creation. Yong argues that three distinctives should characterize pentecostal theology: (1) a biblical hermeneutic informed particularly by Luke-Acts, (2) pneumatology as an orienting motif and christology as a thematic motif, and (3) an experiential basis that unites theology and worship.

In *Theology and Down Syndrome* (2007), Yong articulates a theology of disability in conversation with biological and social-scientific accounts of disabilities. After arguing that physical and intellectual disabilities are partially real conditions and partially social constructions that should be subjected to ongoing interpretation, Yong calls for models of disability theory that give priority to the self-understanding of persons with disabilities. Yong then considers aspects of such self-understanding along with other theological accounts of disabilities in order to construct a Christian theology that is fully informed by disability perspectives. In the process, Yong reshapes the theology of creation, ecclesiology, soteriology, and eschatology in light of some of the critical questions raised by disability perspectives. In *The Bible, Disability, and the Church* (2011), Yong addresses many of the same concerns as in *Theology and Down Syndrome*, but to a theologically informed lay audience rather than to academicians. Instead of a contribution to disability studies per se, the book is an exercise in biblical theology that rereads certain biblical texts from the perspective of a disability hermeneutic.

In *Hospitality and the Other* (2008), Yong returns to his abiding interest in Christian theology of religions, this time with a particular emphasis on the performative nature of theology and on Christian practices toward members of other religions, both descriptively and prescriptively. Yong argues primarily that the Christian is obligated to show hospitality to and receive hospitality from members of other religions. Based in part on several narrative scenes from Luke-Acts, he develops a theology of hospitality centered on concrete practices guided by the Holy Spirit, whom, in this context, Yong calls "the welcoming Spirit."[6]

In *In the Days of Caesar* (2010), Yong addresses political theology in light of the basic logic of foundational pneumatology's commitment to address all concerned interlocutors. Engaging persons in the public square who are outside the church directly raises the issue of political theology inasmuch as it invites questions about the societal implications of a Christian theology that is fully public. Yong examines both the dominant paradigms in political theology and the political logic implicit in certain pentecostal practices. This may be the only book in which Yong's most important contribution comes in the form of his descriptive accounts rather than in his constructive proposals. His extensive global phenomenology of current pentecostal practices in the public sphere silences once for all the dismissive criticism that pentecostals are preoccupied with individual salvation to the exclusion of social concern.

In *The Spirit of Creation* (2011), Yong affirms the interdisciplinary posture of the dialogue between religion and science, while seeking to make a pentecostal contribution to the dialogue. Believing that all truth is God's truth wherever and by whomever it is found, he argues that religion and science are ultimately complementary, even in light of the various inquiries and discourses within each. In the process, he develops an account of divine action in the world in conversation with laws of nature, as well as a pneumatological cosmology that cautiously draws on insights from parapsychology to inform questions about demonology. As does much of the religion and science dialogue, Yong implicitly reminds readers that what is now considered "natural science" was once called "natural philosophy" and that the boundaries between philosophical (and theological) and scientific perspectives are not hard and fast and that the respective disciplines are not necessarily incommensurable.

In *Pneumatology and the Christian-Buddhist Dialogue* (2012), Yong organizes his investigations according to the structure of divine presence, activity, and absence first introduced in *Discerning the Spirit(s)*. Since the category of divine presence is intimately related to the Spirit's work of creating things to be what they are, Yong points toward the possibility of a three-way dialogue among Christianity, Buddhism, and science. Although Yong uses scientific categories like relationality, emergence, and mental causation to translate theistic concepts (Christianity) into a nontheistic context (Buddhism) in an attempt to discern the Spirit's presence, science functions primarily as a facilitator between the other two primary dialogue partners. Concerning divine activity and absence, Yong offers a comparative theology of Christianity's and Buddhism's respective soteriologies (divine activity) and demonologies (divine absence). Science plays no significant role in his discussions of divine activity and absence. However, in *The Cosmic Breath* (2012), Yong brings the three-way conversation ("trialogue") among Christianity, Buddhism, and science to the foreground, and science assumes a voice equally constitutive of the conversation as the voices of Christianity and Buddhism. The result is a theology of nature informed by all three conversation partners.

In *Spirit of Love* (2012), Yong adopts a pentecostal perspective on a pneumatological theology of love, including considerations of God as love and creation as participating in divine love. Conceding that the pentecostal tradition has associated the Holy Spirit far more frequently with "power" than with "love," he attempts to make pentecostal pneumatology's implications for a theology of love explicit. Building in part on recent social-scientific investigations of benevolence among certain pentecostal faith communities, Yong argues that pentecostal practices of divine *power*, such as spiritual gifts, can also be seen as encounters with divine *love*. After exploring Lukan, Pauline, and Johannine texts, he concludes that Spirit, gift, and love come together to suggest that God's gift of the Spirit at Pentecost is a gift of both power and love and, in turn, that manifestations of divine power through spiritual gifts are God's gift of love through the Spirit.

While the pneumatological orientation of Yong's theology is broadly similar to that of Frank D. Macchia's, my claim that they represent two sufficiently distinctive methodological types is justified for at least two reasons. First, Macchia's theology has only recently come to bear a decidedly pneumatological shape, although pneumatology in itself has always been one of his theological concerns. On the other hand, pneumatology shapes Yong's theology from first to last, a characteristic due in part to his being a member of a younger generation of pentecostal scholars who have benefited from the prior work of theologians such as Macchia. Second, Yong's theology contains more elements of philosophical theology and fundamental theology than does Macchia's. Yong engages in philosophical theology by addressing theoretical and speculative questions about God's nature and relationship to the world and by frequently incorporating philosophical insights and reasoning into his constructive theology, including reflections on metaphysics, epistemology, and hermeneutics.[7] Yong engages in fundamental theology by addressing questions about first theology, including human experience and the sources of human knowledge in relation to methodological and hermeneutical considerations, as well as their implications for Christian theology.[8] Yong's theology follows a methodology characterized by philosophical and fundamental theology from a pneumatological perspective.

THEOLOGICAL HERMENEUTICS AND A "PNEUMATOLOGY OF QUEST"

Yong's theological program rigorously follows the logic he articulates in his theological method and hermeneutic. Consisting of a foundational pneumatology and a pneumatological imagination that resist foundationalism and are open to correction, Yong's hermeneutic is truly a "pneumatology of quest" that acknowledges the provisional character of all human knowing.[9]

Foundational Pneumatology

In its most basic sense, Yong's foundational pneumatology is an account of the relationship between God and the world from a decidedly pneumatological perspective. The primacy of pneumatology—hence, foundational *pneumatology* rather than, for example, foundational *christology* or (more generally) *theology*—owes to Yong's contention that "Holy Spirit" is the most fundamental symbol of, and therefore, most appropriate category for referring to God's agency in the world.[10] The respective ideas of God and the world are correlated such that God is capable of acting in the world and the world is capable of receiving God's presence and activity.[11] While it is in part a theology of the Holy Spirit, one should not confuse foundational pneumatology with a *systematic* pneumatology, that is, pneumatology as merely a *locus* of systematic theology. According to Yong, the latter is a coherent theological account of the Holy Spirit, constructed primarily in light of scripture and tradition and directed primarily within the confines of the Christian church. Foundational pneumatology, however, addresses questions of fundamental theology and engages all interlocutors in the public domain pursuing questions concerning divine presence and agency in the world, even persons outside the church.[12] This difference between systematic and foundational pneumatology implies that truth claims about pneumatology meet not only the criterion of coherence (inasmuch as they are elements of a single system of thought) but also the criterion of correspondence (inasmuch as they are claims about reality that are believed to maintain universally, not simply within a single—in this case, ecclesial—context).[13] The criterion of correspondence invites an engagement of truth claims between competing ideological frameworks, not only a consideration of them within a single system of thought.[14] Yong bases his desire for such engagement on a "chastised optimism" about the possible existence of a "universal rationality and grammar."[15] The qualifier "foundational" does not imply epistemic foundations in the hard sense of incorrigible beliefs. Rather, foundational pneumatology invites inquiry from any community of interpreters that wishes to address its tenets. Because it does not draw heavily on a priori necessity in its quest for universal truth claims, foundational pneumatology is subject to correction by empirically driven processes of verification and falsification.[16]

Yong's foundational pneumatology includes the construction of a metaphysic and ontology that are characterized by relationality. Yong predicates both the metaphysic and ontology on his doctrine of the Trinity,[17] which consists of an integration of an Irenaean model of Spirit and Word as the two hands of God[18] with an Augustinian model of the Spirit as the bond of love between Father and Son.[19] It is in Yong's discussion of these two trinitarian models that he most poignantly establishes from a pneumatological perspective the relationality of all reality and being.[20] For Yong, the two-hands model suggests a mutuality of Spirit and Word that leads logically to the notion of the coinherence of the divine persons. Coinherence, which is an affirmation of the reciprocity and interrelationality of the divine persons and a denial of any degree of ontological subordination or division among them, creates the conceptual space for three subsistent relations indwelling each other as one God. Coinherence makes trinitarian confession possible by preserving both God's plurality and unity.[21] Relationality is even more prominent in Yong's appropriation of the Augustinian model of the Spirit as the mutual love between Father and Son.[22] As mutual love, the Spirit relates the Father to the Son and the Son to the Father, eternally in the immanent Trinity and temporally in the economic Trinity.[23] In addition to the relations of the divine persons, both the two-hands model and the mutual-love model provide accounts of God's relationship to the world and of the relationships of the plurality of things in the world to each other. From the perspective of the two-hands model, everything in the world exists by virtue of being created by God through Spirit and Word; therefore, things are what they are because they are created as such by both Spirit and Word. The Spirit establishes the relatedness of things to each other, and the Word establishes the determinateness of things that distinguishes them from all other things that exist.[24] From the perspective of the mutual-love model, the Spirit not only relates Father and Son to each other but also relates God to the world, inasmuch as the Father loves the Son by bestowing the Spirit on him in the economy of salvation, that is, in the world. Likewise, the Spirit relates the world to God, inasmuch as the Son—from within the economy of salvation—returns that love to the Father.[25] All of reality, then, is inherently relational, and the idea of "spirit" itself refers to the quality of relationality that holds together various things in their integrity without the dissolution of their individual identities. In the divine life, the Spirit joins Father and Son; in the world, the Spirit constitutes the relationships among the many things in the world and between God and the world.[26] An interdependence that amounts to "symbiotic relationality" characterizes both God and the world.[27] Crucial to Yong's claim that reality is inherently relational is his insistence that relations are part of the real identities of things, rather than mere categories that human minds employ when interpreting reality. In short, things in the world exist as such because they are products of the creative activities of Spirit and Word and because their relationships to other things constitute them as such.[28]

In addition to relationality, Yong's metaphysic and ontology are also characterized by rationality, as supported by the biblical witness to the Spirit as both source and communicator of rationality. According to Yong, the Spirit's hovering over the waters at creation suggests the Spirit's role in bringing order out of chaos through God's spoken words. In fact, human beings are rational creatures precisely because the Spirit creates them in the image of God. Further, Wisdom of Solomon associates the Spirit with attributes such as intelligence and particularity. Also, while the New Testament tends to connect wisdom more with

Christ than with the Spirit, it does at times relate the Spirit to the divine mind. In I Corinthians 1, specifically, the Spirit searches the depths of God, solely comprehends what is God's, and enables humans to understand the gifts they have received from God. Similarly, in John 14, the Spirit is the one who will lead Jesus' followers into all truth. Just as the Spirit relates created things to each other, the Spirit also makes created thing intelligible.[29]

Finally, in addition to relationality and rationality, Yong's metaphysic and ontology are characterized by dynamism, understood as the Spirit's life-giving activity in the world. From creation to consummation, the Spirit spawns life, heals the fractures stemming from finitude and fallenness, and sustains God's creative act. The Spirit also directs the flow of history to its end and fulfillment and will ultimately triumph over sin and death.[30] Dynamism is Yong's way of affirming a process ontology, according to which the Spirit constantly transforms created things, keeping them from being static entities. However, Yong modifies Whitehead's process ontology in light of an important criticism. He states that Whitehead's notion of "prehension" as the process that drives each thing's movement through successive occasions does not maintain because of its adoption of nominalism. Prehension, then, does not have the enduring ontological identity necessary to be the very creative force that drives other things from one occasion to the next.[31] Therefore, Yong's notion of dynamism functions within a process ontology that explicitly rejects nominalism.

Pneumatological Imagination

Only implicit in my discussion so far, but crucial to Yong's program, is that his metaphysic and ontology are realist, meaning that things exist apart from their being known by humans and that the order of being is distinct from, although related to, the order of knowing.[32] For Yong, the gap between the two is spanned by the pneumatological imagination, which is an orientation to God and the world that the pentecostal-charismatic life in the Spirit continually nurtures and shapes. As the divine mind, the Spirit illuminates the rationality of the world and makes it intelligible to human minds.[33] Yong describes the pneumatological imagination as a root metaphor, or, a symbol that both sustains a worldview and functions normatively in assessing realities outside the scope of that worldview. In so doing, a root metaphor either accounts for such realities in terms of the worldview itself or is corrected by such realities if it cannot adequately account for them. Pneumatological imagination observes the phenomena of the world and, rather than assessing only their plurality and individuality, attempts to discern reality. The Spirit, then, both creates the world as rational and makes its rationality accessible to human knowing.[34]

According to Yong, the pneumatological imagination understands truth as pragmatic, correspondence, and coherence.[35] On the pragmatic score, the truth of a proposition depends in part on its meaningfulness and is judged by its ability to predict the behavior of a thing. Correct predictions over time lead to the establishment of habits concerning a thing and, therefore, connections between human knowing and things in the world, that is, between the orders of being and knowing. Truth as correspondence refers to the real distinction and representational connection between things in the world and human knowing. While external realities exist apart from human minds, propositions can reflect those realities accurately, in the sense of approximate correlation rather than exact congruence. Truth as coherence refers to a proposition's dependence on consistency with other statements within the same thought system. The coherence criterion presumes comprehensive investigation of all relevant data. Yong states that rather than choosing one of these criteria of truth over the other, the pneumatological imagination strives to meet all three criteria in its accounts of reality.[36]

One of the most significant aspects of the pneumatological imagination is its commitment to epistemic fallibilism. While the orders of knowing and being are correlated, one must make truth claims with great humility because all human knowledge is fallible in at least three senses. First, knowledge is partial inasmuch as it is both indirect and semiotic. Nothing is known immediately—not even the self—but rather mediated through signs that are abstracted from the things experienced. Second, knowledge is perspectival. Human knowing is always situated in a particular time and place and marked by attending social and cultural dimensions that impinge on the hermeneutical enterprise. Third, knowledge is finite. Finitude stems both from being creatures and from being embedded in a sinful world.[37] It is because of the pneumatological imagination's fallibilism that foundational pneumatology exhibits a chastised optimism about the possibility of a universal rationality and grammar.[38] Summarizing the basic contours of foundational pneumatology and the pneumatological imagination, Yong writes that

> knowledge and interpretation is ultimately of reality—our engaging it and our
> being corrected by it. Reality is therefore the measure of our interpretations
> and misinterpretations. In this sense, metaphysics and ontology precedes

epistemology and interpretation itself. Now certainly all metaphysics is hermeneutically discerned, and truth in the robust sense is therefore necessarily eschatological. Equally certain, human knowledge is fallible for a variety of reasons. But this does not lead to epistemological skepticism or relativism in the here and now because we do engage reality, our engagement is more or less truthful, and it is normed by reality itself.[39]

According to Yong, hermeneutics neither displaces nor nullifies the possibilities of metaphysics or epistemology,[40] but rather augments and complements them. The combination of metaphysical realism and epistemic fallibilism both makes interpretation possible (inasmuch as there is a real world to interpret in the first place) and requires interpretation to continue until the eschaton (inasmuch as incomplete knowledge invites ongoing attempts to account for reality).[41]

Communal Interpretation

Within Yong's triadic construct of Spirit-Word-Community, community is the context within which Spirit and Word come together. All metaphysics and epistemology are necessarily hermeneutical, inasmuch as all human attempts to know reality arise within interpretive communities.[42] Yong's commitment to the dynamic of communal discernment is an avoidance of two polar extremes: naïve realism and epistemological pluralism. That is, his vision of communal interpretation both grants the perspectival nature of all human knowing and denies that interpretive communities are insulated intellectual ghettos that could somehow be normed only by their own parochial concerns.

In the broadest sense, then, community refers to the global human community, which is neither monolithic nor separated by clearly delineated, impenetrable borders. According to Yong, an informed theology of culture is characterized by the understanding that the

> insider-outsider distinctions with regard to communities of participation are no longer watertight. Each of us is an insider to one or more traditions to a greater or lesser extent, and an outsider to others in equally greater or lesser extents. Yet, being outsiders does not mean being cut off from those traditions. . . . The fact is undeniable: each theological interpreter negotiates membership in multiple intellectual, national, socio-political and cultural-religious communities, each of which have identities that are shaped by specific canons, narratives rituals, and the like.[43]

For Yong, because communal borders are not "watertight" and persons participate in multiple interpretive communities, the ongoing process of interpretation contains the theoretical possibility of leading to consensus. Encountering
others who participate primarily in traditions different from one's own is not
an encounter of pure alterity, at least not hermeneutically speaking. All humans live in the same world and attempt to give account of the same mind-
independent reality. Although they do so from within their respective
interpretive communities, it is ultimately the same Spirit who both enables
human minds to understand the one world in which they all live and who
drives the discourse, exchange, and dialogue necessary to pursue consensus.

Yong's theological method and hermeneutic form the logic by which the
rest of his theological program operates. In order to illustrate the need for
theology to draw on a plurality of perspectives and to make them intelligible in a number of different contexts, Yong highlights the imagery of the
"many tongues" of Pentecost (Acts 2), in which a plurality of tongues are
spoken and heard by a number of different people groups. He makes these
"many tongues" a metaphor that summarizes the salient points of foundational pneumatology, pneumatological imagination, and communal interpretation. I now turn to the facets of his thought that most clearly
demonstrate this logic: his theology of religions, his proposals for a global
theology, his treatment of certain *loci* in systematic theology, and his contributions to the dialogue between religion and science.

PNEUMATOLOGICAL THEOLOGY OF RELIGIONS

From the publication of *Discerning the Spirit(s)* (2000) until the present,
Yong has been one of the most vocal theologians encouraging pentecostals
to develop a theology of religions as well as a consistent advocate of pentecostal involvement in interreligious dialogue. He bases his own theology of
religions—the most comprehensive offered by a pentecostal to date—
firmly on the foundational pneumatology and pneumatological imagination.[44] This basis surfaces in his discussions of discernment and his empirical
investigations of two religious traditions in comparison to Christianity.

Discernment of and by the Spirit

Integral to Yong's theology of religions is his account of discerning the
presence, activity, and absence of both the Holy Spirit and other spirits
in various religious traditions. Two factors drive Yong's efforts toward a

theology of discernment: (1) his desire to cultivate a pneumatological orientation in theology of religions and (2) foundational pneumatology's assumptions about the Spirit's relationship to the created order. Concerning the first, Yong states that the respective economies of Spirit and Word in the world are distinct, although intimately related.[45] This distinction affords the potential of affirming the Spirit's presence and activity in arenas in which Christ is not explicitly proclaimed or professed, inasmuch as the Spirit's economy is not restricted to the Word's economy.[46] The upshot for interreligious dialogue is that participants can temporarily postpone the christological question of whether Jesus is the only savior or merely one savior among others in order to pursue pneumatological questions first.[47] This allows participants to establish greater mutual understanding between the two religious traditions before arriving at the debate over Jesus' particularity, a possible impasse that threatens to terminate dialogue.[48]

Concerning the second driving force behind Yong's determination to discern the Spirit within other religions, he connects his theology of religions directly to some of the metaphysical conclusions he reaches about foundational pneumatology. Building on the premises that the Holy Spirit is God's way of being present to and active within the world and that the norms and values of all created things are determined by the Spirit in relation to all other created things, Yong suggests that pentecostals should assess the Spirit's presence within non-Christian religions both ontologically and concretely. On the ontological level, the elements within world religions such as texts, myths, rituals, and moral codes are what they are precisely as creations of the Spirit. On the concrete level, the degree to which these elements represent themselves authentically and are situated coherently within their respective religious traditions attests to the Spirit's presence within those religious traditions to a greater or lesser degree.[49] However, not all symbols and rituals convey divine presence to practitioners. Those symbols that destroy rather than promote social relationships and human authenticity indicate divine absence, or, the demonic.[50]

While Christians may legitimately expect to find the Spirit at work in various religious beliefs and practices, the possibility that the demonic may also be at work requires Christians to develop a theology of discernment that functions as the scheme for interpreting religious symbols.[51] For Yong, discerning spirits is a two-part process involving both interpretation and comparison. First, practitioners of the religious tradition in question offer interpretations of their own symbols and rituals by articulating the symbols' and rituals' value and utility. As long as the symbols and rituals accomplish what they are supposed to accomplish without deviating significantly from their habits and norms, then one can affirm the Spirit's presence and activity in those symbols and rituals to a limited degree. After all, it is the Spirit who enables a thing's authentic representation relative to other constituent things in a given symbol system. Second, one devises comparative categories for judging claims within the religion in question and then between religious traditions. To a certain extent, then, discerning the spirits is an exercise in comparative theology, the hermeneutical process of classifying and interpreting similarities and differences in symbols between religious traditions. In a pneumatologically guided theology of religions, Yong states, discernment's comparative dimension would proceed along the lines of finding within the non-Christian tradition analogies to a Christian account of the Holy Spirit in order to engage the comparative task in an attempt to discern the Spirit's presence (or absence) in the non-Christian religion. In respect to symbols and rituals specifically, the comparative task might involve determining whether they accomplish in the practitioners of the non-Christian religion goals similar to what the Holy Spirit accomplishes in practitioners of Christian rituals. The importance practitioners ascribe to rituals becomes a measure by which one can discern the Spirit.[52]

Yong proposes that the two-part process of interpretation and comparison should be carried out on three different levels: the phenomenological-experiential, the moral-ethical, and the theological-soteriological.[53] The phenomenological-experiential pertains primarily to the realm of religious experience and all of the phenomena of accompanying symbols and rituals. At this level, discernment is concerned less with the symbols and rituals themselves than with how they influence practitioners. The issue is how practitioners interpret and respond to certain symbols and rituals. While discernment at this level might be sufficient to lead to the initial conclusion that the Spirit is present and active in a non-Christian religion, Yong insists that discernment must proceed to the moral-ethical realm, which pertains to questions of religious utility and outcome.[54] At this level, discernment is concerned with whether and how the symbols and rituals transform practitioners. The issue is whether the symbols and rituals achieve in practitioners their desired effects. While one can attribute similarities between Christianity and another religion on the moral-ethical front to the work of the Spirit, Yong argues that discernment at this level should not be determinative on its own. One still has to discern the referents of the symbols and rituals and render judgment on their relationship to the transcendent. At the level of the theological-soteriological, then, one must still determine whether the transcendent realities behind symbols and rituals are the Holy Spirit or another, perhaps demonic, spirit.

Discerning the Concrete: Umbanda and Buddhism

In addition to describing discernment abstractly, Yong repeatedly explores the particularities of religious traditions in order to test his ideal descriptions.[55] His examinations of Umbanda and Buddhism[56] illustrate how his concrete explorations follow the logic of the pneumatological imagination, which is characterized by empirical investigation and fallibilism.

Yong's first exercise in testing his theology of discernment is his dialogue in *Discerning the Spirit(s)* with Umbanda, an Afro-Brazilian religious tradition.[57] After establishing sufficient phenomenological similarities between Umbanda and pentecostalism to justify the dialogue,[58] Yong focuses on the Umbandist practice of inviting spirits to possess mediums temporarily to assist practitioners with benefits ranging from practical advice to physical and spiritual healings.[59] He observes that there seem to be sufficient utilitarian grounds to suggest that the Spirit may be present and active in at least some Umbandist practices. Benefits from encounters with spirit mediums, as attested by Umbandists themselves, include resolutions to problems, healings, greater senses of peace and tranquility, and assistance assuming personal responsibility in one's day-to-day life. On the basis of the criterion that rituals achieve what they are intended to achieve for their practitioners, Yong states that the Spirit seems to be at work to some degree in Umbandist practices.[60] He is quick to point out, however, that while the Christian engaging in comparative theology or interreligious dialogue may make such a conclusion about Umbandist practices, it is not an element of Umbandist self-understanding. Just as Umbandists should have the prerogative to interpret and describe their own symbols and rituals for the purpose of dialogue and discernment, they should also have the prerogative to reach their own conclusions about the transcendent realities to which their symbols and rituals ultimately refer. In other words, Yong concludes, the ambiguity within the Umbandist self-understanding, especially as pertains to the status of certain possessing spirits, is an obstacle to Christian discernment about whether the Holy Spirit is the operative transcendent reality of Umbandist practices.[61] After all, it is the Umbandist self-understanding that Christian comparative theologians must take seriously if they are to avoid imposing on Umbanda Christian theological categories that Umbanda would resist. This ambiguity alone is enough to necessitate ongoing discernment and dialogue between Umbanda and pentecostalism.[62]

Yong concludes his considerations of Umbanda with a brief dialogue with pentecostalism focused on how the two traditions might mutually inform each other. He suggests, on the one hand, that pentecostals could learn from Umbanda in respect to the latter's diverse responses to the transcendent, a view of ancestors that promotes communal healing, and the ambiguous nature of the finite's interaction with the infinite. He suggests, on the other hand, that Umbandists could learn from pentecostalism with respect to discerning the operations of spirits in human possession, the social and ethical dimensions of healing and wholeness, and the task of combating destructive spirits.[63] In the end, the comparative categories derived from Yong's foundational pneumatology highlight sufficient similarities between the two traditions to suggest that they might learn from each other, while honestly acknowledging the differences that delineate them as two distinct religious traditions.[64]

Yong's determination to engage similarities without dissolving differences in religious traditions also surfaces in his writings on Buddhist-Christian dialogue. In fact, he is so insistent that participants not gloss over the differences between the two that he calls for dialogue to include what he refers to as a "civilized polemics" or "interreligious apologetics." Since both traditions have their own sets of exclusive claims and since it is ultimately truth that is at stake in competing claims, the dialogue partners should not shy away from attempts to persuade each other of their respective truth claims. Alluding to the Spirit's agency in rational communication, as developed in his foundational pneumatology, Yong states that this kind of interreligious interaction presumes the Spirit's activity of enabling communication between dialogue partners.[65]

Within the context of similarities and differences between Christianity and Buddhism, Yong's comparison of Eastern Orthodoxy's notions of *theosis* and Theravada Buddhism's notions of enlightenment deserve attention.[66] For this exercise, he employs three comparative categories— phenomenological and practical, psychological and epistemological, and theological and pneumatological—and highlights similarities and differences between the two traditions within each category.[67] Concerning the phenomenological and practical category, Yong points to similar emphases on mortifying the flesh and achieving detachment from the things of the world. Also similar are the concrete ascetical practices, such as fasting, used to achieve these goals. However, ascetic dimensions are also a point of divergence, inasmuch as Orthodox spirituality is concerned more with resisting the devil's temptations via the flesh, while the Theravadin tradition sees spirituality more in terms of deliverance from the self than in terms of union with God.[68]

Concerning the psychological and epistemological category, Yong contends that each tradition aspires to the illumination and sanctification of the mind, not only the disciplining of the flesh. For the Orthodox, the goal is to overcome the *logismoi* that distract spiritual progress and to come to see reality as it actually is. For the Theravadin, the goal is to center the mind and to reach a state of consciousness (*samadhi*) that is aware of the integration of all of reality and is no longer influenced by passions.[69]

Concerning the theological and pneumatological category, Yong admits that there are vast differences between the two traditions, not the least of which is Theravada Buddhism's rejection of the idea of divinity.[70] These kinds of differences between religious traditions, he suggests, have usually prompted two responses from Christians. Either the non-Christian religion is denounced for its failure to align with Christian standards and the differences are attributed to the demonic, or both traditions are granted equal legitimacy with the understanding that each is shaped by different religious grammars. Rejecting each of these approaches as insufficient, Yong writes that there is still a significant similarity between Orthodoxy and Theravada Buddhism in theological categories, namely, that practitioners of both receive salvation through transcendental experience.[71] In response to this similarity, the comparative theologian can either assume a priori that the Holy Spirit is at work in both traditions (since the Spirit is to some degree the creative source of all things) or one can be open to the possibility of the Spirit's presence in other religions and attempt to discern the Spirit. Yong prefers the latter approach, which assumes foundational pneumatology's account of God's presence with the world and which is directed by the pneumatological imagination's commitment to empirical investigations of concrete religious practices.[72]

Yong's discussions of Christian-Buddhist dialogue also demonstrate poignantly some of the finer points of his pneumatological theology of religions. First, Yong does not advocate relativism of the religions' competing claims. Their normative statuses are not of equal value and require adjudication in light of the pneumatological imagination's epistemic fallibilism. All religious truth claims are subject to scrutiny according to the criteria of pragmatics, coherence, and correspondence.[73]

Second, Yong's account of Christian-Buddhist dialogue illustrates that the pneumatological orientation of his theology of religions changes the questions one is most likely to ask concerning non-Christian religions. Yong writes,

> So whereas previous thinking about the religions focused on whether or not they were or are salvific, a pneumatological theology of religions asks whether or not and how, if so, the religions are divinely providential instruments designed for various purposes. Further, while earlier debates focused on whether or not the religions were or are the results of common grace or

natural revelation, a pneumatological *theologia religionum* asks other kinds of questions, such as, what is the relationship of religion and culture, or of religion and language? How does religion function to sustain life and community? What role does religion play vis-à-vis the other dimensions and domains of life, whether it be the arts, politics, economics, etc.?[74]

Here, Yong indicates that the upshot of a pneumatological theology of religions is not primarily to give different answers to standing soteriological questions usually oriented to christological and ecclesiological concerns. If this were the case, one's pneumatological theology of religions might involve little more than simply affirming a robust pneumatology and becoming a comfortable inclusivist on the basis that the Spirit works outside the confines of the church.[75] On the contrary, for Yong, a thoroughly pneumatological theology of religions—particularly as informed by foundational pneumatology's conclusions about the Spirit's relationship to all created things, including the religions—prompts different questions besides those related strictly and directly to soteriology, christology, and ecclesiology.

PNEUMATOLOGY, PENTECOSTALISM, AND THE POSSIBILITY OF "WORLD THEOLOGY"

One component of Yong's foundational pneumatology (vis-à-vis pneumatology as merely a *locus* of systematic theology) is its alliance with fundamental theology and the need to engage truth claims in the public domain outside the immediate confines of ecclesial contexts. In keeping with this premise, Yong takes up the question of the possibility of constructing a truly global theology, on the basis that the Holy Spirit is being poured out on all flesh (Joel 2:28; Acts 2:17).[76] He contends that Christian theology still has much to contribute amid the endless complexities and pluralities of the global context that characterizes the late modern world and that it should not shy away from making global claims. At the same time, by remaining attuned to and informed by those very pluralities, Yong wishes to avoid the oversimplified ideas of homogenization that often accompany ideas of globalization. In order to accentuate the sensitivity that he wants to give to various global contexts, Yong prefers the term "world theology" to describe his theological aims.[77]

Yong offers two separate accounts of several of systematic theology's traditional *loci*, each informed by foundational pneumatology and driven by pneumatological imagination. The first takes the form of a small-scale systematic theology from a pentecostal perspective;[78] the second, that of systematic *loci* informed by a theology of human disabilities.[79]

Pentecostal Theology and Systematic *Loci*

Yong claims that because pentecostalism spans the globe, it provides unique resources for shaping a Christian theology that can address all people groups without minimizing the differences among the various cultural instantiations of Christianity.[80] In order to establish the complexities of the various cultures in which pentecostalism flourishes, he surveys pentecostal traditions in Latin America, Asia, and Africa.[81] Guided by the pneumatological imagination's concerns for the empirical investigation of concrete religious expressions, Yong acknowledges the vast differences among the many pentecostal traditions while arguing for a recurring theological theme, namely, an emphasis on the concrete nature of salvation as attested by the Spirit's works in physical, social, and political dimensions. Yong makes soteriology the thematic starting point of his exploration of pentecostal systematic *loci*. At the same time, his efforts are ultimately oriented to pneumatology, for salvation comes precisely as the *Spirit* is poured out on all flesh.[82]

Pneumatological Soteriology

According to Yong, the contours of salvation include at least the following seven dimensions: (1) *personal*, the transformation of an individual into the image of Christ marked customarily by repentance, baptism, and reception of the Holy Spirit; (2) *familial*, the conversion of entire households, clans, or tribes; (3) *ecclesial*, baptism into the body of Christ and, thus, into a new communal way of living; (4) *material*, healing of body, soul, and mind; (5) *social*, deliverance from structural evils resulting in race, class, and gender reconciliation; (6) *cosmic*, redemption of the entire creation; and (7) *eschatological*, the final consummation of the other six dimensions.[83] Yong offers these seven aspects of salvation as an expansion of the tenets of the fivefold gospel.[84] He writes, "[W]e can give preliminary articulation to the pentecostal intuition of the fivefold gospel: Jesus is Savior precisely as healer, sanctifier, and baptizer, all in anticipation of the full salvation to be brought with the coming kingdom."[85]

In addition to these seven dimensions of salvation, Yong draws on four primary resources to develop his pneumatological soteriology.[86] First, he reclaims the early church's understanding of Christian initiation, marked by a sustained process of catechesis and culminating in baptism and reception of the Holy Spirit.[87] Second, Yong broadens the pentecostal metaphor of baptism in the Holy Spirit beyond the narrow confines of empowerment for Christian service to include also justification and sanctification.[88] Third, he adopts a Wesleyan approach to the *ordo salutis* as a *via salutis*, which acknowledges more fluidity in salvation's various crisis experiences than does the traditional pentecostal emphases on twofold or threefold soteriological patterns.[89] Fourth, Yong expands the notion of conversion from a restricted idea involving only a once-for-all spiritual reorientation to include also ongoing moral, affective, and social dimensions.[90]

These four resources briefly demonstrate Yong's ability to expand the boundaries of established pentecostal theology and to conduct his theological investigations from a pentecostal perspective in conversation with early, modern, and contemporary Christian theology. His discussions of some traditional Christian atonement models in light of a pneumatological soteriology further demonstrate this ability.[91] First, a pneumatological soteriology, as derived from foundational pneumatology, bolsters ransom theories of atonement by placing additional emphasis on the category of the demonic vis-à-vis divine presence and activity. It also underscores deliverance from such powers as one aspect of material salvation. Second, pneumatological soteriology recasts satisfaction and substitution theories of atonement by emphasizing the Spirit's empowerment of Jesus to make his sacrificial offering. When the atonement is seen as a fully trinitarian event, rather than as a transaction involving only Father and Son, charges that satisfaction and substitution promote so-called divine child abuse can be more easily answered. Third, pneumatological soteriology maintains the concern of moral-influence theories for moral transformation and character rehabilitation, while also offering Jesus as the standard that should measure such progress. For Yong, the coupling of Luke's Spirit-christology with the "Spirit-soteriology" of Acts is a model of how Spirit-filled Christians are to imitate the life and works of the Spirit-anointed Jesus.

Pneumatological Ecclesiology

Yong observes that pentecostals have not historically discussed ecclesiology in detail and that, when they have, they have not usually done so in explicit connection with soteriology. He argues, however, that pentecostal soteriology and ecclesiology are intimately—even if only implicitly—related, inasmuch as pentecostalism has always been a missiological movement. As Yong states, questions about what it means to be saved necessarily raise questions about the church's nature.[92]

Before proposing how pentecostals might begin to explore ecclesiology more explicitly in connection with soteriology, Yong rehearses some of the different ways that the Christian tradition has articulated the relationship between soteriology and ecclesiology.[93] In conversation with church models ranging from those that define entrance into the church in terms of baptism, confession of Christ's lordship, or spiritual union with Christ, to those that describe the church as an alternative community distinguished by its core practices, he proposes elements of a pneumatological ecclesiology on the fronts of baptism and eucharist. Concerning baptism, Yong states that water and Spirit baptism should be closely related due to the witness of the New Testament, the early church's expectations for believers to receive the Spirit in connection with baptism, and the fact that Oneness pentecostals already closely associate the two.[94] Further, Yong contends that the invocation of the Holy Spirit should be central to the pentecostal practice of baptism, with the understanding that the Spirit is the active sacramental agent, not consecrated water.[95] In addition, he suggests that baptism is the enactment of our participation in Christ's death and resurrection and the representation of the reception of the Spirit.[96] Also, he states that pentecostals should allay their fears about sacramental language in respect to baptism since, at the very least, it realizes new life in the Spirit through conformity to Christ's death and resurrection and, at the most, it is a transforming ritual that conveys grace to those who receive it in faith.[97]

Concerning eucharist, Yong describes five dimensions of its transforming effects on worshipping communities. First, eucharist is a physical act of eating and drinking that some pentecostals associate with physical healing, inasmuch as they believe healing to be provided in Jesus' atoning death.[98] For Yong, this notion follows from the idea that the material elements of bread and wine mediate Christ's presence through the Spirit, a belief that pentecostals have not usually held but that they are in a position to embrace given their existing belief that physical healing can be mediated through physical means such as the laying on of hands.[99] Second, just as the Spirit makes Christ present to us, the Spirit also makes us present to Christ in the eucharist. Through the relationship established by the Spirit, eucharist becomes an interpersonal encounter between Christ and his body. Third, as the climax of the church's liturgy, eucharist promotes reconciliation among members of Christ's body. In this way, eucharist is truly the fellowship in the Spirit of the church catholic. Fourth, eucharist is a political act that promotes a radically alternative way of living. This aspect of eucharist resists the privatization of one's religious impulses by encouraging public living that derives from the eucharist as a prophetic act. Fifth, eucharist is an event in which Christians anticipate the final resurrection in the power of the Spirit. It involves both remembering (*anamnesis*) and looking forward.[100]

While Yong does not develop a full-scale ecclesiology, his treatments of baptism and eucharist encourage pentecostals to address soteriology and ecclesiology in conjunction with each other. By describing baptism and eucharist as integral components of a Christian liturgy understood as performative rites that redeem and transform, Yong accentuates the soteriological dimensions of two important elements of ecclesiology.[101]

Theology of Disability and Systematic *Loci*

Yong's *Theology and Down Syndrome: Reimagining Disability in Late Modernity* (2007) is first and foremost a contribution to disabilities studies from a theological perspective.[102] Nonetheless, its final section is a consideration of various systematic *loci* in light of a reconsideration of intellectual disabilities. While it may not be obvious at first glance how such a study fits within the specifically pneumatological logic that governs Yong's theological program, close inspection reveals that the same foundational pneumatology and pneumatological imagination that direct Yong's theology of religions and quest for a world theology also guide his theology of disability, resulting in a Christian theology informed by disabilities perspectives.[103] Inasmuch as the Spirit holds together disparate things without compromising each thing's identity and integrity, the pneumatological imagination is attuned to the many contextual voices in our pluralistic world in order to be informed by them without silencing one voice by conflating it to another. Just as Yong wishes to interpret the "many tongues" of the various cultural manifestations of global pentecostalism, he also wishes to be attentive to the "diverse tongues" of persons with intellectual disabilities, both in allowing them to articulate their own self-understandings and in allowing their insights to shape Christian theology.

Creation from a Disabilities Perspective

Yong's investigations of the impact of experiences of intellectual disabilities on a theology of creation yield notable results for theological anthropology. He focuses particularly on how such experiences both complicate traditional Christian accounts of human creation in the image of God and invite reformulation.[104] Yong states that the difficulty with the substantive view, which locates the *imago Dei* in the human's analogical reflection of God's rational and moral capacities, is its implication that persons with intellectual disabilities bear the *imago Dei* to a lesser degree and/or are not fully human. Also, Yong claims that the functional view, which locates the *imago Dei* in the human's ability to exercise authority and dominion over the rest of creation, implies similar problems as the substantive view because persons with intellectual disabilities frequently exhibit diminished capacities for making decisions and taking responsibility for themselves and others.[105] Most promising, according to Yong, is the relational view, which locates the *imago Dei* in the human's capacity for relationships with God and with fellow humans, something that intellectual disabilities do not necessarily diminish.[106]

Yet, for Yong, even the relational view needs supplementation from a stronger emphasis on the embodied nature of human life in order to understand the *imago Dei* as the *imago trinitatis*, which underscores human interdependence and interrelationality.[107] A theology of embodiment can account for the particularity of creation by seeing the Holy Spirit as the creating and sustaining force that allows a plurality of human body types to exist.[108] Coupled with an emergentist account of the human soul, in which the soul arises from the material complexity of the human body but is not identical with it, a theology of embodiment explains how persons with disabilities can relate to God in spite of their diminished intellectual capacities. The soul is able to commune with God because it is not merely the human brain.[109]

Resurrection from a Disabilities Perspective

Since a theology of embodiment highlights the significance of one's physical body for identity and sense of self, it raises poignant questions about the continuity of human persons in relation to eschatology, especially from the perspective of the resurrection of the body as the removal of all deformity.[110] As Yong points out, a purely physical disability with no intellectual effects might not be obviously constitutive of the person in any meaningful sense, but an intellectual disability like Down Syndrome is more likely to shape drastically one's being in the world and one's self-perception. The question then arises, if the resurrected body were to be transformed to a state that did not include Down Syndrome, would the human self in question truly have endured such transformation? In other words, to what extent can one affirm personal continuity in the eschaton for persons with intellectual disabilities?

While Yong acknowledges that not all persons with disabilities believe that their disabilities will somehow be preserved in the eschaton, he states that the challenges concerning personal continuity from a disabilities perspective warn against quickly accepting the notion that all deformity will be removed from resurrected bodies as well as invite a more dynamic eschatology than has typically been conceived in the Christian tradition.[111] To do this, Yong dialogues with Paul and Gregory of Nyssa. First, Yong offers a reading of I Corinthians 15 that preserves personal continuity without undermining the eschatological transformation of the resurrected body. Second, he adapts Gregory's notion of the perpetual progress of the soul toward God (*epectasis*). Taking both of these elements in pneumatological perspective, Yong describes the Holy Spirit as the force of continuity between current embodied life and the life of the resurrected body. Thus, Yong describes a dynamic eschatology that takes seriously disability perspectives about personal continuity by setting the resurrected human self against the backdrop of perpetual transformation in pneumatological perspective.

RELIGION AND SCIENCE IN THE LATE MODERN WORLD

Most recently, Yong has turned his attention to dialogue between religion and science. While his proposals on this front are new and at the initial stages of development, it is already clear that they also stem from the logic of Spirit-Word-Community. Foundational pneumatology's tenets about the God-world relationship, the pneumatological imagination's empirical processes of verification and falsification, and the hermeneutical sensitivity to the wider human community all combine to set the stage for interdisciplinary pursuits of many kinds.[112] In this case, among the "many tongues" to which theology must listen are the natural, social, and human sciences. The plurality of methodologies in religious discourse, the sciences themselves, and approaches to conversations between the two are both consonant with and able to be explicated by the "many tongues" metaphor.[113]

Foundational pneumatology's tenets about the role of the Spirit in the God-world relationship leads to a pneumatological view of nature that avoids reductionistic accounts of the world. Yong's foray into religion and science is in part an explication of underlying themes of divine agency in foundational pneumatology, but with direct engagement of the claims and technical vocabularies of the natural sciences.[114] The pneumatological imagination's commitment to epistemic fallibilism also surfaces in the conversation between religion and science. Yong brings to the table a pneumatological perspective shaped by pentecostal ethos that in turn attempts to shape the conversation by giving an account of topics such as creation, divine action in the world, and emergence theory. Yet, this attempt does not proceed along the line of a priori necessities that may unduly privilege a particular kind of theological reasoning over scientific methodologies. Rather, it is open to be corrected by reliable scientific data, all of which must be hermeneutically discerned as theologians and scientists give their respective accounts of the one world in which they live.[115]

Although Yong's explicit entry into the religion and science dialogue is relatively recent, all signs indicate that it is going to be a continuing interest for him. In fact, he is already incorporating aspects of the dialogue into his abiding interest in theology of religions and into a new exploration into a theology of love in pneumatological perspective. Concerning theology of religions, Yong focuses on Christian accounts of *pneuma* and Buddhist accounts of *shunyata* (emptiness/emptying) in connection with the neurosciences. With respect to *pneuma*, he interfaces an emergence model of mind-brain relations with a pneumatological reading of the creation accounts in Genesis to suggest that (1) inasmuch as mental processes are dependant on brain activity, humans are truly dependent on "the dust of the earth"; (2) the mind is affectively and emotively constituted by the body, and these dimensions manifest in the emergent self that the Spirit constitutes as irreducibly particular according to its unique fields of activity; (3) the mind also exhibits "top-down" influence on the body that is consonant with the interactivity attested between the Spirit and creation; and (4) humans are intersubjective selves who interact with other persons and other aspects of creation that are equally dependent on the divine Spirit.[116] With respect to *shunyata*, Yong observes that emptying occurs through empirical particularities in such a way that objects are empty precisely in their interdependence with other objects. Further, subject-object relations are transformed as each emerges together through an encounter or experience.[117] Concerning a theology of love, Yong engages the neurosciences for insights into the ontological nature of love and the social sciences for perspectives on human experiences of love. These sciences inform his argument for the possibility of genuinely altruistic forms of love.[118]

INFLUENCES AND CONTINUITIES

While Yong engages hundreds of interlocutors in his writings, a few figures are especially important for the elements of his thought that I have highlighted. First, American pragmatist philosopher C. S. Peirce is a significant influence on Yong's theological method and hermeneutic. Continuities with Peirce surface in Yong's adoption of the pragmatic criterion of truth, a relational metaphysic, the fallibilistic character of human knowing, semiotic interpretation, critical realism, and the strong commitment to considering empirical data to discern the true reality of phenomena.[119] Peirce's triadic account of reality also accords well with Yong's trinitarian hermeneutic.

Second, Yong articulates his foundational pneumatology in close conversation with Donald L. Gelpi. In *The Divine Mother*, Gelpi constructs his own foundational pneumatology, also informed by C. S. Peirce and other figures in the North American philosophical tradition.[120] Yong's foundational pneumatology is similar to Gelpi's with respect to its penchant for fallibilism over hard foundationalism and its refusal to rely heavily on a priori necessity in theological method. At the same time, it differs by working in conjunction with the pneumatological imagination in a way that does not presuppose an inquirer's conversion to Christianity in order for the pneumatological imagination to guide her. Gelpi serves in part as an indirect source through which Peirce's influence reaches Yong. Of course, Gelpi's influence brings Peirce's broadly philosophical concerns to bear specifically on particular theological concerns. Yong follows Gelpi's example of incorporating aspects of Peirce's philosophy into his own theological lines of inquiry.[121]

Third, Yong's claims about the various public arenas to which Christian theology should be addressed draws on David Tracy's descriptions of the nature of fundamental, systematic, and practical theology.[122] Concerning these three public arenas, Tracy writes,

> In terms of primary reference groups, *fundamental* theologies are related primarily to the public represented but not exhausted by the academy. *Systematic* theologies are related primarily to the public represented but not exhausted in the church, here understood as a community of moral and religious discourse and action. *Practical* theologies are related primarily to the public of society, more exactly to the concerns of some particular social, political, cultural or pastoral movement or problematic which is argued or assumed to possess major religious import.[123]

Based in part on Tracy's account of these three distinctions within theology, Yong concludes that theology must address the academy (fundamental), ecclesial self-understanding (systematic), and ecclesial praxis (practical), each of which is correlated with the three criteria of truth—correspondence, coherence, and pragmatic, respectively.[124] The acceptance of these distinctions also forms the basis of Yong's commitment to formulate a foundational pneumatology for debate in the public arenas outside the Christian church, not merely pneumatology as a *locus* of systematic theology. Yong's adoption of Tracy's various "publics" is a significant driving force in his decision to include world religions, the sciences, North American philosophical traditions, and persons with intellectual disabilities in his quest for truth wherever it may be found.

ASSESSMENT

A number of Yong's theological achievements deserve explicit observation. First, Yong follows a method of biblical interpretation that improves drastically on the "Bible doctrines" methodological type described in chapter 1. Rather than reading all biblical texts as equivalent data that require equivalent representation in his theological schema, he allows certain biblical texts to take interpretive authority over other texts and to become more formative in his theology than other texts. Summarizing the method of biblical interpretation proposed in *The Spirit Poured Out on All Flesh*, Yong writes,

> In this volume, a Lukan hermeneutic will be developed. . . . I see as unavoidable such an open acknowledgement of approaching the whole of Scripture through a part of the whole: no one can be merely and fully biblical in the exhaustive sense of the term. Better to concede one's perspective up front, since this better protects against a naïve biblicism that often results in aspirations to be "biblical."[125]

While Yong's choice to privilege Luke-Acts specifically may be debatable, his methodological posture toward the interpretation of the Christian canon for theological purposes is better able to acknowledge the diversity of witnesses it contains than an approach that attempts a purely inductive investigation of the canon in order to weigh all data equally. At the same time, Yong's approach does not preclude the comprehensive study of scripture for theology; it simply concedes that an interpretive lens—unavoidably, from his perspective—shapes such comprehensive study.[126]

Second, more than any other pentecostal scholar, Yong demonstrates awareness that hermeneutics encompasses far more than simply biblical interpretation. In some conservative evangelical, including some pentecostal contexts, "hermeneutics" is simply a synonym for "biblical exegesis."[127] This characteristic among pentecostals is due in part to the fact that scripture scholars preceded (and still outnumber) systematic theologians and philosophers among pentecostal academicians.[128] Yong's articulation of a theological hermeneutic and method through engagement with the broader senses of philosophical hermeneutics on issues such as re-alism, semiotics, fallibilism, and language philosophy encourages pente-costal theologians to explore the wider dimensions of hermeneutics—of which biblical interpretation should be only one facet—and the roles that they should play in future constructive theology.

Third, and closely related to the second, Yong's theology includes exten-sive engagement with abiding and contemporary philosophical issues. While he has not crafted an explicit statement on the relationship between theology and philosophy, he assumes that philosophical discourse is one of the "many tongues" that must be heard in constructive theology, as well as one of the public arenas to which theology must be addressed in the quest for truth in a pluralistic world. Future pentecostal theologians should not ignore Yong's philosophical work to develop a relational metaphysic and ontology and a fallibilist epistemology from a theological perspective. His engagement with philosophical and fundamental theology also sets a prec-edent that pentecostal theologians can either follow, modify, or reject, but they cannot afford to dismiss it.

Fourth, Yong is the pentecostal theologian who reflects on theological method most conscientiously and explicitly. I am aware of no other pente-costal who has devoted an entire monograph to theological method and hermeneutics as Yong has in *Spirit-Word-Community*. This distinguishing trait bears at least two additional characteristics. First, his method is rigor-ously consistent and governs the whole of his theology. As such, it is truly a pneumatological theology throughout.[129] Second, he discusses theolog-ical method in a way that preserves a close relationship between the form and content of theology. While recognizing the importance of method in theology, he does not stop at prolegomena at the expense of taking up other theological themes. This is illustrated most clearly in the relationship between *Spirit-Word-Community* and *The Spirit Poured Out on All Flesh*; the treatment of systematic *loci* in the latter follows the methodological logic of the former.

Nonetheless, there are at least two related issues integral to Yong's theological method and hermeneutic that need to be addressed. I am inter-ested primarily in whether these two issues are ultimately coherent with other aspects of Yong's thought. First, there are some unresolved tensions between Yong's metaphysical tenets in relation to some of his theological formulations. For example, he assumes at a number of different places in *Spirit-Word-Community* that a metaphysic predicated on the category of substance is no longer tenable in the late modern world.[130] Nevertheless, he continues to trade on theological categories such as intra-trinitarian processions, *filioque*, and *perichoresis*, which are imbedded in substance metaphysics. This raises the following related questions: What precisely does it mean to say that within the immanent Trinity the Father begets the Son and that the Father (in the West, *filioque*) breathes forth the Spirit if it does not mean that the Father in eternity imparts the divine essence to the Son and to the Spirit? Similarly, what meaning does a notion like *perichoresis* hold if it is not the coinherence that the divine persons enjoy precisely on the basis of their sharing the one divine essence? Yong's shift from a static metaphysic of substance to a relational metaphysic raises these questions, for it seems that a departure from the substance categories that support these notions requires theologians to thoroughly rework them.[131] That is, Yong's shift to a relational metaphysic removes from notions like intra-trinitarian processions, *filioque*, and *perichoresis* the content that they possess within the context of a metaphysic of substance, and Yong has not stated explicitly what new content is to be invested in these notions within the context of a relational metaphysic. My point is not to assume the abandonment of these notions along with a metaphysic of substance but to question the coherence of their use within a relational metaphysic.

Second, there is tension between Yong's theology of Spirit and Word (read: "Logos," not "scripture") as proposed throughout his corpus and his Lukan hermeneutic of biblical interpretation as proposed in *The Spirit Poured Out on All Flesh*. Throughout his discussions of pneumatological theology, Yong makes clear that he wishes neither to subordinate the Spirit to the Word nor the Word to the Spirit; rather, pneumatological theology leads to a robust trinitarian theology.[132] Yet, in *The Spirit Poured Out on All Flesh*, he suggests that pentecostal theologians should allow Luke-Acts to serve as an interpretive lens for the rest of scripture. It seems, however, that a Lukan hermeneutic might in fact invite a logical priority of the Spirit over the Word, given that in Luke-Acts there is no mention of the incarnate Word and the Spirit brings about Jesus' conception. Again, my concerns are over the issue of coherence. I do not assume that christology should give logical priority to the Spirit over the Word but am inquiring about the compatibility of Yong's theology of the Spirit and the Word with a Lukan hermeneutic. Precisely how a Lukan hermeneutic leads to an egalitarian relationship between Spirit and Word requires further explanation.

SUMMARY AND CONCLUSION

I have demonstrated that Yong engages in philosophical and fundamental theology from a pneumatological perspective by developing a metaphysic, ontology, and epistemology. In so doing, he gives accounts of the God-world relationship (foundational pneumatology) and of the processes of human knowing (pneumatological imagination). I have also shown that all of the other major points of Yong's theology derive from this pneumatological basis. First, Yong's theology of religions depends on foundational pneumatology's claims about the Spirit's presence and activity in the world and on the pneumatological imagination's insistence on ongoing interpretation of religious "others." Second, in his quest for a truly global theology, Yong joins foundational pneumatology's tenets about the Spirit's universal presence and activity with the traditional pentecostal emphasis on the Spirit's being poured out on all flesh. Yong also employs the pneumatological imagination's penchant for empirical investigation in order to establish pentecostalism's diverse instantiations and their potential for contributing to a global theology. Third, in his treatment of systematic *loci*, Yong allows foundational pneumatology to inform soteriology and ecclesiology and follows the pneumatological imagination's lead in listening to diverse contextual voices, including persons with intellectual disabilities. Fourth, foundational pneumatology and pneumatological imagination also lead to interdisciplinarity, seen most clearly in Yong's contributions to the dialogue between religion and science. All in all, Yong is the most successful pentecostal theologian at developing a thoroughly and consistently pneumatological theology.

Yong posits a triadic theological hermeneutic that is attentive to the interplay of Spirit, Word, and Community. He also very briefly sketches a model of the relationship between Christian beliefs and practices. However, this brief sketch fails to explain to what extent pentecostals should allow popular devotion to influence their doctrinal formulations and, therefore, leaves the door open for uncritical acceptance of aspects of pentecostal spirituality within a reciprocal relationship between beliefs and practices. It also fails to offer a test case of precisely how the relationship between beliefs and practices could give rise to a particular doctrinal *locus*. In chapter 5, I attempt to improve on Yong by providing safeguards against uncritical appropriations of popular devotion and by offering a case study of a particular doctrinal *locus*, the Lord's supper.

CHAPTER 5

✧

"Regula Spiritualitatis, Regula Doctrinae"

A Contribution to Pentecostal Theological Method

INTRODUCTION

Pentecostals have not always been quick to perceive the significant impact that theological method can have on the content of one's theology. For example, Steven M. Studebaker demonstrates this problem in his study of pentecostals' dependence on Protestant scholasticism in their attempts to relate christology to pneumatology in their soteriologies. Studebaker shows not only that pentecostals have developed soteriologies with similar content to some Reformed soteriologies, but also that they have borrowed certain methodological structures that have shaped their theologies by yielding results that are in fact quite contrary to their intentions.[1]

Part of the purpose of this book is to show that this inattentiveness to theological method among pentecostals is receding. I have discussed in detail methodological approaches centered on the implications of pentecostal experience for biblical interpretation (Arrington), the relationship between theology and Christian spirituality (Land and Chan), the kingdom of God (Macchia), as well as foundational pneumatology, pneumatological imagination, and communal interpretation (Yong)[2]—all of which indicate that pentecostal theologians are now suggesting points of orientation for their theologies that demonstrate their increased awareness of the necessity to be both conscious of and intentional about theological method. I wish to encourage further this awareness by proposing that pentecostals give careful consideration to the contributions that a form of *lex orandi, lex credendi* could make as one facet of theological method in systematic theology. Here, I reiterate that my contribution is not a fifth methodological type but rather a proposal for an element of pentecostal theological method that has not yet been sufficiently developed within the four types.[3] After describing the method, I will offer the Lord's supper as an exercise in the performance of the method.[4] Throughout this chapter, I will indicate, mostly in the notes, continuities and discontinuities between my proposals and the theologies of the figures considered in previous chapters.[5]

One of my own presuppositions for the following discussion is that it is crucial to the life and health of pentecostal communities for their theologians to engage in doctrinal theology. I essentially agree with Chan's observation that the struggle pentecostals are experiencing in their attempts to pass on their core values to successive generations is in part a failure in systematic theology.[6] When their children have asked them about the "Whys" and "Whats" of their beliefs and practices, pentecostals have always been able to take their children to meetings of corporate worship for them to experience those particulars firsthand. The question still remains, however, concerning the extent to which pentecostals will be able to give critical and convincing theological rationales for their beliefs and practices. While the preceding chapters make it clear that work on this front is already under way, additional work is needed. The challenges posed by the question "What are we going to teach our children?" should further motivate pentecostals to theologize systematically and constructively.

LEX ORANDI, LEX CREDENDI

Recent considerations of *lex orandi, lex credendi* are numerous,[7] but I will limit my discussion to the insights of Geoffrey Wainwright and Maurice Wiles. Literally translated as "law of praying, law of believing," the axiom *lex orandi, lex credendi* (or some form of it) goes back within the Western theological tradition at least to the semi-pelagian controversy of the fifth century, at which time the Augustinian monk Prosper of Aquitaine wrote that "the law of supplication should determine the law of faith."[8] In keeping with Prosper's statement, *lex orandi, lex credendi* is often shorthand for the indissoluble relationship between Christian worship and Christian belief.

There are, however, different opinions about precisely how that relationship should operate. Geoffrey Wainwright, in his commendable undertaking to write a systematic theology from the perspective of Christian liturgy and doxology,[9] notes that there are at least two ways to interpret *lex orandi, lex credendi*. First, it can mean that the law of prayer norms the law of belief, in which case what one prays determines what one should believe. Wainwright suggests that Roman Catholics usually understand the axiom in this sense. But the phrase can also mean that the law of belief norms the law of prayer, in which case what one believes determines what one should pray. Wainwright suggests that Protestants usually understand the phrase in this sense, that is, when they intentionally make use of the method at all.[10] Wainwright carefully notes that both Roman Catholics and Protestants know both appropriations of *lex orandi, lex credendi*, but goes on to say,

> It is rare that the Roman Catholic church prunes its liturgy in any doctrinally substantial way. On the other hand, the origins of Protestantism lie in a critical confrontation with existing liturgy and doctrine, and the original Protestant search for purity of worship and belief is prolonged in the notion of *ecclesia semper reformanda*. Protestantism does not consider its worship or its doctrine infallible, whereas the Roman Catholic church makes that claim of its dogma and, in essentials, its liturgy. The agreement and difference may be put as follows. Both Catholicism and Protestantism consider that there is properly a complementary and harmonious relation between worship and doctrine, and that it is the business of worship and doctrine to express the Christian truth. They tend to differ on the question of which of the two, doctrine or worship, should set the pace, and they differ profoundly on the question of whether either or both—the Church's worship or its doctrine—may fall into error.[11]

Also, Wainwright states that it is rare to find Protestant theologians who have addressed at length the questions involved in the interplay between worship and doctrine, even though the interplay undeniably takes place in Protestant churches. He notes that the Reformers were determined to control worship with doctrine and that doctrine's primacy in relation to liturgy remains characteristic of Protestantism.[12]

In *The Making of Christian Doctrine*,[13] Maurice Wiles addresses the issue of early doctrinal development and considers the role of *lex orandi* in doctrinal formulation.[14] He contends that early doctrinal controversies were not matters of intellectual argument alone and that ideas such as Arianism and subordinationism were defeated on an official doctrinal level largely because they failed to do justice to the early Christian view that the Son is a fitting object of worship. He continues by stating that amid the debate over the status of the Holy Spirit the most important factor was the established institution of triple immersion at baptism into the names of Father, Son, and Holy Spirit.[15]

However, in regard to the christological controversy, Wiles says that the influence of worship that contributed to the siding for Nicene theology over against Arius was the pattern of popular devotion, not the pattern of ordered liturgical development. His belief that the influence of worship in the earliest doctrinal development was at times that of "untutored popular devotion"[16] causes Wiles to warn that theologians not accept uncritically the validity of the influence of *lex orandi*. Wiles concludes that while the practice of prayer *has had* an effect on doctrine and *should continue* to do so, the practice of prayer has *not* always had the effect on doctrine that it *should have had*.[17]

THE RULE OF SPIRITUALITY AND THE RULE OF DOCTRINE

I now want to state the specific points of a pentecostal appropriation of *lex orandi, lex credendi* informed by Wainwright and Wiles that I call "the rule of spirituality and the rule of doctrine." I will then offer two examples that implicitly illustrate the relationship between the two, one from the New Testament and one from fourth-century Greek pneumatology. I will conclude this section with a brief survey of three aspects of pentecostal spirituality that should figure prominently in any attempt to articulate a relationship between spirituality and doctrine.

Relationship between Spirituality and Doctrine

These insights from Wainwright and Wiles lead to two specific guidelines that pentecostals should follow when relying on *lex orandi, lex credendi* as an aspect of theological method. First, while Wainwright's characterization of Protestant and Roman Catholic reliance on the relationship between *lex orandi, lex credendi* is by his own admission a generalization, his descriptions can serve as a heuristic device for developing a pentecostal approach to the relationship between the two. Such an approach should involve granting a reciprocal relationship between *lex orandi* and *lex credendi* rather than one ordered in either direction. That is, pentecostals could acknowledge that each unavoidably influences the other, and they could encourage the interplay between worship and beliefs in their formulation of doctrinal theology. They would intentionally employ the rule of prayer in order to influence the rule of belief, and they would intentionally employ the rule of belief in order to influence the rule of prayer.

Second, a pentecostal appropriation of *lex orandi, lex credendi* should also involve giving careful attention to the role of what Wiles calls untutored popular devotion in doctrinal development. That is, pentecostal practices should have a formative role in doctrinal formulation, but pentecostals should not accept their practices uncritically. Rather, pentecostals must engage in a serious discerning process about precisely which practices they should embrace and transmit and which practices they might need to revise or jettison. They should not pass on everything that they have received.[18]

I propose an appropriate form of *lex orandi, lex credendi* for pentecostals that I call *regula spiritualitatis, regula doctrinae,* "the rule of spirituality and the rule of doctrine." As its name indicates, the axiom says something about the relationship between spirituality and doctrine. I broaden "law of prayer" (*lex orandi*) to "rule of spirituality" because on the whole pentecostals do not tend to place much emphasis on scripted liturgy in their worship, although I do not deny that "liturgy" can also refer to worship in a broader sense. This is not to say that pentecostals *should not* place more emphasis on scripted liturgy than they usually do—I have no doubt that they could benefit from such an increased emphasis. However, to limit this methodological principle to scripted liturgy would be to sabotage it from the start. "Rule of spirituality" better captures the realities of pentecostal practices as well as formative experiences that lie outside the boundaries of corporate worship.[19] Walter Principe expresses some of my intention by the phrase "rule of spirituality" when he refers to the existential nature of spirituality as related to one's lived experience.[20] "Rule of doctrine" refers to the consciously formulated and adopted teachings of pentecostal communities expressed in a systematic fashion that explores how those doctrines relate to each other. I intentionally avoid describing doctrine as the official teaching of a denomination or fellowship of churches, although this may be a legitimate approach for other contexts.[21] My purpose for using the phrase "rule of doctrine" is to distinguish between, on the one hand, general theological beliefs that might be almost indistinguishable from the ethos of a spirituality and, on the other hand, particular theological views that have been acknowledged, scrutinized, and carefully articulated with sensitivity to broader systematic relationships between it and other acknowledged, scrutinized, and carefully articulated theological views. Every Christian tradition struggles with the difficulty that its most skilled theologians are not always the ones who make ecclesiastical decisions about the content of official teaching, and pentecostals are no exception. Because they do not assume that the Spirit will necessarily keep their official doctrinal decisions from error and because they do not rely on a magisterium to judge their theological developments,[22] detailed and astute theological positions often flourish among pentecostals even though they do not enjoy the status of official authoritative teaching. These kinds of theological articulations are what I mean by "doctrine." I also change the phrases from the use of "law" (*lex*) to the use of "rule" (*regula*). On the one hand, *lex* implies something that is binding and, therefore, would effectively communicate my belief that the mutual influence of spirituality and doctrine is binding and unavoidable. On the other hand, I prefer *regula* in order to underscore the reality that responsible doctrinal formulation requires the discipline associated with following a community rule. At its best, doctrinal theology is an ascetic practice carried out in community that involves the rigorous training of all of one's faculties for the greater glory of God. In short, doctrinal theology is itself a spiritual discipline that one practices with detail and determination and in fellowship with other believers.

Unlike those who may tend to choose an either-or approach to *lex orandi*, *lex credendi*, pentecostals can adopt a both-and understanding of the rule of spirituality and the rule of doctrine. Just as spirituality has something to say about doctrine, doctrine also has something to say about spirituality. If pentecostal theologians allow spirituality and doctrine to stand in a proper relationship with each other, the results can be the articulation of doctrines that are not antagonistic to the aspects of spirituality that are intentionally embraced by a pentecostal community, as well as doctrine that can in turn inform and if necessary correct aspects of a pentecostal community's spirituality that need to be adjusted.[23] The movement back and forth between the two could look something like the following. First, what pentecostals assume about God and the world in various facets of spirituality will inform the process of doctrinal articulation. These insights will not be able to provide the entire content of a given doctrine, of course, but they will at least provide a framework for reflection and a point of reference for doctrinal claims. This doctrinal formulation, then, will be in part a verbalization of the implications of the more general and sometimes amorphous theological views that pentecostals already presuppose (at times unconsciously) within their spirituality. Second, the doctrine in question, having been informed by pentecostal spirituality, will then reach a higher level of clarity and specificity and will be able to correct undesirable aspects of the community's spirituality.

Concerning this mutually informing process, I need to state two important qualifications. First, I realize that there is no single pentecostal spirituality shared by all pentecostal communities.[24] I simply use the singular form because I find it more euphonic than "spiritualities." I can only trust that theologians in contexts other than my own will take it upon themselves to determine whether my claims about spirituality and doctrine are useful where they theologize. Second, no pentecostal community in the twenty-first century ever engages in practices that are not *already* influenced by theological beliefs or ever evaluates beliefs that are not *already* influenced by spirituality. Existing theological viewpoints mediate every experience or concrete manifestation of spirituality. No experience is merely passive but rather is a construction involving interpretations rooted in these as well. Therefore, one must speak of more than simply a relationship between spirituality and general or overarching theological views, for in a sense these two exist simultaneously. The relationship that I propose is specifically between spirituality and doctrine, with each understood as described previously. There can be no serious doubt that practices serve as part of the hermeneutical lens through which we view and evaluate beliefs, and vice versa. Neither beliefs nor practices exist as if one were derived solely from the other. Instead, part of the theological task is to become more sensitive to the already existing mutual influence between beliefs and practices and to encourage the active interplay between them with an eye toward the ramifications for both spirituality and doctrine. Since the mutual influence is hermeneutically unavoidable, pentecostals would do well to find a way for it to work for the benefit of both spirituality and doctrine. This is what I hope to achieve through this back and forth movement in theologizing.[25]

The New Testament contains at least one example of this kind of relationship between spirituality and doctrine. In Galatians 3:1–5,[26] Paul rhetorically asks the Galatians if their reception of the Spirit and the Spirit's working of mighty deeds among them stem from works of the law or from faith. Because these things are the results of faith, Paul argues, the Galatians have no need for circumcision or for following the whole law. One way to couch Paul's appeal is to say that he is asking the Galatians to come to a theological viewpoint that is consistent with their spirituality and what they already implicitly assume on the basis of it. According to Paul, their spirituality tells them that their reception of the Spirit and the Spirit's activity among them are due to faith rather than to works of the law. Paul is asking the Galatians to adopt consciously the theological viewpoint that they unconsciously presuppose in their spirituality. Their conscious theological view about the place of works of the law (and of circumcision, specifically) should be consistent with their spirituality. In turn, the theologically sound outlook, once achieved, should inform the spiritual practices of the Galatians. That is, they should refuse circumcision because it is not a means to righteousness. In other words, Paul offers the Galatians' experiences of the Spirit as a means through which to reach a theological conclusion. The conscious theological view then becomes the means through which the Galatians should reach a decision about their practices.

Basil of Caesarea's *On the Holy Spirit*[27] serves as a similar example. At the beginning of this treatise, Basil states that certain persons objected to his occasional amendments to the doxology. Instead of consistently closing the doxology with "Glory to the Father through (διὰ) the Son in (ἐν) the Holy Spirit," the accepted phrase, Basil sometimes concludes with "Glory to the Father with (μετὰ) the Son along with (σὺν) the Holy Spirit."[28] Refuting his objectors, Basil claims that it is entirely appropriate to place the Holy Spirit "along with" (σὺν) the Father and the Son, as is the case in the latter formula. The point of interest for me is that Basil makes this statement on the basis of the established baptismal formula, according to which baptism takes place "in the name of the Father and the Son and the Holy Spirit."[29] Basil continues,

> What makes us Christians? "Our faith," everyone would answer. How are we saved? Obviously through the regenerating grace of baptism. How else could we be? We are confirmed in our understanding that salvation comes through Father, Son, and Holy Spirit. Shall we cast away the standard teaching we received?[30]

Since the Holy Spirit is as much the source of regenerating grace as the Father and the Son (Basil's point here), it is proper to give glory to the Holy Spirit "along with" (σὺν) the Father and the Son. Basil's argument can be accurately summarized as follows: Basil appeals to the common reality of accepted spiritual practice (the baptismal formula, which assumes that the Holy Spirit is also the source of saving grace) in order to support the theological claim that it is fitting to give glory to the Spirit "along with" (σὺν) the Father and the Son. This theological outlook, then, informs the liturgical practice, inasmuch as "Glory to the Father with (μετὰ) the Son along with (σὺν) the Holy Spirit" is an appropriate conclusion to the doxology.

Both Paul and Basil appeal to spirituality to inform theology, Paul to the works of the Holy Spirit and Basil to the practices of corporate Christian worship. Each endeavors to employ spirituality to make explicit an implicit theological belief. For Paul, the belief is that reception of the Spirit depends on faith rather than works of the law, and for Basil, the belief is that the Spirit is equally worthy of glory with the Father and the Son. Each argument also suggests a concern for coherence between practices and implicit beliefs now made explicit. For Paul, the practice is circumcision—namely, the refusal of it—and for Basil, the practice is praying the doxology. The rule of spirituality and the rule of doctrine should, likewise, involve making implicit beliefs explicit and establishing coherence between beliefs and practices.

Some Core Aspects of Pentecostal Spirituality

"We drink from our own wells." This is the phrase that Gustavo Gutiérrez uses to describe the practice of drawing on the experiences of Latin Americans to inform liberation theology.[31] Pentecostals are increasingly drawing intentionally upon other Christian traditions in their theologizing, and this has tremendous potential to benefit their doctrinal theologies.[32] But as they do so, they must not neglect to drink from their own wells also. I want to highlight three facets of pentecostal spirituality—the Spirit's transforming work, eschatology, and the universality of the Spirit's work—in order to draw upon them for a discussion of the Lord's supper. Then, I will reverse the perspective and examine other components of pentecostal spirituality from the view of a doctrine of the Lord's supper. These three components are by no means exhaustive of pentecostal spirituality, but I choose them because of their importance for a doctrine of the supper. Since many pentecostal communities share them, I assume that my suggestion of them is not innovative or controversial and, therefore, discuss them briefly.

First, it is axiomatic to pentecostal spirituality that the Holy Spirit is present among the people of God to transform them, especially during corporate worship. Pentecostal soteriology places heavy emphasis on rebirth and renewal in the Spirit and the sanctifying work of the Spirit. Whether conceived primarily in ontological categories that emphasize perceived similarities with Eastern Orthodox ideas of *theosis*[33] or in more practical theological categories,[34] the transforming dimension of the Holy Spirit among the people of God can hardly be overstated.

This transforming dimension of the Spirit's activity is one way of speaking about the Holy Spirit being poured out on the people of God. This brings me to the second and third aspects of pentecostal spirituality, both of which are intimately related to the first. The second is that pentecostal spirituality has an eschatological orientation. The kingdom of God, many early pentecostals believed, had broken into history, and the gospel had to be preached with urgency in all of the world because Jesus' second coming was imminent.[35] In short, the Spirit cultivates eschatological longing and fervor.

The third aspect of pentecostal spirituality is the notion that the transforming activity of the Holy Spirit is available equally and to the same extent to all members of the believing community. The outpouring of the

Spirit is upon all flesh—male and female, sons and daughters, young and old, slave and free (Acts 2:17–18). To the extent that pentecostalism is faithful to this tenet of its spirituality, there is no concept of any person within the community of faith having greater capacity for the Spirit than any other person within the community. This does not mean, of course, that everyone exhibits exactly the same gifts or degrees of maturity and formation. The point here regards potential, not necessarily actuality.

A DOCTRINE OF THE LORD'S SUPPER IN LIGHT OF PENTECOSTAL SPIRITUALITY

The following is an application of the method described previously in an attempt to give more extensive theological content to a doctrine of the Lord's supper for pentecostals in light of their own spirituality. This is by no means an exhaustive formulation of all components needed for a robust doctrine of the supper. Because this discussion is an exercise in the particular theological method at hand, I discuss only those facets of a doctrine of the supper that follow from the three aspects of pentecostal spirituality I have sketched. In respect to the Lord's supper, I discuss the role of remembrance, the question of divine presence, the importance of eschatology, and the question of who is qualified to preside over the supper's celebration.[36]

More Than Remembrance

Whatever else the Lord's supper may be, it is at very least a commemoration for the believer of Jesus' death on his or her behalf. Indeed, this is the exclusive attitude with which many pentecostals celebrate the Lord's supper.[37] However, a doctrine of the supper that emphasizes solely the concept of remembrance overlooks the transforming potential of the pneumatological and eschatological dimensions of pentecostal spirituality. Since openness to the transforming work of the Spirit at any time characterizes the spirituality, the celebration of the supper should not be an exception. And since pentecostal spirituality is eschatologically oriented, this sense should find emphasis in the supper as well. Remembrance should be part of the event, but it should hardly be the dominating theme. Of all of the passages in the New Testament that refer to the supper (Matt 26:26–30; Mark 14:22–26; Luke 22:14–20; I Cor 10:14–22, 11:23–34),[38] only two of them mention ἀνάμνησις (Luke 22:19 and I Cor 11:24). Each of these two passages simply states that Jesus instructed those with him to eat the meal in his remembrance, without any elaboration on what those subsequent acts of remembrance should involve or what their effects might be.[39]

To the extent that pentecostals stand within interpretive traditions that have been suspicious of some of the excesses of a sacramentally oriented soteriology, it is easy to understand why many of them see the Lord's supper as no more than an act of remembrance. To eat the meal in remembrance of Jesus is an important act of obedience that should not be overlooked, but the idea that the supper is nothing more than a time of remembering and that nothing else is to be gained from its observation is an example of what Maurice Wiles calls untutored popular devotion.[40] That is, it is a widely held and partially reactionary idea that pentecostal theologians have yet to scrutinize adequately. Therefore, it is necessary to subject this notion to serious theological inquiry while both granting that it is the most common approach to the supper among pentecostals and asking whether this should continue to be the case. I contend that, in spite of this established track record, pentecostals should not continue to celebrate the supper solely as a time of remembrance. They need to consider other aspects of the supper, and they should be ready for the task because they have the ability to draw insights from their own spirituality to deepen the significance of the supper for their communities.

Divine Presence in the Supper

A doctrine of the supper that is faithful to the realization that the Spirit transforms the people of God will necessarily address the question of divine presence in the supper, and there is hardly any doubt that in the history of theology this controversial issue has been focused primarily on the question of the nature and means of the presence of *Christ* in the supper. But should this be the first or primary question for pentecostals about divine presence in the supper?

In another context, D. Lyle Dabney writes,

Moreover, as a movement that has arisen at the end rather than at the beginning or in the middle of the era of Christendom, Pentecostalism is not a tradition that represents yet another answer to the question of Christendom, the question of How?, but is rather implicitly the emergence of a claim about a different question entirely, a new posing of the question of What?: What is the gospel of Jesus Christ? What is the grace of God in Christ all about? What is the redemption of which we speak and in which we hope?[41]

The importance of Dabney's statement for my purposes is simply this: pentecostals should not avoid returning to basic theological questions of "What?" that may have been settled for so long in the Christian tradition that the only questions still being asked in relation to them are questions of "How?" That is, they must not shy away from theologically engaging at fundamental levels theological issues whose content (the question of "What?") may be so settled in the larger Christian tradition that questions now arise merely about mode or agency (the question of "How?"). I suspect that in at least some instances pentecostals might discover that they do not share the dominant views about the content of a theological issue and that they must ask for themselves "What?" before they can address issues of mode or agency by asking "How?" If pentecostal theologians are to ask anew fundamental theological questions in order to address new situations, then they must be open to the possibility that some within the theological tradition might have misplaced some of their theological emphases or that their categories might have been altogether appropriate for their contexts but are insufficient for our own.

Perhaps pentecostals should ask again at least one fundamental question about the Lord's supper. The dominant question concerning the supper, at least since the ninth-century writings of Paschasius Radbertus and Ratramnus,[42] has been the question "How?"—that is, "How is Christ present in the supper?" Most Christian traditions assume that Christ is in fact present; the dispute is over mode rather than fact. Most Christian traditions agree on the question of "What?"; however, they disagree on the question of "How?" Rather than becoming immediately entangled in questions about the means or agency of Christ's presence in the supper, pentecostals can first ask anew "What"—or rather—"Who is present in the supper?" Or, better, "Into whose presence are we first and foremost inquiring when we pose the question of divine presence in the supper?" Much more than semantic nuance, this is a shift from inquiring about the mode of an assumed reality to inquiring about the very content of the reality itself. If according to pentecostal spirituality it is the Holy Spirit who is active among the people of God to transform them, then for pentecostals the question of the Spirit's presence in the supper could take precedence over the question of Christ's presence in the supper. Since most pentecostals do not take literally Jesus' words that the bread and wine are his body and blood (Matt 26:26–28; Mark 14:22–24; Luke 22:20), they are in position to see that little if anything else in any of the relevant New Testament texts prioritizes the question of Christ's presence in the supper.

For example, in the Last Supper passages from the Synoptic Gospels, the context of the meal is not Jesus' *presence* but his *absence*. Jesus is preparing his disciples for his departure, and they will thereafter eat the meal in his remembrance because he will not be present with them in the meal until he eats it again with them in the kingdom of God (Matt 26:29; Mark 14:25; Luke 22:16). By this point in the narratives, the readers of all three Synoptic Gospels have already been warned that the unthinkable will take place, namely, the departure of the bridegroom (Matt 9:14–15; Mark 2:18–20; Luke 5:33–35).[43] To the extent that fasting often accompanied mourning, there is nothing surprising in Jesus' assertion that the time of the bridegroom's *presence*—a time of joy and feasting—is not the time for fasting. The shock is in his claim that the bridegroom will depart, during which time his followers will fast in his *absence*.[44] The Last Supper passages are a similar preparation for Jesus' departure, although one that carries even more urgency given its closer proximity to his death.

In addition, I Corinthians 10:16[45] does not refer to mystical union with Christ's body and blood, which are believed to be somehow present in the Lord's supper. Paul rhetorically appeals to the idea that the celebration of the supper creates "fellowship" (κοινωνία) between the participant and Christ's body and blood in order to parallel that fellowship with the fellowship between those who sacrifice to idols and the demons to whom such sacrifices are ultimately made (10:19–20),[46] all in order to convince the Corinthians that they should avoid idolatry (10:14).[47] This fellowship with Christ's body and blood refers to the common interest (another sense of κοινωνία) that all of the Corinthians have in Jesus' suffering and death,[48] a Pauline soteriological metaphor also found in Romans 6:3–5[49] and Philippians 3:8–11.[50] Paul follows his rhetorical questions by stating that the many who share in the one bread are one body (I Cor 10:17)[51] with a common stake in and commitment to Jesus' death,[52] which the Corinthians should demonstrate by celebrating the supper only after all have assembled (11:33–34).[53] In short, neither the Synoptic Gospels nor I Corinthians points to Christ's *presence*, but rather to his *absence*.[54]

Eschatological Passions

A doctrine of the Lord's supper that is faithful to the eschatological orientation of pentecostal spirituality could involve the view that celebrating the supper is a catalyst that enlivens eschatological passions. Each celebration can inspire hope for the coming kingdom of God in its fullness, but it can also cause groaning that cannot be expressed in words (Rom

8:26) as the people of God struggle under the tension of anticipation for ultimate redemption, a tension fueled by the realization that once again the Lord's supper is being observed without the fullness of the kingdom. The supper can have a proper eschatological orientation for pentecostals only if when observing the meal they remember that Jesus is still absent and that they still anticipate his coming. The supper does not dissolve the distinctions between present and future;[55] rather, it accentuates these distinctions. The supper reminds us that what is expected in the future is by very fact not realized in the present, for who waits in hope for what she sees? (Rom 8:24). After all, we still live in a world of injustice and seemingly gratuitous evil, and we still celebrate the supper until he comes (I Cor 11:26).[56] The kingdom is still not here in its fullness, and Jesus is still absent; therefore, we groan. Only once emphasis shifts from Christ's eucharistic presence to the Spirit's presence can the supper have its full effect in deepening eschatological passions, for this shift allows the supper to be seen as a celebration that takes place in the presence of the Spirit, who is present in the very absence of the Son. The presence of the Spirit in the absence of the Son is a characteristic of Christian existence, and it is precisely in Jesus' absence that we rely on the Spirit's presence when celebrating the supper.

The Presence of a Minister

I have already suggested that a consequence of the pentecostal notion of the Spirit being poured out on all flesh is that no one in the community of faith has a greater capacity for the Spirit than another member of the community. If this is so, then there is no place in a pentecostal doctrine of the Lord's supper for the particular distinctions between clergy and laity that would exclude laity from leading a celebration of the Lord's supper or that would require a representative of the clergy to be present in order for the supper to be celebrated. Yet, some pentecostals operate with these restrictions while offering little theological rationale for them.[57] It is clear why a priest or an ordained minister within a tradition that affirms the consecration of the bread and wine into Christ's body and blood must be present for the supper, for only he or she can effect the consecration. But why would pentecostals, who do not operate with a theology of consecration, enforce these requirements?

It may be that these requirements are simply an uncritical continuation of the precedent of older Christian traditions. If this is the case, perhaps pentecostals should not continue to maintain a conclusion whose premises they have already rejected. If a priest or an ordained minister is not needed to consecrate the bread and wine, then his or her presence is not essential to a celebration of the supper. Or, perhaps these requirements among pentecostals stem from a commendable desire to maintain order and reverence in the supper. If so, then Paul's approach related to similar concerns in I Corinthians 11:17–34 provides a helpful model for consideration. When addressing the many improprieties of the Corinthians' celebrations of the supper, Paul does not correct them by requiring that certain persons always be present to ensure an orderly celebration. Instead, he attempts to impress upon *all of the Corinthians* the gravity of the meal by stating that one can eat and drink unworthily by failing to discern the body, and thereby show hostility against the body and blood of the Lord.[58] Given the immediate context of 11:17–22, 33–34, the phrase "discerning the body" (v. 29) probably refers in part to giving necessary considerations to the assembled body of believers, hence Paul's instructions to wait for each other before eating the meal (11:33–34).[59] But given his comments in 10:14–22, it could also refer to the fact that eating the bread and drinking the cup should not be casual actions because of their association with Christ's body and blood (10:16). Paul's hope is that a more thorough understanding of the solemnity of the supper—in respect to both the body of believers in the Corinthian community and the body and blood of the Lord—will produce an orderly celebration. The presence of any particular persons does not guarantee a more reverent celebration of the supper if, as in Corinth, there is rampant misunderstanding about its seriousness. Similarly, the presence of an ordained pentecostal minister does not necessarily result in all of those participating—the minister included—discerning both the assembled body of believers and the body and blood of the Lord. Only discipleship and theological instruction can ensure the necessary reverence for the supper.

PENTECOSTAL SPIRITUALITY IN LIGHT OF A DOCTRINE OF THE LORD'S SUPPER

Having made some suggestions concerning a doctrine of the Lord's supper, I wish to consider aspects of pentecostal spirituality from the perspective of the doctrine of the supper I have described. This is an exercise in "the rule of doctrine" now influencing "the rule of spirituality." The first point is related to eschatology in general, and the remaining points are related to the actual celebration of the supper itself.

"Realized Eschatology"

Both Land and Macchia insist that pentecostals must maintain an "already-not yet" tension in their eschatology. How might a doctrine of the Lord's supper correct this tendency in pentecostal spirituality toward realized eschatology? Primarily, it could work against ideas of the kingdom's full realization in the present by underscoring Jesus' absence rather than his presence. If Jesus is still absent, then the kingdom must also be understood as somehow still absent, even if it has drawn near (Mark 1:15). The idea that the church can make Christ to be present eucharistically whenever it sees fit to celebrate the supper and that the supper effects mystical union with Christ will always have the potential to encourage forms of realized eschatology. To an extent, Christ's presence is domesticated and housed at the will of the church. As pentecostals seek a developed doctrine of the Lord's supper, it will be important for them to avoid this hazard by giving priority to the question of the Spirit's presence in the supper in order to resist undue preoccupation with the question of Christ's eucharistic presence. A celebration of the supper that reinforces Jesus' absence can help maintain the "not yet" of the "already-not yet" tension.

Acknowledging Jesus' absence and rejecting realized eschatology can encourage pentecostals to take evil more seriously and address it through both theologizing and concrete social action. The celebration of the Lord's supper as an opportunity for the Spirit to orient believers to Jesus' death, in which all humans have a common stake (κοινωνία), can serve as additional impetus for social action. Larry W. Hurtado writes of the paradigmatic nature of Jesus' death in the New Testament and highlights the implications of passages such as Mark 10:42–45 for service and self-giving.[60] In this passage, Jesus states that those who are great among the Gentiles exert authority over each other, but the ones among Jesus' followers who wish to become great will become servants and slaves because they follow Jesus' example. Jesus came to serve rather than to be served and to give his life as a means of redemption for many. Jesus' followers cannot give their lives as ransoms, but they can imitate his service.[61]

William T. Cavanaugh argues that celebrations of the Lord's supper have political ramifications. In his consideration of its practice by Roman Catholic Chileans during the Pinochet regime (1973–1990), Cavanaugh calls the celebration of the supper an act of resisting torture, the regime's program for dismantling faith communities. He writes, "The torturer extracts a confession of the unlimited power of the state. The Eucharist requires the confession that Jesus is Lord of all, and that the body belongs to him."[62] Yet, as Walter Brueggemann points out (in reference to Cavanaugh), the need in

North America, especially in the United States, is less for celebrations of
the Lord's supper that empower the tortured to resist the state's oppression and more for celebrations that promote the resistance of "commodity
satiation."[63] Viewed pneumatologically and in light of Jesus' absence, the
Lord's supper could become for pentecostals a constant reminder that they
must actively engage the brokenness and suffering of the world in which
they live. As Jesus' death, the ultimate example of service, is repeatedly
placed before them through the supper, they could be challenged to serve
rather than to be served and to play their parts in making provisions for
others. It was by the Spirit that Jesus offered himself to God on our behalf
(Heb 9:14), and it is only through the mortifying work of the Spirit that we
will offer ourselves with similar abandonment to others. The supper can be
a time in which the Spirit turns our attention to others and empowers believers for this self-giving. Herein, one sees how a pneumatological priority
in a theology of the Lord's supper leads to one of the most important christological dimensions of the supper. By focusing on the Spirit's presence,
pentecostals can become more sensitive to the need to devote themselves
to others in Jesus' absence after the pattern of his self-surrender. The need
for focusing on the Holy Spirit with respect to divine presence in
the supper is not in order to evacuate christology per se from a theology of
the supper. On the contrary, it invigorates the christological dimension by
shifting the questions from Christ's eucharistic presence to the believer's
imitation of his self-giving to others. It makes pneumatology the entry
point into considering the christological dimensions of the supper.[64] Pentecostals would do well to adopt a post-communion prayer that underscores
the sense of mission that is so intimately connected to the Lord's supper.
For example, until pentecostals write their own liturgies, perhaps a portion
of the following post-communion prayer from the *Book of Common Prayer*
would suffice for their celebrations of the supper:

> Send us now into the world in peace, and grant us strength and courage to love
> and serve you with gladness and singleness of heart; through Christ our Lord.
> Amen.[65]

Frequency of Celebration

Given the realization that the Lord's supper is far more significant than
merely a time of remembering Jesus' death, pentecostals should consider
both celebrating it more frequently and in a manner that makes it more
central to corporate worship.[66] They have long known the value of waiting

in the Spirit's presence. The supper could become another opportunity to pause with openness to the Spirit's work of orienting them to the brokenness, suffering, and death of the crucified Jesus and of the present world, as well as to enliven their eschatological passions by reinforcing Jesus' absence and thereby fueling their desperate longing for his return and the redemption of the entire world. If pentecostals are committed to maintaining their emphasis on eschatology, then the supper can play a formative role in their attempts to reformulate this emphasis.[67] With so much at stake in a pneumatologically based approach to the Lord's supper, a celebration at every gathering of believers is certainly in order.[68]

My argument that the presence of an ordained minister is not necessary for a legitimate pentecostal celebration of the supper is by no means an arbitrary dismissal of authority. In addition to the reasons discussed previously, the fact that such a view can become an obstacle to frequent celebrations of the supper also motivates my argument. With an ever-increasing number of small group meetings focused on discipleship, which take place in addition to traditional weekly worship services and often in the homes of church members, there is great opportunity for pentecostals to increase the frequency of their celebrations of the supper. They should not hinder this potential simply because an ordained minister is not always present at such gatherings.

Deepening Understanding of the Supper's Significance

If the average pentecostal is to have a deepened understanding of the significance of the Lord's supper for Christian existence, then some preaching on the matter that is both theologically informed and accessible is required. One of John Calvin's discussions of the nature of a sacrament serves as a helpful model. Making what is now a virtually irrelevant polemical point, he argues against the use of Latin instead of the vernacular in the Roman mass. Yet, in doing so, he establishes a mutual interdependence between sacraments and proclamation. Sacraments visibly display the truths that one might be too slow to grasp through preaching alone, and preaching explains the importance of the sacraments as visible signs of the fulfillment of God's promises. The Latin words of consecration—unintelligible to most of their hearers—do not make a sacrament efficacious for the recipients; rather, it is intelligible preaching that leads to understanding, and therefore, to the benefits of the sacrament. Calvin concludes, "Therefore, when we hear mention made of the word that accompanies a sacrament, let us understand it to be the promise, which, having been proclaimed in a loud voice by the minister, leads the people by the hand to that to which the sign directs and sends us."[69]

My point is not that pentecostals should adopt all of the details of a Reformed approach to the relationship between gospel and promise or between Word and sacrament. Nevertheless, they should carefully consider Calvin's claims about the indispensability of preaching to the effectiveness of a sacrament. If pentecostals would be willing to make celebrations of the Lord's supper central to more of their worship gatherings, then there would be both opportunity and need for proclamation of a robust doctrine of the supper. This could involve teaching about why they celebrate the supper and what participants might expect the Holy Spirit to impress upon them during its celebration, including the eschatological orientation and impetus to social engagement discussed previously. The supper's significance is not self-evident; preachers, teachers, and theologians who make disciples within the body of Christ bear the responsibility of explaining its significance. The explication of a doctrine of the supper through theologically sound preaching could enhance the celebration of the supper, and the supper could reinforce those things preached.

SUMMARY AND CONCLUSION

I have argued that a form of *lex orandi, lex credendi* can serve as a valuable methodological tool for pentecostal theologians in their attempts to formulate doctrine in light of spirituality and to inform spirituality from the perspective of doctrine. Called *regula spiritualitatis, regula doctrinae,* "the rule of spirituality and the rule of doctrine," the approach involves intellectual honesty about the influence that worship and beliefs unavoidably have on each other. I also argued that great theological benefit can come from consciously placing spirituality and doctrine in conversation with each other. I recommended this aspect of theological method to pentecostals because it (1) exhibits the traditional pentecostal emphasis on both pneumatology and eschatology, (2) establishes a strong relationship between theology and spirituality in the process of formulating doctrine, (3) is attentive to the hermeneutical matrix constituted by the worshipping communities in which pentecostal theologians are situated, and (4) gives a prominent place to biblical interpretation in systematic theology.

In application of the method, I drew on three facets of pentecostal spirituality (the Spirit's transforming work, eschatology, and the universality of the Spirit's work) to construct a doctrine of the Lord's supper that makes pneumatological emphases the entry point into christological questions, gives greater emphasis to the supper as an eschatological catalyst, and claims that the presence of a credentialed ministers is not necessary for the supper to be effective. From the perspective of a doctrine of the supper, I then critiqued some facets of pentecostal spirituality, including realized eschatology, infrequent celebrations of the supper, and the lack of theological instruction that sometimes accompanies celebrations of the supper.

Conclusion

Instead of summarizing all that has preceded, I want to conclude by explaining and briefly reflecting on the phrase found on the book's dedication page: The battle's not mine, said little David. The metaphor "Saul's armor" has been used to describe pentecostals' theological maturation process, with the implication that they have at times encumbered themselves with some theological interests of other Christian traditions that do not ultimately serve their own theological interests.[1] Like David facing Goliath, the metaphor continues, pentecostals need to discard the armor and weaponry that encumber them and take up the stones and sling needed to slay Goliath. That is, they need to forsake some of the trappings of the theological tradition in order to address the theological task in the twenty-first century with their own insights, rather than solely with insights borrowed from other traditions.

I trust that this book, especially the logic of chapter 5, makes it clear that I see some important heuristic value in this metaphor, even while I by no means think that pentecostals should insulate themselves from other theological traditions.[2] I also hope it is clear, especially in the concluding portions of chapters 1 through 4, that pentecostal systematic theologians *have not* insulated themselves from other traditions or currents in theological method. It remains to be seen whether rising pentecostal theologians will consider the perspectives of figures like Hodge and Warfield, Wesley and Hauerwas, Barth, Moltmann, and Tillich, and Gelpi, Peirce, and Tracy as "Saul's armor" or as "David's stones and sling." Whatever the verdicts on these particular figures turn out to be, pentecostals would do well to consider a couple of things. First, if I may continue to play with the metaphor, David slaying his "tens of thousands" does not obviate Saul slaying his "thousands." There is much to praise in pentecostal systematic theology, just as there is much reason to be optimistic about its future. Pentecostal theologians should remember that it is not necessary to minimize or demean the theological accomplishments of others for their own to emerge. After all, it is the hyperbolic couplet sung after Goliath's defeat that first pits Saul—whom David himself recognizes as the Lord's anointed—against David, only a very few verses after David learns to soothe Saul by playing the lyre. Second, while David certainly fought more adroitly without "Saul's armor," he is not as unschooled in "royal warfare" as an isolated reading of I Samuel 17 might suggest, inasmuch as he has already entered Saul's service and become, ironically enough, his armor-bearer.[3] It is necessary for pentecostals to continue to engage currents in theological method, both to inform them and to be informed by them, to ask old questions and new ones. Saul's armor may be a hindrance to David, but he at least tries it on to find out, rather than dismissing it out of hand.

The battle may not "be David's," since he faces his foe in the name of the Lord of hosts, but he is nonetheless on the scene, equipped and ready to fight. I am confident that such an approach to the theological task can slay many Goliaths—perhaps tens of thousands—and bring great joy!

NOTES

INTRODUCTION

1. Other points of origin include Topeka, KS, and Appalachia, in addition to a number of locations outside the United States in which pentecostalism is indigenous rather than the result of missionary expansions from North America. For an introduction to the events of Azusa Street and their aftermath, see Cecil M. Robeck, Jr., *The Azusa Street Mission and Revival: The Birth of the Global Pentecostal Movement* (Nashville, TN: Thomas Nelson, 2006); William K. Kay, *Pentecostalism: A Very Short Introduction* (Oxford: Oxford University Press, 2011), 17–34.

2. Vinson Synan, *The Holiness-Pentecostal Tradition: Charismatic Movements in the Twentieth Century* (Grand Rapids, MI: Eerdmans, 1997).

3. Grant Wacker, *Heaven Below: Early Pentecostals and American Culture* (Cambridge, MA: Harvard University Press, 2001).

4. Kenneth J. Archer, *A Pentecostal Hermeneutic for the Twenty-First Century: Spirit, Scripture, and Community* (London: T & T Clark, 2003), especially chapters 2–4.

5. Donald W. Dayton, *Theological Roots of Pentecostalism* (Peabody, MA: Hendrickson, 1987); D. William Faupel, *The Everlasting Gospel: The Significance of Eschatology in the Development of Pentecostal Thought* (Sheffield: Sheffield Academic Press, 1996); Douglas Jacobsen, *Thinking in the Spirit: Theologies of the Early Pentecostal Movement* (Bloomington, IN: Indiana University Press, 2003).

6. Walter J. Hollenweger, *The Pentecostals: The Charismatic Movement in the Churches* (London: SCM Press, 1972).

7. Harvey Cox, *Fire from Heaven: The Rise of Pentecostal Spirituality and the Reshaping of Religion in the Twenty-First Century* (Reading, MA: Addison-Wesley, 1995).

8. Robert Mapes Anderson, *Vision of the Disinherited: The Making of American Pentecostalism* (Oxford: Oxford University Press, 1979).

9. Frederick Dale Bruner, *A Theology of the Holy Spirit: The Pentecostal Experience and the New Testament Witness* (Grand Rapids, MI: Eerdmans, 1970); James D. G. Dunn, *Baptism in the Holy Spirit: A Re-Examination of the New Testament Teaching on the Gift of the Spirit in Relation to Pentecostalism Today* (Philadelphia, PA: Westminster Press, 1970); Henry I. Lederle, *Treasures Old and New: Interpretations of "Spirit-Baptism" in the Charismatic Renewal Movement* (Peabody, MA: Hendrickson, 1988); Matthew S. Clark and Henry I. Lederle et al., *What Is Distinctive about Pentecostal Theology?* (Pretoria: University of South Africa, 1989).

10. Charles W. Conn, *Like a Mighty Army: A History of the Church of God, Definitive Edition* (Cleveland, TN: Pathway Press, 1996); Edith L. Blumhofer, *The Assemblies of God: A Chapter in the Story of American Pentecostalism*, 2 vols. (Springfield,

MO: Gospel Publishing House, 1989); Margaret M. Poloma, *Charisma and Institutional Dilemmas* (Knoxville, TN: University of Tennessee Press, 1989); Anthea D. Butler, *Women in the Church of God in Christ: Making a Sanctified World* (Chapel Hill, NC: University of North Carolina Press, 2007); Estrelda Alexander, *The Women of Azusa Street* (Cleveland, OH: Pilgrim Press, 2005); Estrelda Alexander, *Limited Liberty: The Legacy of Four Pentecostal Women* (Cleveland, OH: Pilgrim Press, 2008).

11. Keith Warrington, *Pentecostal Theology: A Theology of Encounter* (London: T & T Clark, 2008).

12. At no time in this book do I employ the term "theological method" as what Merold Westphal calls "an algorithm for cranking out theorems." The term does not refer to a mechanistic procedure with a definitive number of steps that guarantees precise theological articulations, but simply to the ways one goes about theologizing. See Merold Westphal, "Hermeneutics and Holiness," in *Analytic Theology: New Essays in the Philosophy of Theology*, ed. Oliver D. Crisp and Michael C. Rea (Oxford: Oxford University Press, 2009), 271.

13. For an introduction to these perspectives, see Rebecca Chopp and Mark Taylor, eds., *Reconstructing Christian Theology* (Minneapolis, MN: Fortress Press, 1994); Serene Jones and Paul Lakeland, eds., *Constructive Theology: A Contemporary Approach to Classical Themes* (Minneapolis, MN: Fortress Press, 2005).

14. See L. William Oliverio, Jr., *Theological Hermeneutics in the Classical Pentecostal Tradition: A Typological Account* (Leiden: E. J. Brill, 2012).

15. Patricia D. Gruits, *Understanding God: A Catechism of Christian Doctrine* (Detroit, MI: Evangel Press, 1962).

16. See, for example, Lisa P. Stephenson, *Dismantling the Dualisms for American Pentecostal Women in Ministry: A Feminist-Pneumatological Approach* (Leiden: E. J. Brill, 2012).

17. J. Rodman Williams, *Renewal Theology: Systematic Theology from a Charismatic Perspective*, 3 vols. (Grand Rapids, MI: Zondervan, 1988–92).

18. See, for example, David K. Bernard, *The Oneness of God*, rev. ed. (Hazelwood, MO: Word Aflame Press, 2001).

19. See, for example, Veli-Matti Kärkkäinen, *One with God: Salvation as Deification and Justification* (Collegeville, MN: Liturgical Press, 2004); Veli-Matti Kärkkäinen, Ad Ultimum Terrae: *Evangelization, Proselytism, and Common Witness in the Roman Catholic-Pentecostal Dialogue (1990–1997)* (New York, NY: Peter Lang, 1999); Veli-Matti Kärkkäinen, Spiritus Ubi Vult Spirat: *Pneumatology in Roman Catholic-Pentecostal Dialogue (1972–1989)* (Helsinki: Luther-Agricola, 1998). Kärkkäinen is preparing a multivolume systematic theology, but the first volume has not yet appeared.

20. As in, for example, David Tracy, *Blessed Rage for Order: The New Pluralism in Theology* (New York, NY: Seabury Press, 1975); Hans W. Frei, *Types of Christian Theology*, ed. George Hunsinger and William C. Placher (New Haven, CT: Yale University Press, 1992).

CHAPTER 1

1. The description "Bible doctrines" is found in Russell P. Spittler, "Theological Style among Pentecostals and Charismatics," in *Doing Theology in Today's World: Essays in Honor of Kenneth S. Kantzer*, ed. John D. Woodbridge and Thomas Edward

McComiskey (Grand Rapids, MI: Zondervan, 1991), 297; Frank D. Macchia, "Revitalizing Theological Categories: A Classical Pentecostal Response to J. Rodman Williams's *Renewal Theology*," *PNEUMA: The Journal of the Society for Pentecostal Studies* 16, no. 2 (1994): 303; Frank D. Macchia, "Theology, Pentecostal," in *The New International Dictionary of Pentecostal and Charismatic Movements*, revised and expanded edition, ed. Stanley M. Burgess and Eduard M. van der Maas (Grand Rapids, MI: Zondervan, 2003), 1123.

2. William W. Menzies, *Anointed to Serve: The Story of the Assemblies of God* (Springfield, MO: Gospel Publishing House, 1971), 172–73; G. W. Gohr, "Pearlman, Myer," in *The New International Dictionary of Pentecostal and Charismatic Movements*, revised and expanded edition, ed. Stanley M. Burgess and Eduard M. van der Maas (Grand Rapids, MI: Zondervan, 2003), 959; Edith L. Blumhofer, *The Assemblies of God: A Chapter in the Story of American Pentecostalism*, vol. 1 (Springfield, MO: Gospel Publishing House, 1989), 318–19; Irene P. Pearlman, *Myer Pearlman and His Friends* (Springfield, MO: Irene P. Pearlman, 1953); Spittler, "Theological Style," 296–98.

3. Myer Pearlman, *Knowing the Doctrines of the Bible* (Springfield, MO: Gospel Publishing House, 1937). The same publisher offered a "revised edition" of the text in 1939, with virtually no changes from the first. The text of the 1937 edition is still in print in English and has been translated into Italian, Korean, Portuguese, and Spanish. Pearlman's other works include *Seeing the Story of the Bible* (Springfield, MO: Gospel Publishing House, 1930); *The Heavenly Gift: Studies in the Work of the Holy Spirit* (Springfield, MO: Gospel Publishing House, 1935); *Through the Bible Book by Book*, 4 vols. (Springfield, MO: Gospel Publishing House, 1935).

4. Douglas Jacobsen, "Knowing the Doctrines of Pentecostals: The Scholastic Theology of the Assemblies of God, 1930–55," in *Pentecostal Currents in American Protestantism*, ed. Edith L. Blumhofer, Russell P. Spittler, and Grant Wacker (Chicago, IL: University of Illinois Press, 1999), 90; David W. Faupel, "The American Pentecostal Movement: A Bibliographic Essay," in *The Higher Christian Life*, ed. Donald W. Dayton (London: Garland, 1985), 89; David Bundy, "The Genre of Systematic Theology in Pentecostalism," *PNEUMA: The Journal of the Society for Pentecostal Studies* 15, no. 1 (1993): 91.

5. For the citations of the Catechism (questions 4, 33, 35, 86, and 87), some of which are completely unacknowledged, see Pearlman, *Knowing the Doctrines*, 50, 225, 226, 228, 237, 253.

6. Pearlman, *Knowing the Doctrines*, 8–11, 181, 326, 334.

7. Ernest S. Williams, "The Life Story of Reverend Ernest S. Williams, 1979–80," Pearlman Memorial Library, Central Bible College, Springfield, MO; Ernest S. Williams, "Pentecostal Origins," interview by James S. Tinney, *Agora* 2, no. 3 (1979): 4–6; C. M. Robeck, Jr., "Williams, Ernest Swing," in *The New International Dictionary of Pentecostal and Charismatic Movements*, revised and expanded edition, ed. Stanley M. Burgess and Eduard M. van der Maas (Grand Rapids, MI: Zondervan, 2003), 1197–98; Menzies, *Anointed to Serve*, 154.

8. E. S. Williams, *Systematic Theology*, 3 vols. (Springfield, MO: Gospel Publishing House, 1953). There is no consensus on whether Williams's work lives up to its name. Robeck calls it "the first systematic theology by a pentecostal" (Robeck, "Williams," 1198). Macchia states that it is "mistakenly titled" (Macchia, "Theology," 1123). Faupel includes Williams's (and Pearlman's) work(s) among three "attempts" at a pentecostal theology (Faupel, "American Pentecostal Movement," 89). Spittler observes that "it might have better been entitled *Notes on Systematic*

Theology" (Spittler, "Theological Style," 299). And Gary B. McGee says "it is more accurately a doctrinal manual" (Gary B. McGee, "Historical Background," in *Systematic Theology*, ed. Stanley M. Horton [Springfield, MO: Logion Press, 1994], 26).

9. Williams's *Systematic Theology* is edited by Frank M. Boyd, who Williams says "has given the most careful attention to every sentence, and, where expressions have been used that might not be clear to those who read, he has sought to make the meaning clear" (Williams, *Systematic Theology*, I:v). It is impossible to be certain of the extent of Boyd's editorial work or whether at any point it compromises the integrity of Williams's notes, but the close similarities with a bound collection of notes taken by one of Williams's students suggests that the three volumes come directly from Williams's lecture materials with little change (see Elmer E. Kirsch, "Systematic Theology II, III, IV by Ernest S. Williams, 1959," Pearlman Memorial Library, Central Bible College, Springfield, MO). Further, Williams states that he has "worked side by side with [Boyd] as he has gone over much of the material" (Williams, *Systematic Theology*, I:v). Boyd (1888–1984) was a pioneer educator in the Assemblies of God who served as the principal of Central Bible College when Williams's *Systematic Theology* was published. See B. M. Stout, "Boyd, Frank Matthews," in *Dictionary of Pentecostal and Charismatic Movements*, ed. Stanley M. Burgess and Gary McGee (Grand Rapids, MI: Zondervan, 1988), 94–95.

10. The observation that Williams's *Systematic Theology* does not treat ecclesiology is, therefore, incorrect. This observation is made in Peter D. Hocken, "Church, Theology of the," in *The New International Dictionary of Pentecostal and Charismatic Movements*, revised and expanded edition, ed. Stanley M. Burgess and Eduard M. van der Maas (Grand Rapids, MI: Zondervan, 2003), 546–47; Macchia, "Theology," 1137.

11. Pearlman is one of Williams's most frequently cited sources. See Williams, *Systematic Theology*, I:84, 155, 176, II:106, 110, 112, 113–14, 139, 185, 186, III:53, 64, 68, 75, 121, 123–24, 153.

12. Williams, *Systematic Theology*, II:5–6, 27. By comparing Pearlman and Williams on this point, I am not suggesting that Pearlman, to the contrary, attempts to "coerce" (to use Williams's word) his readers to adopt his personal views; rather, I illustrate only that Pearlman does not demonstrate as extensive an awareness as Williams that there are multiple interpretive traditions that address various theological themes, all of which claim to be "biblical."

13. Williams, *Systematic Theology*, I:vii–viii.

14. Williams, *Systematic Theology*, II:137–40, 259–63.

15. Williams, *Systematic Theology*, II:161–69.

16. Williams, *Systematic Theology*, III:185–87.

17. Williams, *Systematic Theology*, III:125–33.

18. Arrington's dissertation is entitled "Paul's *Aeon* Theology in I Corinthians," published under the same title (Washington, DC: University Press of America, 1978).

19. French L. Arrington, *Christian Doctrine: A Pentecostal Perspective*, 3 vols. (Cleveland, TN: Pathway Press, 1992–94).

20. Arrington, *Christian Doctrine*, I:57–60, 82.

21. See Arrington, *Christian Doctrine*, I:11. The (general editor's) foreword states that the volumes are offered in part for the benefit of "scholars," but it is clear that they are written on a level that allows for popular consumption. In some respects, the reading level is pre-high school, such as the repeated italicizing of key sentences that distill the main points of their paragraphs. Arrington demonstrates the depth of his scholarly abilities much more clearly in some of his other publications. See

especially French L. Arrington, *The Acts of the Apostles: An Introduction and Commentary* (Peabody, MA: Hendrickson, 1988); French L. Arrington, *The Ministry of Reconciliation: A Study of 2 Corinthians* (Grand Rapids, MI: Baker Book House, 1980); French L. Arrington, *Paul's Aeon Theology in I Corinthians*. More popular publications since *Christian Doctrine* include French L. Arrington, *Encountering the Holy Spirit: Paths of Christian Growth and Service* (Cleveland, TN: Pathway Press, 2003); French L. Arrington, *Exploring the Declaration of Faith* (Cleveland, TN: Pathway Press, 2003); French L. Arrington, *Unconditional Eternal Security: Myth or Truth?* (Cleveland, TN: Pathway Press, 2005); French L. Arrington, *The Spirit-Anointed Jesus: A Study of the Gospel of Luke* (Cleveland, TN: Pathway Press, 2008).

22. See Arrington's citations of Georges Florovsky (*Christian Doctrine*, I:53) and the Athanasian Creed (*Christian Doctrine*, I:127), as well as his reference to John Wesley (*Christian Doctrine*, II:231). Unlike Pearlman and Williams, Arrington includes a bibliography for further reading after each doctrine, although he does not explicitly engage these sources in the text. It is also rare for Arrington to present varying perspectives on a theological issue. For a few examples of the latter, see Arrington, *Christian Doctrine*, I:189–90, II:84–86, 138–41, 265–69.

23. Arrington, *Christian Doctrine*, I:13.

24. Williams, *Systematic Theology*, I:vii.

25. Arrington, *Christian Doctrine*, I:13.

26. On the influence of common sense realism in American theology, see Mark A. Noll, *America's God: From Jonathan Edwards to Abraham Lincoln* (Oxford: Oxford University Press, 2002), 93–113. On the influence of common sense realism on early pentecostal biblical interpretation, see Grant Wacker, *Heaven Below: Early Pentecostals and American Culture* (Cambridge, MA: Harvard University Press, 2001), 75–76; Kenneth J. Archer, *A Pentecostal Hermeneutic for the Twenty-First Century: Spirit, Scripture, and Community* (London: T & T Clark, 2004), 35–40, 72–93.

27. Arrington states, "The true Pentecostal interpreter avoids spiritualizing and giving allegorical interpretations to Scripture" (Arrington, *Christian Doctrine*, I:79). Among the few passages that all three writers read allegorically are Isaiah 14 and Ezekiel 28, which they suppose to describe the fall of Satan. See Pearlman, *Knowing the Doctrines*, 85–86; Williams, *Systematic Theology*, I:131–35; Arrington, *Christian Doctrine*, II:121.

28. Arrington, *Christian Doctrine*, I:34. See also French L. Arrington, "The Use of the Bible by Pentecostals," *PNEUMA: The Journal of the Society for Pentecostal Studies* 16, no. 1 (1994): 101–07. Arrington writes, "Although the truth of the Bible does not depend on our answering historical and literary questions, such study can enlarge and make more precise our understanding of Scripture as the Word of God and how it has been given to humankind. The danger is that it places the Bible in the laboratory of the expert and takes it out of the hands of the ordinary person who can lay no claim to methodological and theological expertise. Grammatical analysis of the text and historical understanding have significance for sound exegesis, but spiritual understanding does not always wait on the acquisition of these tools. It is God who opens eyes of faith and illuminates his Word to the human heart" (103).

29. Some of the words they scrutinize include "atonement," "redemption," "propitiation," "regeneration," "anthropology," and the nine "*charismata*" in I Cor 12:8–11. See Pearlman, *Knowing the Doctrines*, 202–11, 242–43, 320–23; Williams, *Systematic Theology*, I:115–16, II:91; Arrington, *Christian Doctrine*, III:129–61.

30. For example, the names and titles for God, Satan, Jesus Christ, the Holy Spirit, and the church. See Pearlman, *Knowing the Doctrines*, 50–52, 57, 86–89, 141–64, 281–90, 345–48; Williams, *Systematic Theology*, I:137–39, III:9–11; Arrington, *Christian Doctrine*, I:97–109.

31. See Pearlman, *Knowing the Doctrines*, 323; Williams, *Systematic Theology*, I:114–16, 133, II:27, 109, 216, 218, III:56, 115, 144–46, 149, 171, 174, 178, 191–92, 246, 247. Occasionally, Pearlman and Williams consult an English dictionary as well. See Pearlman, *Knowing the Doctrines*, 20; Williams, *Systematic Theology*, I:73, 159, 169, 173, 193.

32. See especially, Pearlman, *Knowing the Doctrines*, 59–65, 84–85, 106–7; Williams, *Systematic Theology*, I:19–22, 200–203, II:82, 140, III:9–11, 154, 224. Arrington's *Christian Doctrine* contains only full, coherent paragraphs, never mere lists of scripture references, but he also offers propositions followed by parenthetical scripture references.

33. Pearlman, *Knowing the Doctrines*, 58–59. Pearlman also addresses Gen 2:7, which suggests that humans are body and soul (read: "material" and "immaterial"), and I Thess 5:23 and Heb 4:12, both of which suggest that humans are body, soul, and spirit. "Both views are correct," he writes, "when properly understood." Humans are bipartite in the sense that they are material and immaterial and tripartite in the sense that soul and spirit constitute two sides of the human's "non-physical substance" (101). Similarly, he resolves the tension between Jesus' commission to baptize in the name of the Father, Son, and Holy Spirit (Matt 28:19) and Peter's admonition to be baptized in the name of Jesus (Acts 2:38) by stating that the former alone constitutes a baptismal formula, while the latter means only that those baptized had acknowledged Jesus as Lord (354). Pearlman also attempts to balance such theological themes as God's immanence and transcendence (57), God's justice and graciousness (201–02), as well as various Reformed and Wesleyan insights on sanctification (252–53, 263–66). On grace and free will, he writes, "The respective fundamental positions of both Calvinism and Arminianism are taught in the Scriptures. Calvinism exalts the grace of God as the only source of salvation—and so does the Bible; Arminianism emphasizes man's free will and responsibility—and so does the Bible. The practical solution consists in avoiding the unscriptural extremes of either view, and in refraining from setting one view in antagonism to the other. For when two scriptural doctrines are set squarely in opposition to each other the result is a reaction that leads to error" (273).

34. Williams, *Systematic Theology*, I:173. In addition, Williams considers whether universal consciousness of sin is effected in humans by the eternal Word (on the basis of Isa 6:1–4 and John 12:41) or the Holy Spirit (on the basis of Gen 1:2 and 6:3). Both views have merit, he says, but what is most important is to realize that God has not abandoned the world to sin (5).

35. Arrington, *Christian Doctrine*, I:59–60. Arrington's practice of comparing scriptures leads him to consider Christ's exaltation to the right hand of God in all power and authority (Eph 1:20–21) and ask whether the eternal Son *already* had all power and authority. He answers, "Yes, He did, for He was God. The essential power and authority of God cannot be increased or decreased. But Scripture teaches that the exalted Christ is both God and Man. Because His deity and humanity are united in His person in heaven, His endowment with authority through His exaltation to heaven was on a different order than His eternal power and authority" (II:104).

36. Pearlman uses "doctrine" and "theology" (when without a preceding adjective such as "biblical" or "systematic") interchangeably (Pearlman, *Knowing the Doctrines*, 8).

37. Pearlman, *Knowing the Doctrines*, 20–24.
38. Pearlman, *Knowing the Doctrines*, 69–70. Elsewhere, Pearlman states that Jesus taught the disciples his "doctrine" before sending the Holy Spirit to remind them of it (287).
39. Pearlman, *Knowing the Doctrines*, 8, 11, 20–21.
40. Pearlman, *Knowing the Doctrines*, 71. One exception to his distinction between "doctrine" and "dogma" may be in his later statement that the "primitive church" formulated the "doctrine" (not dogma) of the Trinity. However, the context does not clarify whether "primitive church" refers to the writers of the New Testament or the post-apostolic church as the formulators of the "doctrine." The statement is preceded by a presentation of the New Testament witness to Jesus as the Son of God and followed by a discussion of a portion of the Nicene Creed (144–46).
41. Pearlman, *Knowing the Doctrines*, 20–21. On the whole, Pearlman approves of the use of creeds in their own right. His concern is that sometimes they become a hindrance because confessing them is "substituted for a living faith" (21) and that "they are recited by many in a formal manner" (146). For a survey of some pentecostal sentiments (both approving and pejorative) about creeds, see Gerald T. Sheppard, "The Nicean Creed, Filioque, and Pentecostal Movements in the United States," *Greek Orthodox Theological Review* 31, nos. 3–4 (1986): 401–16.
42. Pearlman, *Knowing the Doctrines*, 8.
43. Pearlman, *Knowing the Doctrines*, 11–12.
44. It would be misguided, however, to think of these three pentecostals as writing biblical theology understood as an enterprise that describes the theological contents of the Bible in conversation with biblical scholarship, as opposed to attempts to authorize contemporary doctrinal positions from scripture or to make those positions seem credible to contemporary interlocutors. I have conflated this description of biblical theology from James Barr, *The Concept of Biblical Theology: An Old Testament Perspective* (Minneapolis, MN: Fortress Press, 1999), 3–7; and G. B. Caird, *New Testament Theology*, completed and edited by L. D. Hurst (Oxford: Oxford University Press, 1994), 1–4.
45. Williams, *Systematic Theology*, I:3–4; Arrington, *Christian Doctrine*, I:13.
46. In this chapter, "theological epistemology" refers simply to accounts or assumptions about how humans come to know about God.
47. Pearlman, *Knowing the Doctrines*, 17. This is an allusion to I Cor 1:21.
48. Pearlman, *Knowing the Doctrines*, 12.
49. Pearlman, *Knowing the Doctrines*, 24.
50. Pearlman, *Knowing the Doctrines*, 21–22.
51. Williams, *Systematic Theology*, I:1–8, 46–47.
52. Williams, *Systematic Theology*, I:73.
53. Williams, *Systematic Theology*, I:44.
54. Arrington, *Christian Doctrine*, I:13–14.
55. Arrington, *Christian Doctrine*, I:37. This is a citation of Job 11:7.
56. Arrington, *Christian Doctrine*, I:40–49.
57. Arrington, *Christian Doctrine*, I:41–42.
58. Arrington, *Christian Doctrine*, I:44.
59. Arrington, *Christian Doctrine*, I:51–52.
60. Arrington, *Christian Doctrine*, I:76–77. See also Arrington, "Use of the Bible," 103–07.
61. Pearlman is the exception to this. While he contends that revelation found in nature is inadequate, he does not refer explicitly to the noetic impact of sin as Williams and Arrington do.

62. In this respect, they commit the error Charles Taylor calls giving epistemology "pride of place." See Charles Taylor, *Philosophical Arguments* (Cambridge, MA: Harvard University Press, 1995), vii–viii, 1–19. Taylor writes, "These are the assumptions Descartes gave articulation to; central is the view that we can somehow come to grips with the problem of knowledge, and then later proceed to determine what we can legitimately say about other things: about God, or the world, or human life. From Descartes's standpoint, this seems not only a *possible* way to proceed, but the only *defensible* way. Because, after all, whatever we say about God or the world represents a kind of knowledge claim. So first we ought to be clear about the nature of knowledge, and about what it is to make a defensible claim. To deny this would be irresponsible" (vii).

63. Pearlman, *Knowing the Doctrines*, 34–46.

64. Williams, *Systematic Theology*, I:159–62. Concerning intuition, which he defines (from an unspecified English dictionary) as "immediate perception of truth without conscious reasoning," Williams writes, "Intuitive knowledge . . . is fundamental; upon it all subsequent knowledge must build. Among all men there is intuitively a knowledge that a Supreme Being exists, and a certain knowledge concerning right and wrong, as there is concerning other things" (I:159). He goes on to say that such intuition is demonstrated when those who do not have the revelation of the Bible instinctively seek divine help during trouble (I:167–68).

65. Arrington, *Christian Doctrine*, I:25.

66. Williams makes only one passing remark about the relationship between theology and religious experience. He warns that experiences can become problematic if they are based solely on religious feelings rather than on the Word of God. Citing another author, he contends that theology must regulate religious feelings rather than vice versa. See Williams, *Systematic Theology*, I:2–3.

67. Pearlman, *Knowing the Doctrines*, 56, 257, 267, 386.

68. Pearlman, *Knowing the Doctrines*, 73–74.

69. Pearlman, *Knowing the Doctrines*, 259–61.

70. Arrington, *Christian Doctrine*, I:28, 50, 60, 76–77.

71. Arrington, *Christian Doctrine*, I:77–78. See also Arrington, "Use of the Bible," 104–05. Here Arrington writes, "The distance between the interpreter and the biblical text has been a hermeneutical problem, and, too, the distance is even greater for a contemporary interpreter in a scientific culture. This distance needs to be respected, but the Holy Spirit overcomes the distance by serving as the common context and bridging the temporal and cultural distance between the original author and the modern interpreter. Put differently, the Spirit establishes a continuum between the written word of the past and the same word in the present, thereby illuminating what the ancient author's words mean to us living in the twentieth century and how they speak to us today. . . . No one but the Holy Spirit provides the bridge that enables the ancient author and modern interpreter to meet and to span the historical and cultural gulf between them. The heart of the biblical text remains ambiguous until it is illuminated by the Holy Spirit. The pneumatic dimension is so crucial to sound hermeneutics."

72. Charles Hodge, *Systematic Theology*, vol. 1 (Grand Rapids, MI: Eerdmans, 1982; first published in 1871–72), 4–9.

73. Hodge, *Systematic Theology*, I:1–2.

74. Hodge, *Systematic Theology*, I:17. For a discussion of these facets of Hodge's theological method, see Ernest R. Sandeen, *The Roots of Fundamentalism: British and American Millenarianism 1800–1930* (Chicago, IL: University of Chicago Press,

1970), 114–31; E. Brooks Holifield, *Theology in America: Christian Thought from the Age of the Puritans to the Civil War* (New Haven, CT: Yale University Press, 2003), 377–89; David F. Wells, "Charles Hodge," in *The Princeton Theology*, ed. David F. Wells (Grand Rapids, MI: Baker Book House, 1989), 37–62; John W. Stewart, "Introducing Charles Hodge to Postmoderns," in *Charles Hodge Revisited: A Critical Appraisal of His Life and Work*, ed. John W. Stewart (Grand Rapids, MI: Eerdmans, 2002), 11–25. For the claim that these ideas (in Hodge's *Systematic Theology*) are not fully representative of his theological method elsewhere, see Noll, *America's God*, 317.

75. Compare, for example, Pearlman's description of a science as an "arrangement of certified facts" (*Knowing the Doctrines*, 8) with Hodge's description of a science as containing not only facts themselves but also "the internal relation of those facts," (*Systematic Theology*, I:1), as well as their respective discussions of the meaning of "religion" and its distinctions from "theology" (*Knowing the Doctrines*, 8; *Systematic Theology*, I:20–21).

76. While it is not certain that Pearlman read Hodge, it is clear that Williams consulted Hodge's first volume. See his quotation of Hodge, *Systematic Theology*, I:503–04 at Williams, *Systematic Theology*, II:38. Hodge's *Systematic Theology* does not appear in Arrington's bibliographies.

77. Hodge is by no means the only theologian to begin his systematic theology or dogmatics with a theological epistemology in the form of a doctrine of scripture or of revelation. See, for example, Herman Bavinck, *Reformed Dogmatics*, vol. 1 (Grand Rapids, MI: Baker Academic, 2003); Louis Berkhof, *Systematic Theology*, 4th ed. (Grand Rapids, MI: Eerdmans, 1941); Henry Thiessen, *Lectures in Systematic Theology* (Grand Rapids, MI: Eerdmans, 1979).

78. Hodge, *Systematic Theology*, I:155.

79. Hodge, *Systematic Theology*, I:154–55. B. B. Warfield, one of Hodge's best-known students and fellow Princeton theologian, continues his teacher's thinking on the distinctions among revelation, inspiration, and illumination. See B. B. Warfield, "Inspiration," in *Selected Shorter Writings of Benjamin B. Warfield*, vol. 2, ed. John E. Meeter (Phillipsburg, NJ: Presbyterian and Reformed Publishing House, 1973), 615–17; B. B. Warfield, "The Biblical Idea of Inspiration," in *The Inspiration and Authority of the Bible*, ed. Samuel G. Craig (Phillipsburg, NJ: Presbyterian and Reformed Publishing House, 1948), 160–62. Warfield also shares the pentecostal theologians' contention that sin renders humans unable to appropriate general revelation properly. See B. B. Warfield, "Christianity and Revelation," in *Selected Shorter Writings of Benjamin B. Warfield*, vol. 1, ed. John E. Meeter (Phillipsburg, NJ: Presbyterian and Reformed Publishing House, 1973), 24–29. Warfield also affirms that it is the original autographs of scripture that were inerrant and uses an analogy between the divine and human aspects of scripture and the two natures of Christ. See B. B. Warfield, "The Inerrancy of the Original Autographs," in *Selected Shorter Writings of Benjamin B. Warfield*, vol. 2, ed. John E. Meeter (Phillipsburg, NJ: Presbyterian and Reformed Publishing House, 1973), 580–87; B. B. Warfield, "Biblical Idea," 162–63. Arrington echoes these last two sentiments from Warfield. See Arrington, *Christian Doctrine*, I:53, 57–58.

80. The observation that pentecostals initially patterned their theologies after existing theological rubrics is made in Faupel, "American Pentecostal Movement," 89; Bundy, "Genre of Systematic Theology," 91; David R. Nichols, "The Search for a Pentecostal Structure in Systematic Theology," *PNEUMA: The Journal of the Society for Pentecostal Studies* 6, no. 2 (1984): 57–76; Terry L. Cross, "Can There be a Pentecostal

Systematic Theology? An Essay on Theological Method in a Postmodern World," *Proceedings of the 30th Annual Meeting of the Society for Pentecostal Studies*, Tulsa, OK, 2001, 145–66; Steven M. Studebaker, "Pentecostal Soteriology and Pneumatology," *Journal of Pentecostal Theology* 11, no. 2 (2003): 248–70; Steven M. Studebaker, "Beyond Tongues: A Pentecostal Theology of Grace," in *Defining Issues in Pentecostalism: Classical and Emergent*, ed. Steven M. Studebaker (Eugene, OR: Pickwick, 2008), 46–68; Steven J. Land, *Pentecostal Spirituality: A Passion for the Kingdom* (Sheffield: Sheffield Academic Press, 1993), 24.

81. Concerning the rise of pentecostal educational institutions at the beginning of the twentieth century in connection with ministerial training, see Christopher A. Stephenson, "Pentecostal Theology: Retrospect and Prospect," *Religion Compass* 5, no. 9 (2011): 490–500.

82. For a few examples of deductive reasoning, see Pearlman, *Knowing the Doctrines*, 17–19, 121–22, 257; Williams, *Systematic Theology*, I:19, 47, 141; Arrington, *Christian Doctrine*, I:31.

83. For example, Pearlman assigns to the realm of mystery the question of whether the believer is first "regenerated" or "converted," a question that is "not to be analyzed with mathematical precision" (Pearlman, *Knowing the Doctrines*, 227). Similarly, he is content that in John 3:6 Jesus did not explain to Nicodemus *how* the new birth takes place, only *why* humans need it (245). Concerning guardian angels, he claims that even on the basis of Matt 18:10–11 and Acts 12:15 one cannot be certain that each believer has his or her own angel (85), and he writes that although Luke 2:49 indicates that Jesus was aware of his divine identity, the question of how and when he became so must remain a mystery (141).

84. For example, after making what he believes to be self-evident observations, Pearlman twice remarks to the effect that "an ounce of common sense" outweighs any amount of philosophy (Pearlman, *Knowing the Doctrines*, 55, 121). These statements suggest both his suspicion about the value of philosophy for theology and his unwitting dependence on a particular philosophical tenet, namely, common sense.

85. The clearest example of this lack of synthesis and clarity is the struggle that each theologian has with presenting the doctrine of the Trinity, due to his lack of appeal to the metaphysics of substance that keeps the orthodox statement that one God exists in three persons from violating the law of non-contradiction. The category of substance clarifies in the orthodox formulation that God is not both one and three *in the same sense*, but one in respect to substance and three in respect to persons. Their failure to employ this category leaves the doctrine of the Trinity as a mathematical mystery that must simply be affirmed because scripture suggests that God is both one and three. See Pearlman, *Knowing the Doctrines*, 68–77; Arrington, *Christian Doctrine*, I:127–41. Citing another author, Williams makes one reference to the distinction between essence and persons, but it is not integrated into his larger discussion of the Trinity (Williams, *Systematic Theology*, I:199–201). For a similar observation of the lack of engagement with philosophy in pentecostal and charismatic theology, see Terry L. Cross, "Toward a Theology of the Word and the Spirit: A Review of J. Rodman Williams's *Renewal Theology*," *Journal of Pentecostal Theology* 3 (1993): 120–22, 127–35.

86. The importance of pneumatology in the history of pentecostalism is widely known, but the importance of eschatology may not be as obvious. Its prominence among early pentecostals is demonstrated most convincingly in D. William Faupel, *The Everlasting Gospel: The Significance of Eschatology in the Development of Pentecostal Thought* (Sheffield: Sheffield Academic Press, 1996).

87. Studebaker argues that pentecostal theologians in fact inadvertently marginalize pneumatology in their soteriologies (Studebaker, "Pentecostal Soteriology").
88. Williams is concerned more with clearly distinguishing between scripture and tradition than between scripture and experience (Williams, *Systematic Theology*, I:35–36).
89. Arrington, *Christian Doctrine*, I:31, 79–80.
90. Elsewhere, Arrington criticizes the notion that the relationship between scripture and experience is "linear" and insists that it is rather "dialogical." He writes, "At every point, experience informs the process of interpretation, and the fruit of interpretation informs experience." Nonetheless, he still maintains that in this dialogical relationship, scripture should remain the "norm" against which experience must be tested. See F. L. Arrington, "Hermeneutics, Historical Perspectives on Pentecostal and Charismatic," in *Dictionary of Pentecostal and Charismatic Movements*, ed. Stanley Burgess and Gary B. McGee (Grand Rapids, MI: Zondervan, 1988), 384.
91. Other recent texts that exhibit the "Bible doctrines" method include Ned D. Sauls, *Pentecostal Doctrines: A Wesleyan Approach* (Dunn, NC: Heritage Press, 1979); John R. Higgins, Michael L. Dusing, and Frank D. Tallman, *An Introduction to Theology: A Classical Pentecostal Perspective*, 2nd ed. (Dubuque, IA: Kendall/Hunt, 1994); Guy P. Duffield and Nathaniel M. Van Cleave, *Foundations of Pentecostal Theology* (Los Angeles, CA: L.I.F.E Bible College, 1983).

CHAPTER 2

1. Other pentecostals had tended toward doctoral emphases in scripture—French L. Arrington (PhD, St. Louis University, 1975), James M. Beaty (PhD, Vanderbilt University, 1963), Gordon D. Fee (PhD, University of Southern California, 1966), R. Hollis Gause (PhD, Emory University, 1975), Russell P. Spittler (PhD, Harvard University, 1971)—or in the history of Christianity—Stanley M. Burgess (PhD, University of Missouri-Columbia, 1971), William W. Menzies (PhD, University of Iowa, 1968), Cecil M. Robeck, Jr. (PhD, Fuller Theological Seminary, 1985), Vinson H. Synan (PhD, University of Georgia, 1967)—or in social ethics—Leonard Lovett (PhD, Emory University, 1979), Robert M. Franklin (PhD, University of Chicago, 1985). Stanley M. Horton acquired an unaccredited ThD in scripture (Central Baptist Theological Seminary, 1959), and Donald N. Bowdle acquired an unaccredited PhD in scripture (Bob Jones University, 1961) and a ThD in the history of Christianity (Union Theological Seminary [VA], 1970). Other pentecostals who obtained doctoral specialization in systematic theology around the same time as Land include Terry L. Cross (PhD, Princeton Theological Seminary, 1991) and Frank D. Macchia (DTheol, University of Basel, 1989). The number of pentecostals trained in systematic or constructive theology has increased exponentially since that time.
2. Charles W. Conn, *Like a Mighty Army: A History of the Church of God, Definitive Edition* (Cleveland, TN: Pathway Press, 1996), 477–78; Steven J. Land, "A Stewardship Manifesto for a Discipling Church," in *The Promise and the Power: Essays on the Motivations, Developments, and Prospects of the Ministries of the Church of God*, ed. Donald N. Bowdle (Cleveland, TN: Pathway Press, 1980), 287.
3. Steven J. Land, *Pentecostal Spirituality: A Passion for the Kingdom* (Sheffield: Sheffield Academic Press, 1993). This is the published version of his doctoral dissertation submitted at Emory University. Myer Pearlman, *Knowing the Doctrines of the*

Bible (Springfield, MO: Gospel Publishing House, 1937). E. S. Williams, *Systematic Theology*, 3 vols. (Springfield, MO: Gospel Publishing House, 1953). I make this claim in part on the basis of a thorough search of papers and articles in the annual conference proceedings of the Society for Pentecostal Studies, *PNEUMA: The Journal of the Society for Pentecostal Studies*, and *Journal of Pentecostal Theology* 1993–2011, as well as other publications cited in this chapter. Among Land's most notable interlocutors outside the pentecostal tradition is Harvey Cox. See Cox's "A Review of *Pentecostal Spirituality: A Passion for the Kingdom* by Steven J. Land," *Journal of Pentecostal Theology* 5 (1994): 3–12, which is followed by Steven J. Land, "Response to Professor Harvey Cox," 13–16.

4. Land, *Pentecostal Spirituality*, 24. Land gives this description in specific reference to Pearlman's *Knowing the Doctrines of the Bible* (among works by others) but makes no mention of Williams's *Systematic Theology*. Land writes before the publication of French L. Arrington, *Christian Doctrine: A Pentecostal Perspective*, 3 vols. (Cleveland, TN: Pathway Press, 1992–94).

5. I discuss Land's use of the terms "apocalyptic" and "eschatology" later in this chapter.

6. Most of *Pentecostal Spirituality*'s content is summarized in Steven J. Land, "Pentecostal Spirituality: Living in the Spirit," in *Christian Spirituality: Post-Reformation and Modern*, ed. Louis Dupré and Don E. Saliers (New York, NY: Crossroads, 1989), 479–99; and also very briefly in Steven J. Land, "Praying in the Spirit: A Pentecostal Perspective," in *Pentecostal Movements as an Ecumenical Challenge*, ed. Jürgen Moltmann and Karl-Josef Kuschel (London: SCM Press, 1996), 85–93. The salient points of Land's constructive proposals are found in Steven J. Land, "A Passion for the Kingdom: Revisioning Pentecostal Spirituality," *Journal of Pentecostal Theology* 1 (1992): 19–46; Steven J. Land, "The Triune Center: Wesleyans and Pentecostals Together in Mission," *PNEUMA: The Journal of the Society for Pentecostal Studies* 21, no. 2 (1999): 199–214 (published simultaneously in *Wesleyan Theological Journal* 34, no. 1 [1999]: 83–100). Successive citations of "Triune Center" correspond to the publication in *PNEUMA*.

7. It is not, however, primarily apologetic. Land distinguishes some such previous works from his own, which is offered instead as "a comprehensive, theological analysis and constructive explication of Pentecostal spirituality" (Land, *Pentecostal Spirituality*, 23–24). For the observation that *Pentecostal Spirituality* is part apology, see Richard Massey's and Stan Tinon's respective reviews in *EPTA Bulletin* 14 (1995): 112 and *Ashland Theological Journal* 27 (1995): 177. For the observation that it is not apology, see Byron D. Klaus's review in *Paraclete* 29, no. 3 (1995): 46. Further, Land distinguishes his own work from others that he feels are pure apologies of pentecostal practices such as glossolalia (Land, *Pentecostal Spirituality*, 23–24). While having a slightly apologetic tone in a few places, *Pentecostal Spirituality* is by no means polemical.

8. See Frederick Dale Bruner, *A Theology of the Holy Spirit: The Pentecostal Experience and the New Testament Witness* (Grand Rapids, MI: Eerdmans, 1970), 56–149. Bruner, a critic from outside the pentecostal tradition, calls pentecostalism "pneumobaptistocentric" (56) and states that pentecostals are concerned far more with the *experience* than with the *doctrine* of baptism in the Holy Spirit. Land argues to the contrary that premillennial eschatology is the inner logic that indicates the decisive theological shift from the Holiness Movement to pentecostalism, that affections rather than emotional experiences govern pentecostal life, and that it is precisely *as* spirituality that pentecostals express their theology (Land, *Pentecostal Spirituality*, 30,

44, 62–63, 74–75, 122–81, 191). Nevertheless, Land's concern for apology does not hinder his concession of certain other criticisms of pentecostalism, which frame some of his constructive proposals (Land, *Pentecostal Spirituality*, 188–90). The claim to the centrality of baptism in the Holy Spirit to pentecostalism is echoed with specific reference to Bruner in Martin E. Marty, "Pentecostalism in the Context of American Piety and Practice," in *Aspects of Pentecostal-Charismatic Origins*, ed. Vinson Synan (Plainfield, NJ: Logos International, 1975), 206–07; Martin E. Marty, *A Nation of Behavers* (Chicago, IL: University of Chicago Press, 1976), 110–11.

9. Land, *Pentecostal Spirituality*, 29–30, 207.

10. Land, *Pentecostal Spirituality*, 31, 37. On the discipleship of pentecostal converts, see also Land, "Stewardship Manifesto."

11. For a scholarly history of the Azusa street events, see Cecil M. Robeck, Jr., *The Azusa Street Mission and Revival: The Birth of the Global Pentecostal Movement* (Nashville, TN: Thomas Nelson, 2006).

12. Land, *Pentecostal Spirituality*, 13, 26, 47, 184–85, 207. Land takes this sentiment about the heart of pentecostalism from Walter J. Hollenweger, "Pentecostals and the Charismatic Movement," in *The Study of Spirituality*, ed. Cheslyn Jones et al. (Oxford: Oxford University Press, 1986), 551–52. For the observation that Land's portrayal of this early period is sometimes idealistic, see Frank D. Macchia, *Baptized in the Spirit: A Global Pentecostal Theology* (Grand Rapids, MI: Zondervan, 2006), 44; Keith Warrington, "Review of *Pentecostal Spirituality: A Passion for the Kingdom*," *Evangelical Quarterly* 68, no. 3 (1996): 273; Cox, "Review," 5.

13. Land, *Pentecostal Spirituality*, 220.

14. Land, *Pentecostal Spirituality*, 13, 41–46, 132–33. For the charge that Land mistakenly identifies the integration of beliefs and practices in the affections as the "essence" of pentecostalism, see Koo Dong Yun, *Baptism in the Holy Spirit: An Ecumenical Theology of Spirit Baptism* (Lanham, MD: University Press of America, 2003), 154.

15. Land, *Pentecostal Spirituality*, 112.

16. Land, *Pentecostal Spirituality*, 18, 23, 55–56, 61–65, 75, 82–96, 185–86.

17. Land, *Pentecostal Spirituality*, 94, 97.

18. Land, *Pentecostal Spirituality*, 30, 34, 41, 97, 123, 183, 192, 218–19.

19. Land, *Pentecostal Spirituality*, 41.

20. For the claim that Land (and others) overlooks the pentecostal roots in sixteenth-century Anabaptism, see Matthew S. Clark, "Pentecostalism's Anabaptist Roots: Hermeneutical Implications," in *The Spirit and Spirituality: Essays in Honour of Russell P. Spittler*, ed. Wonsuk Ma and Robert P. Menzies (London: T & T Clark, 2004), 194–98, 202.

21. Land, *Pentecostal Spirituality*, 19, 35–36, 47–55, 58–59, 66, 73, 81, 83–89, 116, 121, 148–55.

22. For recent scholarly discussions of the relationship between beliefs and practices, see Catherine Pickstock, *On the Liturgical Consummation of Philosophy* (Malden, MA: Blackwell, 1998); Reinhard Hütter, *Suffering Divine Things: Theology as Church Practice* (Grand Rapids, MI: Eerdmans, 2000); *Knowing the Triune God: The Work of the Spirit in the Practices of the Church*, ed. James J. Buckley and David S. Yeago (Grand Rapids, MI: Eerdmans, 2001); *Practicing Theology: Beliefs and Practices in Christian Life*, ed. Miroslav Volf and Dorothy C. Bass (Grand Rapids, MI: Eerdmans, 2002).

23. Land situates himself in the traditions of John Wesley and Jonathan Edwards in respect to his claim to the centrality of the affections to spirituality (Land, *Pentecostal Spirituality*, 132–33).

24. Land, *Pentecostal Spirituality*, 120–21. Observing the centrality of affections to Land's project Ralph Del Colle writes, "If Karl Barth could define dogmatics as 'the scientific self-examination of the Christian Church with respect to the content of its distinctive talk about God' and Friedrich Schleiermacher describes the same discipline as 'the science which systematizes the doctrine prevalent in a Christian Church at a given time' with doctrine understood as 'accounts of the Christian religious affections set forth in speech' then Land may be said to propose Pentecostal theology as 'the scientific self-examination of the Christian religious affections as they embody speech about God.'" See Ralph Del Colle, "Pentecostalism and Apocalyptic Passion: A Review of Steve Land's *Pentecostal Spirituality: A Passion for the Kingdom*: A Roman Catholic Response," *Proceedings of the 25th Annual Meeting of the Society for Pentecostal Studies*, 12–13, Toronto, 1996. For Del Colle's references to Barth and Schleiermacher, see Karl Barth, *Church Dogmatics*, trans. Geoffrey W. Bromiley (Edinburgh: T & T Clark, 1936), vol. 1, pt. 1, 3–11; Friedrich Schleiermacher, *The Christian Faith* (Edinburgh: T & T Clark, 1928), 76–78, 88–93.

25. Land, *Pentecostal Spirituality*, 30, 44, 74–75, 131.

26. Land, *Pentecostal Spirituality*, 134–36.

27. Land indicates that he is not reducing pentecostal affections to these three alone but offering them as representatives. Even these three stand for clusters of affections rather than singular ones. Gratitude includes praise and thanksgiving; compassion, love and longing; and courage, confidence and hope (Land, *Pentecostal Spirituality*, 138).

28. On the whole, Land conflates justification and regeneration without explanation (Land, *Pentecostal Spirituality*, 82–88, 125, 139). This conflation may be due in part to pentecostals' more frequent claim to be "saved"—as demonstrated in the five-fold gospel—rather than specifically to be "justified" or "regenerated," although they are certainly familiar with the latter terminology. "Saved" carries the weight both of being forgiven of sins and being delivered from the power of sin through birth to new life, and thus, encompasses aspects of both justification and regeneration as often conceived in Protestant theology. Furthermore, because of its assumption of human free will, pentecostal theology has not traditionally needed the conceptual distinction between justification and regeneration predicated by some streams of Reformed theology on the distinction between God's work to enable one's otherwise impotent human will to believe (regeneration) and God's work to forgive sins (justification). On the "mingling of the terms justification and regeneration" among pentecostals, see Nils Bloch-Hoell, *The Pentecostal Movement: Its Origin, Development, and Distinctive Character* (Oslo: Universitetsforlaget, 1964), 122–23.

29. Land, *Pentecostal Spirituality*, 139–61.

30. Land, *Pentecostal Spirituality*, 35–36, 134, 165–73, 218–19.

31. Land, *Pentecostal Spirituality*, 136–37. Furthermore, the affections are themselves one component of the triadic structure that also includes beliefs and practices, which correspond to orthopathy, orthodoxy, and orthopraxy, respectively; and to metaphysics, epistemology, and ethics, respectively (41).

32. Land, *Pentecostal Spirituality*, 175–77. The primacy of affections in spirituality and this governing passion explain Land's title, *Pentecostal Spirituality: A Passion for the Kingdom*. At one point, Land defines theology itself as "a kind of passion for God" (219).

33. For an adaptation of Land's notion of affections toward the ends of a pneumatological theology of love, see Yong, *Spirit of Love*, 76–80.

34. These uses are taken from John J. Collins, *The Apocalyptic Imagination: An Introduction to Jewish Apocalyptic Literature*, 2nd ed. (Grand Rapids, MI: Eerdmans, 1998), 1–14. See also the opening essays by Collins in *Apocalypse: The Morphology of a Genre*, ed. John J. Collins (Missoula, MT: Scholars Press, 1979; *Semeia* 14).
35. Land, *Pentecostal Spirituality*, 61, 65, 192.
36. Land appears to take this sense of "apocalyptic" from Ernst Käsemann, "The Beginnings of Christian Theology," in *New Testament Questions of Today*, trans. W. J. Montague (London: SCM Press, 1969), 102, from which he borrows the notion of apocalyptic as the "mother" of Christian theology and applies it to pentecostal theology (Land, *Pentecostal Spirituality*, 15, 63). In "On the Subject of Primitive Christian Apocalyptic," in the same volume, Käsemann states that in the former essay he uses "primitive Christian apocalyptic [*urchristlicher Apokalyptik*] to denote the expectation of an imminent Parousia" (109). For the German, see "Die Anfänge christlicher Theologie," *Zeitschrift für Theologie und Kirche* 57 (1960): 162–85, and "Zum Thema der urchristlichen Apokalyptik," *Zeitschrift für Theologie und Kirche* 59 (1962): 257–84. For Land's references to Käsemann, see Land, *Pentecostal Spirituality*, 15, 63.
37. It should be noted that Land sometimes uses "apocalyptic" and "eschatology" separately and seemingly interchangeably. In other words, Land does not employ "eschatology" in any sense other than as "apocalyptic," that is, as characterized by the belief in Jesus' imminent second coming. In keeping with this pattern, I use the terms interchangeably when referring to Land. For an articulation of the distinction between "apocalyptic" and "eschatology," see Christopher Rowland, *The Open Heaven: A Study of Apocalyptic in Judaism and Early Christianity* (New York, NY: Crossroads, 1982), 23–48.
38. Land, *Pentecostal Spirituality*, 22–23, 29, 56–64, 72–73, 80, 94–95. Land claims that eschatological urgency is also the reason that early pentecostals saw very few matters of faith as negotiable. Because the coming of the Lord was near, there was no time for indifference or compromise (65–66, 102).
39. Land, *Pentecostal Spirituality*, 15–16, 56, 98–110, 194–96, 212, 222.
40. In light of Land's multiple associations of apocalyptic with Jesus' imminent return, Peter Althouse's claim (in respect to eschatology) that Land has "shifted the emphasis from the soon return of Christ to the delayed *parousia*" may need qualification. See Peter Althouse, *Spirit of the Last Days: Pentecostal Eschatology in Conversation with Jürgen Moltmann* (London: T & T Clark, 2003), 162.
41. Land, *Pentecostal Spirituality*, 23, 53, 58–60, 66, 72, 95.
42. Land, *Pentecostal Spirituality*, 64.
43. Land, *Pentecostal Spirituality*, 41, 96, 196.
44. Land, *Pentecostal Spirituality*, 23. Elsewhere, Land states that in *Pentecostal Spirituality* he attempts "to locate the starting point of theology in the Holy Spirit" (Land, "Response," 13). His claims about pentecostal spirituality and theology having their starting point in the Holy Spirit are tempered, however, by his concession elsewhere that the fivefold gospel makes the Spirit "merely instrumental" (Land, *Pentecostal Spirituality*, 96). Land's claim that the pneumatological basis of pentecostal spirituality and theology in fact demonstrates its christological basis is unclear and receives no elaboration.
45. Land, *Pentecostal Spirituality*, 32–33, 35–36.
46. Land, *Pentecostal Spirituality*, 38, 61, 74, 184, 220.
47. Land, *Pentecostal Spirituality*, 78–79.
48. Land, *Pentecostal Spirituality*, 75, 80–93, 117–19.

49. For a subsequent argument that pentecostals should be distinguished from fundamentalists, see Russell P. Spittler, "Are Pentecostals and Charismatics Fundamentalists? A Review of American Uses of These Categories," in *Charismatic Christianity as a Global Culture*, ed. Karla Poewe (Columbia, SC: University of South Carolina Press, 1994), 103–16.

50. On the Wesleyan quadrilateral, see Donald A. D. Thorsen, *The Wesleyan Quadrilateral: Scripture, Tradition, Reason, and Experience as a Model of Evangelical Theology* (Grand Rapids, MI: Asbury Press, 1990); Michael Lodahl, *The Story of God: Wesleyan Theology and Biblical Narrative* (Kansas City, MO: Beacon Hill Press, 1994).

51. Land, *Pentecostal Spirituality*, 220–22.

52. Land, *Pentecostal Spirituality*, 47, 182–92.

53. Land, *Pentecostal Spirituality*, 197. The practice of constructing a social doctrine of the Trinity in search of implications for the church or society can be found also in Jürgen Moltmann, *The Trinity and the Kingdom: The Doctrine of God*, trans. Margaret Kohl (Minneapolis, MN: Fortress Press, 1993), 161–90; Miroslav Volf, *After Our Likeness: The Church as the Image of the Trinity* (Grand Rapids, MI: Eerdmans, 1998), 191–257; Colin E. Gunton, *The Promise of Trinitarian Theology*, 2nd ed. (Edinburgh: T & T Clark, 1997), 56–82.

54. Land, *Pentecostal Spirituality*, 197–208; the quotations are from 197, 199, 203, 205, 206.

55. Land, *Pentecostal Spirituality*, 41.

56. Land acknowledges Dayton's and Faupel's works as the primary historical foundations for his own study (Land, *Pentecostal Spirituality*, 8, 28–29). See Walter J. Hollenweger, "The Critical Tradition of Pentecostalism," *Journal of Pentecostal Theology* 1 (1992): 7–17; Walter J. Hollenweger, "After Twenty Years' Research on Pentecostalism," *International Review of Mission* 75, no. 297 (1986): 3–12; Walter J. Hollenweger, "Pentecostals and the Charismatic Movement," in *The Study of Spirituality*, ed. Cheslyn Jones et al. (Oxford: Oxford University Press, 1986), 549–54; Walter J. Hollenweger, "The Black Pentecostal Concept: Interpretations and Variations," *Concept* 30 (1970): 1–70; Donald W. Dayton, "Yet Another Layer of the Onion: Or Opening the Ecumenical Door to Let the Riffraff In," *Ecumenical Review* 40, no. 1 (1988): 87–110; Donald W. Dayton, *Theological Roots of Pentecostalism* (Peabody, MA: Hendrickson, 1987); D. William Faupel, "The Everlasting Gospel: The Significance of Eschatology in the Development of Pentecostal Thought" (PhD diss., University of Birmingham, 1989); D. William Faupel, "The Function of 'Models' in the Interpretation of Pentecostal Thought," *PNEUMA: The Journal of the Society for Pentecostal Studies* 2, no. 1 (1980): 51–71. Land writes before the published form of Faupel's dissertation with the same title (Sheffield: Sheffield Academic Press, 1996), to which my citations correspond.

57. Hollenweger, "Pentecostals and the Charismatic Movement," 551–52; Land, *Pentecostal Spirituality*, 29–31, 45, 52, 110–17, 181, 185–92.

58. Dayton, *Theological Roots*, 17–28, 173–79; Land, *Pentecostal Spirituality*, 18, 23, 55–56, 61–65, 82–96, 185–86. Land calls the fivefold gospel "the core of early Pentecostal orthodoxy" (183).

59. Faupel, *Everlasting Gospel*, 41–43, 307–09, and passim; Land, *Pentecostal Spirituality*, 58–121. Land's emphasis on eschatology is broadly compatible also with Robert Mapes Anderson, *Vision of the Disinherited: The Making of American Pentecostalism* (Oxford: Oxford University Press, 1979), but Faupel's work figures much more prominently for Land than does Anderson's. See Land's references to Anderson at *Pentecostal Spirituality*, 28–29, 63, 188, 208.

60. Dayton articulates the difference between himself and Faupel as follows: "I am arguing here that eschatology is *a* crucial element, but not *the* central theme of Pentecostalism" (Dayton, *Theological Roots*, 33, n. 44).
61. For this recognition, see Land, *Pentecostal Spirituality*, 41–47.
62. Land cites Karl Barth, *Evangelical Theology: An Introduction*, trans. Grover Foley (Grand Rapids, MI: Eerdmans, 1963), 160–64, but expresses his understanding of Barth on prayer by paraphrasing Don E. Saliers, "Prayer and Theology in Karl Barth," in Karl Barth, *Prayer*, ed. Don E. Saliers (Philadelphia, PA: Westminster Press, 1985), xviii–xx. See Land, *Pentecostal Spirituality*, 35–37.
63. Land cites Philip J. Rosato, *The Spirit as Lord: The Pneumatology of Karl Barth* (Edinburgh: T & T Clark, 1981), v, 47–52. See Land, *Pentecostal Spirituality*, 168.
64. Land quotes Barth, *Church Dogmatics*, IV.3, 183–84, as cited in David R. Nichols, "The Search for a Pentecostal Structure in Systematic Theology," *PNEUMA: The Journal of the Society for Pentecostal Studies* 6, no. 2 (1984): 67. See Land, *Pentecostal Spirituality*, 42. In addition to his discussion of orthodoxy, Land cites Barth's insistence that the theological task must involve invoking the Spirit (Barth, *Evangelical Theology*, 58; Land, *Pentecostal Spirituality*, 53, 171).
65. Notwithstanding, Land occasionally relies on secondary accounts for his understanding of Moltmann, such as his references to A. J. Conyers, *God, Hope, and History: Jürgen Moltmann and the Christian Concept of History* (Macon, GA: Mercer University Press, 1988), 77; Melvin E. Dieter, "The Development of Nineteenth Century Holiness Theology," *Wesleyan Theological Journal* 20, no. 1 (1985): 61–77. See Land, *Pentecostal Spirituality*, 70, 198.
66. Land draws on Moltmann, *Trinity and the Kingdom*; Jürgen Moltmann, "The Fellowship of the Holy Spirit—Trinitarian Pneumatology," *Scottish Journal of Theology* 37, no. 3 (1984): 287–300; Jürgen Moltmann, *The Church in the Power of the Spirit: A Contribution to Messianic Ecclesiology*, trans. Margaret Kohl (New York, NY: Harper and Row, 1977), 289–336. See Land, *Pentecostal Spirituality*, 41–42, 197–208. For an assessment of Land's appropriations of Moltmann, see Althouse, *Spirit of the Last Days*, 61–66, 158–97.
67. Land cites Theodore H. Runyon, "The Importance of Experience for Faith," in *Aldersgate Reconsidered*, ed. Randy L. Maddox (Nashville, TN: Kingswood Books), 93–107; Don E. Saliers, *The Soul in Paraphrase* (New York, NY: Seabury Press, 1980); Don E. Saliers, *Worship and Spirituality* (Philadelphia, PA: Westminster Press, 1984); Henry H. Knight III, *The Presence of God in the Christian Life* (Metuchen, NJ: Scarecrow Press, 1992); Gregory S. Clapper, *John Wesley on Religious Affections: His Views on Experience and Emotion and Their Role in the Christian Life and Theology* (Metuchen, NJ: Scarecrow Press, 1989). See Land, *Pentecostal Spirituality*, 33–35, 41–44, 47–48, 54–55, 95, 118, 132–33, 143–44, 178, 184, 186, 200, 202, 207, 212, 220–21.
68. See preceding note. Elsewhere, Land acknowledges that his thoughts on the prominence of prayer and on affections stem from dialogue with Saliers, in addition to Barth and Wesley (Land, "Response," 14), and that his appropriations of Moltmann are shaped by Dieter and Knight (Land, "Triune Center," 199–200). Saliers, Knight, and Runyon were members of Land's dissertation committee (Land, *Pentecostal Spirituality*, 9–10).
69. It should be noted that Frei is not mentioned by name in the body, footnotes, bibliography, or index of *Pentecostal Spirituality*. This does not discount, however, the continuities between their theologies. For Land's subsequent acknowledgment of Frei's influence on him, see Land, "Response," 14. On the difficulties

of determining precisely which theologians are rightly considered "postliberal" and navigating the diverse expressions of postliberal theology, see George Hunsinger, "Postliberal Theology," in *The Cambridge Companion to Postmodern Theology*, ed. Kevin J. Vanhoozer (Cambridge: Cambridge University Press, 2003), 42–57. In spite of these interpretive complexities, virtually everyone agrees that Frei should be numbered among postliberal theologians. For a critical assessment of Frei's relationship to postliberalism, see Paul J. DeHart, *The Trial of the Witnesses: The Rise and Decline of Postliberal Theology* (Malden, MA: Blackwell, 2006).

70. Land, *Pentecostal Spirituality*, 34–35, 55–56, 63, 71–94. For a popular rehearsal of these themes, see R. Lamar Vest and Steven J. Land, *Reclaiming Your Testimony: Your Story and the Christian Story* (Cleveland, TN: Pathway Press, 2002).

71. See Hans W. Frei, *The Eclipse of Biblical Narrative: A Study in Eighteenth and Nineteenth Century Hermeneutics* (New Haven, CT: Yale University Press, 1974), 1–16 and passim. For an early introduction to narrative theology, see *Why Narrative? Readings in Narrative Theology*, ed. Stanley Hauerwas and L. Gregory Jones (Grand Rapids, MI: Eerdmans, 1989).

72. Frei, *Eclipse of Biblical Narrative*, 3.

73. Chan's unpublished doctoral dissertation is entitled "The Puritan Meditative Tradition, 1599–1691: A Study of Ascetical Piety."

74. Simon Chan, *Spiritual Theology: A Systematic Study of the Christian Life* (Downers Grove, IL: InterVarsity Press, 1998); Simon Chan, *Pentecostal Theology and the Christian Spiritual Tradition* (Sheffield: Sheffield Academic Press, 2000); Simon Chan, *Liturgical Theology: The Church as Worshipping Community* (Downers Grove, IL: InterVarsity Press, 2006); Simon Chan, *Pentecostal Ecclesiology: An Essay on the Development of Doctrine* (Blandford Forum: Deo, 2011).

75. Chan, *Spiritual Theology*, 9–18.

76. Chan, *Pentecostal Theology*, 7–12.

77. Chan, *Liturgical Theology*, 9–17. Chan insists that if evangelicals are to return to "historic Christianity" as stated in the "The Chicago Call: An Appeal to Evangelicals" (1977), they must develop a thorough ecclesiology. His determination to introduce evangelicals to the liturgical tradition attests to his conviction that evangelicals need to heed the tenets of "The Chicago Call." Leanne Van Dyk cites Chan as a representative of many evangelical theologians with a growing conviction that evangelicalism desperately needs a "coherent ecclesiology." See Leanne Van Dyk, "The Church in Evangelical Theology and Practice," in *The Cambridge Companion to Evangelical Theology*, ed. Timothy Larsen and Daniel J. Treier (Cambridge: Cambridge University Press, 2007), 129.

78. The earliest academic work by a pentecostal (of which I am aware) advocating the strengths of traditional liturgical worship is Jerald J. Daffe, "An Introduction to Worship for Bible College Ministerial Students" (DMin diss., Western Conservative Baptist Seminary, 1983).

79. Chan, *Spiritual Theology*, 16–20; Chan, *Liturgical Theology*, 147–66. Chan adopts Jordan Aumann's definition of spiritual theology as "that part of theology that, proceeding from the truths of divine revelation and the religious experience of individual persons, defines the nature of the supernatural life, formulates directives for its growth and development, and explains the process by which souls advance from the beginning of the spiritual life to its full perfection" (Chan, *Spiritual Theology*, 18). See Jordan Aumann *Spiritual Theology* (London: Continuum, 2006; first published in 1980), 22.

80. For a pointed criticism of failures in Asian theology to balance God's transcendence and immanence properly, see Simon Chan, "The Problem of Transcendence and Immanence in Asian Contextual Theology," *Trinity Theological Journal* 8 (1999): 5–18. The themes stated there are developed further in Simon Chan, "Problem and Possibility of an Asian Theological Hermeneutic," *Trinity Theological Journal* 9 (2000): 47–59. For the charge that Chan's construction of transcendence and immanence involves a problematic dichotomization of the natural and the supernatural, see Amos Yong, "The Future of Asian Pentecostal Theology: An Asian American Assessment," *Asian Journal of Pentecostal Studies* 10, no. 1 (2007): 24–25.

81. Chan, *Spiritual Theology*, 24; Simon Chan, "Theological Education and Spirituality," *AETEI Journal* 3, no. 1 (1990): 24. Chan borrows the category "evocability" from Ian T. Ramsey, *Religious Language: An Empirical Placing of Theological Phrases* (London: SCM Press, 1957).

82. Chan defines "Western" as typified by ideals such as individualism, rationalism, and egalitarianism, which are not bound to any single geographic location but rather are widespread characteristics of modernity (Chan, *Spiritual Theology*, 11). For an early and critically qualified affirmation of contextual theology, see Simon Chan, "Second Thoughts on Contextualization," *Evangelical Review of Theology* 9, no. 1 (1985): 50–54. For a discussion of the unique dynamics that Chan feels must be considered in Asian contexts, see Chan, "Problem of Transcendence and Immanence," 5–17; Chan, "Problem and Possibility," 47–58. For the claim that much Asian contextual theology is implicit and needs to be made more explicit through formal theological writings and doctrinal statements, see Simon Chan, "Evangelical Theology in Asian Contexts," in *The Cambridge Companion to Evangelical Theology*, ed. Timothy Larsen and Daniel J. Treier (Cambridge: Cambridge University Press, 2007), 229–34. For an observation of Chan's contributions to contextual theology in Asia, see *Asian Christian Theologies: A Research Guide to Authors, Movements, Sources*, vol. 2, ed. John C. England et al. (Delhi: Claretian, 2003), 318–19.

83. Chan states clearly that in this context "personal" is not to be understood as "individual" as opposed to "communal." He intends rather to affirm a commitment to the resurrected Jesus of Nazareth that takes place within the environment of historically concrete church communities (Chan, *Spiritual Theology*, 16, 34–35).

84. For the charge that Chan mistakenly identifies the element of surprise as the "essence" of pentecostalism, see Yun, *Baptism in the Holy Spirit*, 154.

85. Chan, *Spiritual Theology*, 20.

86. Chan, *Spiritual Theology*, 17–20; See also Chan, "Theological Education and Spirituality," 24. For the charge that Chan's distinctions between systematic and spiritual theology constitute a false dichotomy that pentecostals should avoid, see Terry L. Cross, "Can There Be a Pentecostal Systematic Theology? An Essay on Theological Method in a Postmodern World," *Proceedings of the 30th Annual Meeting of the Society for Pentecostal Studies*, 158–60, Tulsa, OK, 2001. Cross writes, "Simon Chan's approach relegates systematic theology to the Scholasticism of the past and thereby denies its true influence on spirituality and . . . denies spirituality's potential influence on theological reflection. Theology is more than a backdrop in the drama of spirituality! To further this analogy, neither theology [nor] spirituality is a backdrop in the drama of Christian living at any time. . . . A fully integrated theology should never place spirituality in the background while a fully integrated spirituality should never jump on stage with energy yet no script!" (159–60). Similar observations are made in Yun, *Baptism in the Holy*

Spirit, 159–60. Cross's and Yun's criticisms do not explicitly acknowledge the fact that Chan's description of the relationship among the branches of theology is a *concession* of what he sees as an undesirable but currently unavoidable scenario.

87. Chan, *Pentecostal Theology*, 25–30. Chan's discussion of the detrimental effects of branches of theology such as systematic, spiritual, and practical relies heavily on the historical narrative in Edward Farley, *Theologia: The Fragmentation and Unity of Theological Education* (Philadelphia, PA: Fortress Press, 1983), especially 1–124.

88. Elsewhere, Chan states that the use of scripture in the liturgical tradition assumes that it is a unity rather than a disparate collection of documents (Chan, *Liturgical Theology*, 136).

89. See Simon Chan, "The Logic of Hell: A Response to Annihilationism," *Evangelical Review of Theology* 18, no. 1 (1994): 20–32. Here, Chan indicates that systematic theology's integrative thinking also requires philosophical considerations. Supporting a position that he calls "eternal punishment," Chan argues in almost exclusively logical terms, developing a reductio ad absurdum against a number of annihilationist tenets, in an attempt to "provide the groundwork for better exegesis" (21). See also John Stott, "The Logic of Hell: A Brief Rejoinder," *Evangelical Review of Theology* 18, no. 1 (1994): 33–34. Stott observes the philosophical tenor of Chan's essay and responds that some of his claims lack a necessary "biblical basis" (33).

90. Chan, *Pentecostal Theology*, 12, 30–32. Here, Chan offers Anselm's *Proslogion* as an example of theology that simultaneously reflects on God and addresses God. Elsewhere, Chan describes the relationship between theology and spirituality as follows: theological education, pertaining particularly to the doctrine of God, is a prerequisite for spirituality because the latter is concerned precisely with one's relationship to God, and spirituality should provide the larger context for theological education, perhaps through following a rule of life or observing canonical hours of prayer. The move from theological education to spirituality takes place through articulating theology with evocability, as described previously ("Theological Education and Spirituality," 23–27).

91. Yee Tham Wan rightly observes that while Chan's *Spiritual Theology* includes considerations of several systematic *loci*, his trinitarian theology and ecclesiology play the largest roles in his spiritual theology. See Wan's book review in *Journal of Asian Mission* 4, no. 1 (2002): 142.

92. Chan, *Pentecostal Theology*, 29.

93. Chan, *Spiritual Theology*, 122.

94. Chan, *Spiritual Theology*, 41–55; Chan, "Problem of Transcendence and Immanence," 5–18.

95. For Chan's suggestion that the traditional dialectic of "church and state" relations should be broadened to consider relations between "the kingdom of God and society," see "Church and Society: A Historical Perspective," in *Church and Society: Singapore Context*, ed. Bobby E. K. Sng (Singapore: Graduates Christian Fellowship, 1989), 38–46.

96. Chan, *Spiritual Theology*, 19, 190; Chan, *Liturgical Theology*, 147–66, 180.

97. Chan, *Spiritual Theology*, 127–28, 137–38, 141–47.

98. Chan, *Spiritual Theology*, 197–98, 239.

99. Chan, *Spiritual Theology*, 84–101. Elsewhere, Chan argues for the compatibility of Protestant piety and Christian mysticism based, in part, on representative sixteenth- and seventeenth-century Puritan views of meditation. See "Protestantism and Mysticism," *Trinity Theological Journal* 2 (1990): 55–76; Chan, "Puritan Meditative Tradition," passim.

100. Chan, *Spiritual Theology*, 239.
101. Chan, *Spiritual Theology*, 191–92.
102. For the criticism that Chan's notion of "traditioning" is inadequate for engaging Christian theology's future horizons, see Yun, *Baptism in the Holy Spirit*, 148.
103. Chan, *Pentecostal Theology*, 11–12.
104. Chan, *Spiritual Theology*, 225–38.
105. Chan, *Pentecostal Theology*, 7–16. Much of Chan's discussion of baptism in the Holy Spirit and glossolalia in *Pentecostal Theology* can also be found, at times with greater detail and more forceful appeals, in his "The Language Game of Glossolalia, or Making Sense of 'Initial Evidence,'" in *Pentecostalism in Context: Essays in Honor of William W. Menzies*, ed. Wonsuk Ma and Robert P. Menzies (Sheffield: Sheffield Academic Press, 1997), 80–95; Simon Chan, "Evidential Glossolalia and the Doctrine of Subsequence," *Asian Journal of Pentecostal Studies* 2, no. 2 (1999): 195–211.
106. Chan, *Pentecostal Theology*, 10–11.
107. For a brief introduction to pentecostal conceptions of glossolalia as the "initial evidence" of baptism in the Holy Spirit, see Gary B. McGee, "Initial Evidence," in *The New International Dictionary of Pentecostal and Charismatic Movements*, revised and expanded edition, ed. Stanley M. Burgess and Eduard M. van der Maas (Grand Rapids, MI: Zondervan, 2003), 784–91. Chan's statement that baptism in the Holy Spirit and glossolalia have the least support in the Christian tradition is based on an important distinction between demonstrating an established history of glossolalia—such as in Kilian McDonnell and George Montague, *Christian Initiation and Baptism in the Holy Spirit: Evidence from the First Eight Centuries*, 2nd revised edition (Collegeville, MN: Liturgical Press, 1994)—and demonstrating specifically that there is an established history of glossolalia *interpreted as initial evidence of baptism in the Holy Spirit*. It is the latter interpretation that Chan rightly observes lacks significant support in the Christian tradition. See Chan, *Pentecostal Theology*, 40; Chan, "Evidential Glossolalia," 195–96.
108. For another example of Chan's seeking scripture's larger "canonical meaning" on a theological issue in direct contrast to relying on isolated biblical texts, see Simon Chan, "Homosexuality: A Theological Perspective," *Church and Society* 1, no. 3 (1998): 79–87; Simon Chan, "The Language Game of Eternal Security," *Church and Society* 2, no. 1 (1999): 23–28. In the former, Chan cites several New Testament texts (Mark 10:2–9, Rom 1:18–32, I Cor 6:12–20, and Eph 5:21–33) and states that they should be understood in relation to a broader theology of creation, which he briefly sketches on the basis of Genesis 1 and 2. In the latter, Chan concludes that debates concerning whether Christians will necessarily persevere in grace or whether they can commit apostasy cannot be resolved on exegetical grounds alone, because proponents of each perspective might interpret the same texts from within their own theological schemas. He then engages in logical evaluations of simplified forms of each perspective in order to reframe the precise points of their disagreement.
109. For his brief description of the early church's process of formulating the doctrine of the Trinity, see Chan, *Pentecostal Theology*, 29–30; Simon Chan, "Communion Spirituality and Its Implications for Holistic Living in a Fragmented World," *Church and Society in Asia Today* 9, no. 2 (2006): 92.
110. See Chan, "The Language Game of Glossolalia," 80–83. Here, Chan states explicitly that the traditional pentecostal formulation of initial evidence "is in tatters" (80) and claims that this is demonstrated by most of the essays in *Initial Evidence:*

Historical and Biblical Perspectives on the Pentecostal Doctrine of Spirit Baptism, ed. Gary B. McGee (Peabody, MA: Hendrickson, 1991). These essays, for example, question the duration of William J. Seymour's commitment to initial evidence (Cecil M. Robeck, Jr.), highlight early pentecostals' diverse views about initial evidence (Gary B. McGee), describe glossolalia as "normal" but reject the notion that it is a "norm" (Larry W. Hurtado), and offer a nonpentecostal critique of initial evidence (J. Ramsey Michaels). This book, one of the first scholarly, collaborative studies of glossolalia, contains primarily biblical and historical considerations. For a criticism of the book's lack of reflection from the perspectives of systematic theology, see Frank D. Macchia, "The Question of Tongues as Initial Evidence: A Review of *Initial Evidence*, Edited by Gary B. McGee," *Journal of Pentecostal Theology* 2 (1993): 127. For a more recent treatment of glossolalia containing biblical, historical, theological, philosophical, psychological, sociological, and linguistic studies, see *Speaking in Tongues: Multi-Disciplinary Perspectives*, ed. Mark J. Cartledge (Waynesboro, GA: Paternoster Press, 2006).

111. For a recent attempt to defend the traditional pentecostal formulation of initial evidence on exclusively biblical and historical grounds, see John A. Lombard, Jr., and Jerald J. Daffe, *Speaking in Tongues: Initial Evidence of Spirit Baptism?* (Cleveland, TN: Pathway Press, 2005).

112. Chan, *Pentecostal Theology*, 40–49, 62–70; Chan, "The Language Game of Glossolalia," 82–83; Chan, "Evidential Glossolalia," 195–97, 202–05. For some brief reflections on Johannine pneumatology, see Simon Chan, "Sharing the Trinitarian Life: John 17:20–26, I John 1:1–4," in *On the Way to Fuller* Koinonia, ed. Thomas F. Best and Günther Gassmann (Geneva: World Council of Churches Publications, 1994), 85–90; Chan, "Communion Spirituality," 91–95.

113. For a brief introduction to the three ways, see the following entries by Thomas D. McGonigle in *The New Dictionary of Catholic Spirituality*, ed. Michael Downey (Collegeville, MN: Liturgical Press, 1993): "Illumination, illuminative way" (529–31), "Purgation, purgative way" (800–02), "Three ways" (963–65), and "Union, unitive way" (987–88). Chan's choice to engage the three ways in relation to pentecostal spirituality illustrates further his contention that growth in the spiritual life is marked primarily by growth in prayer, inasmuch as the three ways are usually employed as measures of growth in prayer. For Chan's claim that meditation specifically is the primary activity of the three ways, see Chan, "Protestantism and Mysticism," 55 and passim. For an apology for meditation as an important spiritual discipline, directed to a popular Christian audience, see Simon Chan, "Hush Your Heart to Listen," *Impact* (June–July 1989): 17–20.

114. On prayer and receptivity, see also Chan, *Pentecostal Ecclesiology*, 99–100. Chan's view of glossolalia as ascetical and passive prayer implies a close relationship between the ascetical and the mystical within the three ways that is broadly compatible with the close relationship between the two articulated in Reginald Garrigou-Lagrange, *The Three Ages of the Interior Life: Prelude of Eternal Life*, 2 vols., trans. M. Timothea Doyle (Rockford, IL: TAN Books, 1989), especially 628–43. For a harder distinction between the ascetical and the mystical, see Adolphe Tanquerey, *The Spiritual Life: A Treatise on Ascetical and Mystical Theology*, 2nd ed. trans. Herman Branderis (Belgium: Society of St. John the Evangelist, 1932), especially 731–37. For the criticism that Chan's *Spiritual Theology* does not give the sufficient consideration to contemplative prayer that its historical significance requires, see J. David Muyskens's book review in *Reformed Review* 53, no. 1 (1999): 84.

115. Chan acknowledges that "evidence" might not be the best category to employ but maintains it in part because he feels the term is valuable for expressing "a distinct sort of experience in which the powerful presence of the Spirit bears a unique relationship to speaking in tongues" (Chan, "The Language Game of Glossolalia," 81). For the claim that glossolalia is for pentecostals more "sacramental" than "evidential," see Frank D. Macchia, "Tongues as a Sign: Towards a Sacramental Understanding of Pentecostal Experience," *PNEUMA: The Journal of the Society for Pentecostal Studies* 15, no. 1 (1993): 68–76. While Chan sees some benefit in Macchia's rejection of "evidence" in favor of a theology of glossolalia more closely related to its sacramental quality and a theology of grace, he states that Macchia does not give sufficient account of how early pentecostals actually *experienced* glossolalia. He writes, "Tongues, for them, were not the means of grace but the *fruit* of grace, the spontaneous response to the *prior* action of God in their innermost being. It is primarily in this aspect of Pentecostal experience that tongues functions as 'evidence' rather than as sacramental sign" (Chan, "The Language Game of Glossolalia," 87; see also Chan, "Evidential Glossolalia," 197–98). Advocating a distinction between glossolalia as initial evidence and glossolalia as a gift of the Spirit for use in public assemblies, Chan suggests that Macchia's notion of glossolalia's sacramental quality is more appropriately applied to glossolalia as gift than to glossolalia as initial evidence (Chan, "The Language Game of Glossolalia," 88, 94–95). For a criticism of Chan's distinction between these two kinds of glossolalia, see Max Turner, "Tongues: An Experience for All in the Pauline Churches?" *Asian Journal of Pentecostal Studies* 1, no. 2 (1998): 250–52. For Chan's defense of the distinction in response to Turner, see Simon Chan, "A Response to Max Turner," *Asian Journal of Pentecostal Studies* 2, no. 2 (1999): 279–81. It should be noted that Chan neither reiterates nor rescinds this distinction between types of glossolalia or its accompanying application to Macchia's theology of glossolalia in the subsequent works "Evidential Glossolalia" and *Pentecostal Theology*. For my discussion of Macchia on glossolalia, see chapter 3.

116. Chan, *Pentecostal Theology*, 57–96; Chan, "Language Game of Glossolalia," 89–90.

117. Chan explicitly frames his *Liturgical Theology* with criticisms and initiatives taken from the following: David Bebbington, *Evangelicalism in Modern Britain: A History from the 1730s to the 1980s* (London: Unwin Hyman, 1989); Donald Bloesch, *The Church: Sacraments, Worship, Ministry, Mission* (Downers Grove, IL: InterVarsity Press, 2002); Stanley J. Grenz, *Revisioning Evangelical Theology: A Fresh Agenda for the Twenty-first Century* (Downers Grove, IL: InterVarsity Press, 1993); Stanley J. Grenz, *Renewing the Center: Evangelical Theology in a Post-theological Era* (Grand Rapids, MI: Baker Academic, 2000); Mark Noll, *Scandal of the Evangelical Mind* (Grand Rapids, MI: Eerdmans, 1995); David Wells, *No Place for Truth* (Grand Rapids, MI: Eerdmans, 1993); David Wells, *God in the Wasteland: The Reality of Truth in a World of Fading Dreams* (Grand Rapids, MI: Eerdmans, 1994). For assessments of some of the above works by pentecostals, see (on Noll) Cheryl Bridges Johns, "Partners in Scandal: Wesleyan and Pentecostal Scholarship," *PNEUMA: The Journal of the Society for Pentecostal Studies* 21, no. 2 (1999): 183–97; James K. A. Smith, "Scandalizing Theology: A Pentecostal Response to Noll's *Scandal*," *PNEUMA: The Journal of the Society for Pentecostal Studies* 19, no. 2 (1997): 225–38; Amos Yong, "Whither Systematic Theology? A Systematician Chimes in on a Scandalous Conversation," *PNEUMA: The Journal of the Society for Pentecostal Studies* 20, no. 1 (1998): 85–93; (on Wells) Amos Yong, "Review of *No Place for Truth* and *God in the Wasteland*," *PNEUMA: The Journal of the Society for Pentecostal Studies* 18, no. 2 (1996): 239–43.

118. For an early criticism of contextual theology's overemphasis on socialization to the neglect of other factors determinative for human identity and behavior, see Chan, "Second Thoughts on Contextualization," 51–52.
119. Chan, *Pentecostal Theology*, 97–101; Chan, *Liturgical Theology*, 21–40. Cf. Chan, *Spiritual Theology*, 77–122. Chan's insistence on the prior existence of the church is clearer in *Pentecostal Theology* and *Liturgical Theology* than in *Spiritual Theology*. In the former two, he is explicit that ecclesiology must logically precede soteriology; whereas in the latter one, he states that human salvation finds its conclusion in ecclesiology. Much of Chan's discussion of ecclesiology in *Pentecostal Theology* (97–119) can also be found, at times with greater detail and more forceful appeals, in Simon Chan, "Mother Church: Toward a Pentecostal Ecclesiology," *PNEUMA: The Journal of the Society for Pentecostal Studies* 22, no. 2 (2000): 177–208.
120. Chan takes the phrase "new ecclesiologies" from Nicholas M. Healy, and echoes some of the guarded affirmations and constructive criticisms of them found in Healy's *Church, World, and the Christian Life: Practical-Prophetic Ecclesiology* (Cambridge: Cambridge University Press, 2000); Nicholas M. Healy, "Practices and the New Ecclesiology: Misplaced Concreteness?" *International Journal of Systematic Theology* 5, no. 3 (2003): 287–308. See Chan, *Liturgical Theology*, 85–98, most of which can also be found in Simon Chan, "The Mystery of the Liturgy: Towards a Theology of Ecclesial Practices," *Trinity Theological Journal* 12 (2004): 93–110.
121. For the claim that some charismatics reduce the primary act of worship to "praise music" and that some evangelicals reduce it to preaching, see Simon Chan, "A Hollowed-Out Spirituality: Spirituality without Theology as Illustrated in the Contemporary Worship Phenomenon," *Church and Society* 2, no. 3 (1999): 56–59.
122. Chan, *Liturgical Theology*, 85–90; Chan, "Mystery of the Liturgy," 93–98.
123. Chan, *Liturgical Theology*, 28–30, 91–92. Here (28–30), Chan favorably cites Augustine's statement that Christians are themselves what they receive in the Lord's supper. See "Sermon 227," in *The Works of Saint Augustine*, III/6, ed. John E. Rotelle and trans. Edmund Hill (New York, NY: New City Press, 1993), 254–56.
124. Chan, *Liturgical Theology*, 36–39; Chan, *Pentecostal Ecclesiology*, 71–73; Chan, "Hollowed-Out Spirituality," 59–62.
125. Chan, *Pentecostal Theology*, 99–108; Chan, *Pentecostal Ecclesiology*, 77–80; Chan, "Mother Church," 180–96.
126. Chan, *Pentecostal Theology*, 108–16; Chan, *Pentecostal Ecclesiology*, 66–67; Chan, "Mother Church," 196–208.
127. Chan, *Pentecostal Theology*, 71.
128. Chan, *Pentecostal Theology*, 33–34. Here, Chan approvingly cites Gordon D. Fee, *God's Empowering Presence: The Holy Spirit in the Letters of Paul* (Peabody, MA: Hendrickson, 1994). On I Cor 12:6, Fee writes, "On the one hand . . . the unity of God dominates [Paul's] thinking in such a way that the Son and Spirit are subsumed under that unity, and their own activities are seen as functionally subordinate" (163).
129. Chan, *Pentecostal Theology*, 34. Chan makes similar statements about the Spirit in Chan, *Pentecostal Ecclesiology*, 90–91, and Chan, "Sharing the Trinitarian Life," 85–87.
130. To say that Chan frames pneumatology with ecclesiology is to say that he gives logical priority to ecclesiology over pneumatology (understood as two different systematic *loci*). One might even summarize Chan's theology as the first pentecostal instantiation of ecclesiology as first theology. This is not to say, however, that Chan gives logical priority to the church over the Spirit (understood as those two

particular realities themselves, as opposed to systematic *loci* about them). Here, the Spirit clearly has logical priority over the church inasmuch as the church is utterly dependent on the outpouring of the Spirit. For an attempt to view pneumatologically the relationships among the Spirit, creation, and the church that nevertheless gives logical priority to ecclesiology, see Chan, *Pentecostal Ecclesiology*.

131. For a discussion of Hauerwas as a postliberal theologian, see William C. Placher, "Postliberal Theology," in *The Modern Theologians: An Introduction to Christian Theology in the Twentieth Century*, 2nd ed., ed. David F. Ford (Oxford: Blackwell Publishers, 1997), 348–49.

132. See Stanley Hauerwas, *A Community of Character: Toward a Constructive Christian Social Ethic* (Notre Dame, IN: University of Notre Dame Press, 1981), 9–86. Also important for Chan is Stanley Hauerwas and William H. Willimon, *Resident Aliens: Life in the Christian Colony* (Nashville, TN: Abingdon Press, 1989).

133. Criticisms of Moltmann are most explicit in Chan, *Spiritual Theology*, 185–89; Chan, "Problem and Possibility," 49, 52. Sympathies for Hauerwas are summarized in Simon Chan, "Introduction," in *Truth to Proclaim: The Gospel in Church and Society*, ed. Simon Chan (Singapore: Trinity Theological College, 2002), v–x. For a description of Hauerwas's political theology vis-à-vis Moltmann's, see Arne Rasmusson, *The Church as* Polis: *From Political Theology to Theological Politics as Exemplified by Jürgen Moltmann and Stanley Hauerwas* (Notre Dame, IN: University of Notre Dame Press, 1995). For the claim that Chan's *Spiritual Theology* borrows too heavily from "narrative theology," see Stephen D. Kovach's book review in *Faith and Mission* 15, no. 2 (1998): 101.

134. For the criticism that Land's *Pentecostal Spirituality* represents an undesirable shift away from the centrality of baptism in the Holy Spirit in pentecostal theology, see Frank D. Macchia, *Baptized in the Spirit*, 23–24, 38–49. While Macchia's observation that Land devotes little space to baptism in the Holy Spirit as traditionally understood by pentecostals is accurate, the prominence of pneumatology in *Pentecostal Spirituality* cannot be denied. The irony in Macchia's criticism is that his own book is an attempt to broaden the notion of "baptism in the Holy Spirit" to a metaphor for the entirety of the Christian life in the Spirit; therefore, the phrase becomes more or less a circumlocution for "pneumatology." The question can be posed, then, whether or not Macchia himself devotes significantly more space than Land to considerations of baptism in the Holy Spirit as traditionally understood by pentecostals.

135. This is due to the significant interpretive hurdle referenced previously, namely, Harvey Cox's claim that Land is not always clear about whether he is offering descriptions of what pentecostal spirituality is like or how he would like it to be (Cox, "Review," 5). In response to Cox, Land writes, "Obviously [*Pentecostal Spirituality*] is three fourths analysis and one fourth revision—unless one counts all the places where I am . . . both describing and prescribing. This is because the deep elements of Pentecostal spirituality are both expressive of and judgments upon particular elements of that spirituality as it is practiced today" (Land, "Response," 15). Whether Land's descriptions of early pentecostalism are accurate is an important question (historically and historiographically), but it is irrelevant to my purposes of assessing how his reading of that history functions for his proposals for contemporary pentecostal spirituality and theology. There is, however, a significant obstacle to assessing precisely those functions, namely, the fact that one of Land's proposals is a critical return to some of this early period's basic elements of spirituality and theology (Land, *Pentecostal Spirituality*, 56). The reader is left

wondering whether *all* approving *descriptions* of the spirituality and theology of pentecostalism's first ten years are also *prescriptions* for contemporary pentecostal spirituality and theology, not just those elements explicitly stated as prescriptions in his final, constructive chapter.

136. Cross does not explicitly acknowledge this in his description of *Pentecostal Spirituality* as "non-systematic" (Cross, "Pentecostal Systematic Theology?" 147, n. 13). Cross's own appropriation of a social doctrine of the Trinity as the orienting motif of theology actually functions quite similarly to Land's.

137. The closest Land comes to this in *Pentecostal Spirituality* is found in statements such as pentecostalism needing "sustained theological discussion" (191–92), theology requiring "discerning discursive reflection" (196), and a re-visioned pentecostal spirituality needing the ability for pentecostals to speak to each other through "international publication[s]" (214). Land is more explicit elsewhere when he writes, "Doctrinally pentecostals need to show how they display their theology in a systematic way and with a comprehensiveness that has been heretofore lacking. . . . The biblical and historical work which has been going on for several decades should continue, but it is time to gather up these results into a more comprehensive proposal" ("Pentecostal Spirituality," 493–94).

138. Land, *Pentecostal Spirituality*, 96. For other pentecostal proponents of the fivefold gospel as the center or integrating motif of theology, see John Christopher Thomas, "Pentecostal Theology in the Twenty-First Century," *PNEUMA: The Journal of the Society for Pentecostal Studies* 20, no. 1 (1998): 3–19; Kenneth J. Archer, "Nourishment for Our Journey: The Pentecostal *Via Salutis* and Sacramental Ordinances," *Journal of Pentecostal Theology* 13, no. 1 (2004): 79–96.

139. On Spirit-christology and the fivefold gospel, see also my assessment of Frank D. Macchia at the end of chapter 3.

140. A recent example of using pentecostal perspectives to broaden conceptual categories within theological and philosophical discourses is found in James K. A. Smith, *Thinking in Tongues: Pentecostal Contributions to Christian Philosophy* (Grand Rapids, MI: Eerdmans, 2010). See especially "At the Limits of Speech" (123–50), where rather than legitimating glossolalia by situating it within the reigning paradigms of philosophy of language, Smith argues that glossolalia demonstrates one of the limitations of the categories currently in use and points to the need for philosophy of language (from phenomenological, hermeneutical, and speech-act perspectives) to include categories that account for the philosophical significance of glossolalia. Regardless of the assessments one makes of the content of Smith's discussion of glossolalia, his approach provides a needed balance to Chan's primary approach.

CHAPTER 3

1. For additional information on pentecostals with the PhD or equivalent in religion, see chapter 2, n. 1.

2. See "Word and Spirit, Church and World: The Final Report of the International Dialogue between Representatives of the World Alliance of Reformed Churches and Some Classical Pentecostal Churches and Leaders, 1996–2000," *PNEUMA: The Journal of the Society for Pentecostal Studies* 23, no. 1 (2001): 9–43; Frank D. Macchia, "Spirit, Word, and Kingdom: Theological Reflections on the Reformed/Pentecostal

Dialogue," in *Theology between East and West: A Radical Heritage*, ed. Frank D. Macchia and Paul S. Chung (Eugene, OR: Wipf and Stock, 2002), 77–91; Frank D. Macchia, "Dialogue, Reformed—Pentecostal," in *The New International Dictionary of Pentecostal and Charismatic Movements*, revised and expanded edition, ed. Stanley M. Burgess and Eduard M. van der Maas (Grand Rapids, MI: Zondervan, 2003), 575–76.

3. See Macchia's biographical information in "The Tongues of Pentecost: A Pentecostal Perspective on the Promise and Challenge of Pentecostal/Roman Catholic Dialogue," *Journal of Ecumenical Studies* 35, no. 1 (1998): 1–18; Frank D. Macchia, "Unity and Otherness: Lessons from Babel and Pentecost," *Living Pulpit* 13, no. 4 (2004): 5–7. Information on his involvement with the Society for Pentecostal Studies can be found in *Commemorating Thirty Years of Annual Meetings, 1971–2001*, ed. Mark E. Roberts (Society for Pentecostal Studies, 2001).

4. Frank D. Macchia, *Spirituality and Social Liberation: The Message of the Blumhardts in the Light of Wuerttemberg Pietism* (Metuchen, NJ: Scarecrow Press, 1993); Frank D. Macchia, *Baptized in the Spirit: A Global Pentecostal Theology* (Grand Rapids, MI: Zondervan, 2006); Frank D. Macchia, *Justified in the Spirit: Creation, Redemption, and the Triune God* (Grand Rapids, MI: Eerdmans, 2010). See the following article reviews of *Baptized in the Spirit* and Macchia's response to them in *Journal of Pentecostal Theology*, 16, no. 1 (2008): Clark H. Pinnock, "Review of Frank D. Macchia's *Baptized in the Spirit: A Global Pentecostal Theology*," 1–4; Henry H. Knight III, "Reflections on Frank Macchia's *Baptized in the Spirit*," 5–8; Jürgen Moltmann, "On the Abundance of the Holy Spirit: Friendly Remarks for *Baptized in the Spirit* by Frank D. Macchia," 9–13; Frank D. Macchia, "Baptized in the Spirit: Reflections in Response to My Reviewers," 14–20.

5. Macchia, *Spirituality and Social Liberation*, 158–72. While acknowledging that some aspects of pentecostal spirituality conflict with evangelicalism, Macchia includes pentecostals under the label "evangelical," which he associates with concerns such as being "born again," proclaiming the gospel, and the urgency of eschatology (158).

6. Macchia, *Spirituality and Social Liberation*, 158–59. Macchia seems to base his description of pentecostal eschatology as "apocalyptic" on its being "premillennial," or, marked by the assumption that Jesus' second coming will *precede* a literal 1,000 year reign on earth. Macchia attributes these categorical descriptions of "apocalyptic" and "prophetic" to Paul D. Hanson, *The Dawn of Apocalyptic: The Historical and Sociological Roots of Jewish Apocalyptic Eschatology* (Philadelphia, PA: Fortress Press, 1975).

7. Macchia, *Spirituality and Social Liberation*, 160–63. On the Blumhardts, see also Frank D. Macchia, "Spirituality and Social Liberation: The Message of the Blumhardts in the Light of Württemberg Pietism, with Implications for Pentecostal Theology," in *Experiences of the Spirit: Conference on Pentecostal and Charismatic Research in Europe at Utrecht University, 1989*, ed. Jan A. B. Jongeneel (Frankfurt: Peter Lang, 1991), 65–84; Frank D. Macchia, "The Spirit and the Kingdom: Implications in the Message of the Blumhardts for a Pentecostal Social Spirituality," *Transformation* 11 (1994): 1–5, 32.

8. Macchia, *Spirituality and Social Liberation*, 166–67. These comments about pentecostals' lack of social engagement must be understood within the context of the time of their publication (1993). Near the time of and since the publication of Macchia's *Spirituality and Social Liberation*, there has been significant increase in the amount of scholarly literature by pentecostals devoted to social ethics and other sociopolitical concerns. See, for example, Eldin Villafañe, *The Liberating*

Spirit: Toward an Hispanic American Pentecostal Social Ethic (Lanham, MD: University Press of America, 1992); Douglas Petersen, *Not by Might nor by Power: A Pentecostal Theology of Social Concern in Latin America* (Oxford: Regnum Books, 1996); Samuel Solivan, *The Spirit, Pathos, and Liberation: Toward an Hispanic Pentecostal Theology* (Sheffield: Sheffield Academic Press, 1998); Robert M. Franklin, *Crisis in the Village: Restoring Hope in African American Communities* (Minneapolis, MN: Fortress Press, 2007); Paul Alexander, *Peace to War: Shifting Allegiances in the Assemblies of God* (Telford, PA: Cascadia, 2009); Amos Yong, *In the Days of Caesar: Pentecostalism and Political Theology* (Grand Rapids, MI: Eerdmans, 2010).

9. For a definition and brief discussion of "initial evidence," see my discussion of Simon Chan in chapter 2.

10. Frank D. Macchia, "Sighs Too Deep for Words: Toward a Theology of Glossolalia," *Journal of Pentecostal Theology* 1 (1992): 47–73; Frank D. Macchia, "Tongues as a Sign: Towards a Sacramental Understanding of Pentecostal Experience," *PNEUMA: The Journal of the Society for Pentecostal Studies* 15, no. 1 (1993): 61–76; Frank D. Macchia, "The Question of Tongues as Initial Evidence: A Review of *Initial Evidence*, Edited by Gary B. McGee," *Journal of Pentecostal Theology* 2 (1993): 117–27; Frank D. Macchia, "Is Footwashing the Neglected Sacrament? A Theological Response to John Christopher Thomas," *PNEUMA: The Journal of the Society for Pentecostal Studies* 19, no. 2 (1997): 239–49; Frank D. Macchia, "Groans Too Deep for Words: Towards a Theology of Tongues as Initial Evidence," *Asian Journal of Pentecostal Studies* 1, no. 2 (1998): 149–73.

11. Macchia makes this observation with poignant criticism in his essay review of *Initial Evidence*. He writes, "It is unfortunate that [the book] does not offer any constructive theological reflections on tongues as initial evidence . . . [and] is designed to present us with little more than historical commentary and biblical hermeneutics. There can be little doubt that Pentecostal scholarship to date has limited itself largely to these fields. This is an understandable trend in the light of our urgent need to reflect on the biblical and historical foundations of our faith, worship and mission. Yet, we must ask, is an engagement in biblical and historical research consistent with the experience and *praxis*-orientation of Pentecostalism without an equally intensive reflection on what such research implies for contemporary Christian experience, belief and *praxis*?" (Macchia, "Question of Tongues as Initial Evidence," 127). Elsewhere, Macchia states more concisely that without genuine theological reflection on initial evidence the biblical and historical scholarship devoted to it "will lack contemporary theological and practical significance" (Macchia, "Groans Too Deep for Words," 150–51).

12. Macchia, "Sighs Too Deep for Words," 47–54.

13. Macchia, "Sighs Too Deep for Words," 56–57.

14. Macchia, "Sighs Too Deep for Words," 57–59.

15. For an assessment of Macchia's use of the category "experience," see John Hiski Ridge, "Dionysus or Apollo: Observations on the Need for a Redefined Pentecostal Epistemology," *Proceedings of the 29th Annual Meeting of the Society for Pentecostal Studies*, 1–25, Kirkland, WA, 2000. Ridge concludes that Macchia's notion of "experience" is ambiguous, but admits to having "played very fast and loose" with Macchia's writings (5). While Ridge raises an issue that could possibly be made to bear fruit, his criticisms of Macchia should be seen within the context of their serving as a foil for Ridge's contention that Bernard Lonergan's theories of human cognition can contribute to a pentecostal epistemology by clarifying the relationship between experience and human knowing.

16. Part of Macchia's fundamental initiative in developing a theology of glossolalia is to surpass its characteristically narrow association with "a self-centered emotional euphoria or a sensationalistic quest for signs and wonders" (Macchia, "Sighs Too Deep for Words," 60).

17. Macchia's conception of the communion of the saints has more to do with the societal connotations of Dietrich Bonhoeffer's *"communio sanctorum,"* which he explicitly invokes, than with a mystical participation of all living and dead Christians with each other in Christ, although he does not explicitly deny the latter and even refers to spiritual *koinonia*.

18. Elsewhere, Macchia broadens this imagery to contend that no single *Christian tradition* possesses fullness of the Spirit—and therefore *koinonia*—on its own, because no single tradition possesses all spiritual gifts on its own. See Frank D. Macchia, "The Struggle for the Spirit in the Church: The Gifts of the Spirit and the Kingdom of God in Pentecostal Perspective," in *Spirit's Gifts—God's Reign*, Theology and Worship Occasional Paper No. 11, Presbyterian Church (U.S.A.) (Louisville, KY: 1999), 4–35.

19. Macchia, "Sighs Too Deep for Words," 65–66.

20. Macchia, "Sighs Too Deep for Words," 68–70. Elsewhere, Macchia states that glossolalia at Pentecost can be seen as a "metaphor of the mission accomplished in the cross and resurrection." See Frank D. Macchia, "Tradition and the *Novum* of the Spirit: A Review of Clark Pinnock's *Flame of Love,*" *Journal of Pentecostal Theology* 13 (1998): 43.

21. Macchia, "Sighs Too Deep for Words," 70–72. Macchia employs the phrase "initial physical evidence" because it is the precise wording contained in the Assembly of God's official doctrinal statement of the relationship between glossolalia and baptism in the Holy Spirit.

22. Macchia, "Tongues as a Sign," 61–66. Concerning recent Roman Catholic sacramental theology, Macchia cites Edward Schillebeeckx, *Christ, the Sacrament of Encounter with God* (London: Sheed and Ward, 1965); Karl Rahner, "Theology of the Symbol," in *Theological Investigations*, vol. 4 (London: Darton, Longman, and Todd, 1966), 221–52. While Macchia employs the term "sign" in this article, he clearly refers to the real participation between a symbol and that which it symbolizes, not to a sign that merely points beyond itself to that which it signifies without participating in that which it signifies.

23. Macchia, "Tongues as a Sign," 68–70. Part of Macchia's concern in establishing the sacramental function of glossolalia is to demonstrate that "Pentecostal spirituality does not advocate an unmediated encounter with God, nor a subjectivistic emotionalism unrelated to an objective means of grace" (76).

24. Most pentecostals use the term "ordinance" to refer to rites such as baptism and the Lord's supper that Jesus instructed his followers to practice as acts of obedience rather than as the means of grace, such as is usually implied by the term "sacrament." For a brief introduction to these terminological distinctions among pentecostals, see Harold. D. Hunter, "Ordinances, Pentecostal," in *The New International Dictionary of Pentecostal and Charismatic Movements*, revised and expanded edition, ed. Stanley M. Burgess and Eduard M. van der Maas (Grand Rapids, MI: Zondervan, 2003), 947–49; David S. Bishop, "The Sacraments in Worship," in *Pentecostal Worship*, ed. Cecil B. Knight (Cleveland, TN: Pathway Press, 1974), 101–03.

25. Macchia, "Is Footwashing the Neglected Sacrament?" 240–42. Macchia's point here is dependent on Tom Driver's claim that pentecostal footwashing, in spite of

terminological debates, is a sacramental act inasmuch as it is concerned with participants being filled with God's presence. See Tom F. Driver, *The Magic of Ritual: Our Need for Liberating Rites that Transform Our Lives and Our Communities* (New York, NY: Harper Collins, 1991), 208.

26. See Tan May Ling, "A Response to Frank Macchia's 'Groans Too Deep for Words: Towards a Theology of Tongues as Initial Evidence,'" *Asian Journal of Pentecostal Studies* 1, no. 2 (1998): 175–83. Ling's response does little more than summarize Macchia's article. It offers no insightful criticism and simply asserts that Macchia's ideas are developed neither "systematically nor satisfactorily" (182).

27. Macchia, "Groans Too Deep for Words," 149–51, 156.

28. In a more recent essay, Macchia writes that Pentecost establishes a unity that does not dissolve diversity. Arguing that the relationship between Babel and Pentecost is one of promise-fulfillment, not merely of curse-reversal as suggested by several scholars, Macchia sees Babel as God's judgment of grace on an idolatrous unity that through the results of Pentecost ends in dispersed peoples being ultimately reunited rather than scattered and separated. See Frank D. Macchia, "Babel and the Tongues of Pentecost: Reversal or Fulfillment?" in *Speaking in Tongues: Multi-Disciplinary Perspectives*, ed. Mark J. Cartledge (Waynesboro, GA: Paternoster Press, 2006), 34–51.

29. Macchia, "Groans Too Deep for Words," 159–61.

30. Macchia, "Groans Too Deep for Words," 163–64. Elsewhere, Macchia states that in addition to prompting the privileged to act on behalf of the oppressed, glossolalia also can give a strong voice in corporate worship to the uneducated and illiterate. See Frank D. Macchia, "Discerning the Spirit in Life: A Review of *God the Spirit* by Michael Welker," *Journal of Pentecostal Theology* 10 (1997): 15.

31. The presidential address is published as Frank D. Macchia, "Justification and the Spirit: A Pentecostal Reflection on the Doctrine by Which the Church Stands or Falls," *PNEUMA: The Journal of the Society for Pentecostal Studies* 22, no. 1 (2000): 3–21. A slightly revised version of this material appears in Frank D. Macchia, "Justification Through New Creation: The Holy Spirit and the Doctrine by Which the Church Stands or Falls," *Theology Today* 58, no. 2 (2001): 202–17. Also important to this discussion is Macchia's assessment of the *Joint Declaration on the Doctrine of Justification* in Frank D. Macchia, "Justification and the Spirit of Life: A Pentecostal Response to the *Joint Declaration*," in *Justification and the Future of the Ecumenical Movement: The Joint Declaration on the Doctrine of Justification*, ed. William G. Rusch (Collegeville, MN: Liturgical Press, 2003), 133–49. See also Macchia, *Justified in the Spirit*. In order to establish the chronological development I trace in Macchia's theology, my discussion of pneumatology and justification follows these articles and essays rather than the subsequent *Justified in the Spirit*. The book is an expansion and culmination of these earlier publications, but it suggests no substantive changes to the structure I describe. When necessary for clarification, I make additional references to *Justified in the Spirit*.

32. Macchia credits Christoph Blumhardt for first prompting him to consider the inadequacy of a purely forensic account of justification and whether such an account "held any promise for Pentecostal theology" ("Justification and the Spirit of Life," 139).

33. Macchia credits a presentation at the 1998 annual meeting of the American Academy of Religion by D. Lyle Dabney for first raising for him questions concerning the relationship of justification with Jesus' resurrection and with the Holy Spirit (Macchia, "Justification and the Spirit," 6; Macchia, "Justification through New

Creation," 209; Macchia, *Baptized in the Spirit*, 130). This presentation is published as D. Lyle Dabney, "'Justified by the Spirit': Soteriological Reflections on the Resurrection," *International Journal of Systematic Theology* 3, no. 1 (2001): 46–68.

34. For an earlier view that does not yet demonstrate awareness of the significance of pneumatology and resurrection for soteriology, see Frank D. Macchia, "Created Spirit Beings," in *Systematic Theology*, rev. ed., ed. Stanley M. Horton (Springfield, MO: Logion Press, 1995), 199–200. Here, Macchia states that Jesus' death is the substitutionary completion of redemption and that his resurrection involves primarily the defeat of Satan.

35. Macchia's pneumatological expansion of justification is offered in explicit distinction from Clark H. Pinnock, *Flame of Love: A Theology of the Holy Spirit* (Downers Grove, IL: InterVarsity Press, 1996), 155–57. While Macchia appreciates some of the ramifications of Pinnock's pneumatological soteriology, he prefers to reshape justification from a pneumatological perspective rather than to focus on other soteriological *loci* that seem to be more readily associated with pneumatology (e.g., union with God) as Pinnock does (Macchia, "Justification and the Spirit," 20–21; Macchia, "Justification through New Creation," 205). Elsewhere, Macchia states explicitly that the reduction of justification to a forensic category should be resisted, rather than simply conceded and situated within a broader soteriology marked by pneumatology and the kingdom of God. See Frank D. Macchia, "Pinnock's Pneumatology: A Pentecostal Appreciation," *Journal of Pentecostal Theology* 14, no. 2 (2006): 167–73. While still desiring to broaden justification, Macchia states elsewhere that baptism in the Holy Spirit and the kingdom of God are the appropriate backgrounds for considering various elements of life in the Spirit, including justification, sanctification, and charismatic empowerment (Macchia, *Baptized in the Spirit*, 89–91).

36. Macchia, "Justification through New Creation," 207–11.

37. Macchia, "Justification through New Creation," 215–17. On the church as a community of justified persons, see Macchia, *Justified in the Spirit*, 258–92.

38. Macchia, "Justification and the Spirit of Life," 136–38.

39. Macchia, "Justification and the Spirit of Life," 147–48. It should be understood that Macchia's contribution to this volume is specifically an assessment of the *Joint Declaration* from a pentecostal perspective, part of the reason for his focus on pneumatology within it. His criticisms should not be read as indications of a general posture of disapproval toward ecumenism. I include these criticisms because they are germane to Macchia's discussion of the relationship between justification and pneumatology, not because they are fully representative on their own of his views of ecumenism. For detailed discussion of Macchia's general support of ecumenical theology, see my assessment at the end of this chapter.

40. Macchia, *Baptized in the Spirit*, 129–30. For Macchia's claim that the Spirit is the "substance" of justification, see Macchia, *Justified in the Spirit*, 15–37. For a criticism of this claim, see Ralph Del Colle, "Frank's *Justified in the Spirit*: The Spirit as the Substance of Justification—'A Bridge too Far,'" *Proceedings of the 40th Annual Meeting of the Society for Pentecostal Studies*, 1–22, Memphis, TN, 2011.

41. Macchia, "Justification through New Creation," 140, 212–14.

42. Jürgen Moltmann, "Was heisst heute 'evangelisch'? Von der Rechtfertigungslehre zur Reich-Gottes-Theologie," *Evangelische Theologie* 57, no. 1 (1997): 41–46. For Macchia's earlier criticism of Moltmann's reliance on Paul to the neglect of Luke-Acts, especially concerning pneumatology, see Frank D. Macchia, "A North American Response," *Journal of Pentecostal Theology* 4 (1994): 32–33, which refers to Jürgen

Moltmann, *The Spirit of Life: A Universal Affirmation*, trans. Margaret Kohl (London: SCM Press, 1992).

43. Macchia, *Baptized in the Spirit*, 131–32.

44. Macchia, *Baptized in the Spirit*, 14–15.

45. Macchia, *Baptized in the Spirit*, 58–59. For Macchia's adoption of canonical-critical hermeneutics, see also Frank D. Macchia, "The Spirit and Life: A Further Response to Jürgen Moltmann," *Journal of Pentecostal Theology* 5 (1994): 125–26; Macchia, "Is Footwashing the Neglected Sacrament?" 243–44. On canonical criticism, see Gerald T. Sheppard, "Canonization: Hearing the Voice of the Same God through Historically Dissimilar Traditions," *Interpretation: A Journal of Bible and Theology* 36 (1982): 21–33; Brevard S. Childs, *Biblical Theology of the Old and New Testaments: Theological Reflection on the Christian Bible* (London: SCM Press, 1992), to all of which Macchia refers. For a criticism of Childs, see Walter Brueggemann, "Canonization and Contextualization," in *Interpretation and Obedience: From Faithful Reading to Faithful Living* (Philadelphia, PA: Fortress Press, 1991), 119–42. For Childs's response to these criticisms, see Brevard S. Childs, *Biblical Theology: A Proposal* (Minneapolis, MN: Fortress, Press, 2002), 40–44.

46. Macchia's criticisms of the *Joint Declaration* are based in part on its call for a trinitarian approach to justification. While Macchia echoes this call, he feels that its lack of pneumatology undermines the call (Macchia, "Justification and the Spirit of Life," passim). On the trinitarian nature of justification, see Macchia, *Justified in the Spirit*, 293–312.

47. Macchia, *Baptized in the Spirit*, 130. Macchia cites Robert Jenson, "Justification as a Triune Act," *Modern Theology* 11 (1995): 421–27.

48. Macchia, *Baptized in the Spirit*, 134–35.

49. Macchia, *Baptized in the Spirit*, 258–60. For an adaptation of Macchia's notion of baptism into divine love toward the ends of a pneumatological theology of love, see Yong, *Spirit of Love*, 85–90.

50. Macchia, *Baptized in the Spirit*, 89. Macchia's fourth chapter is entitled "Christ as the King and the Spirit as the Kingdom" (Macchia, *Baptized in the Spirit*, 89–154). He adapts this phrase (via Kilian McDonnell, *The Other Hand of God: The Holy Spirit as the Universal Touch and Goal* [Collegeville, MN: Liturgical Press, 2003], 226) from Gregory of Nyssa's third sermon on the Lord's prayer. See St. Gregory of Nyssa, *The Lord's Prayer, The Beatitudes*, trans. Hilda C. Graef. Ancient Christian Writers, 18 (New York, NY: Ramsey Press, 1954), 52–56. Here, Gregory equates the kingdom with the Spirit based on a poorly attested variation of the Our Father in Luke 11:2 that reads "May your Holy Spirit come upon us and cleanse us," instead of "May your kingdom come" as in Matt 6:10. For a brief discussion of Gregory's account of Christ and the Spirit in this passage, see Michel René Barnes, *The Power of God: Δύναμις in Gregory of Nyssa's Trinitarian Theology* (Washington, DC: Catholic University of America Press, 2001), 303–05.

51. I say that *Baptized in the Spirit* is an initial step because Macchia himself describes the book as a consideration of baptism in the Holy Spirit as an organizing principle for theology. He writes, "Moreover, this is not a systematic theology but rather a description of its organizing principle and a testing of the waters as to how this might relate to certain prominent theological *loci*. A systematic theology must have a number of other components lacking here and would be organized differently" (Macchia, *Baptized in the Spirit*, 17).

52. Macchia, *Baptized in the Spirit*, 27–57. Macchia cites several contributing forces to this recent neglect. Concerning (1): Donald W. Dayton, *Theological Roots of Pentecostalism*

(Peabody, MA: Hendrickson, 1987); D. William Faupel, *The Everlasting Gospel: The Significance of Eschatology in the Development of Pentecostal Thought* (Sheffield: Sheffield Academic Press, 1996). Concerning (2): *The Globalization of Pentecostalism*, ed. Byron D. Klaus et al. (Irvine, CA: Regnum, 1999); Harvey Cox, *Fire from Heaven: The Rise of Pentecostal Spirituality and the Reshaping of Religion in the Twenty-First Century* (Reading, MA: Addison-Wesley, 1995); Walter J. Hollenweger, *The Pentecostals: The Charismatic Movement in the Churches* (London: SCM Press, 1972). Concerning (3): Steven J. Land, *Pentecostal Spirituality: A Passion for the Kingdom* (Sheffield: Sheffield Academic Press, 1993). Concerning (4): Walter J. Hollenweger, "Priorities in Pentecostal Research: Historiography, Missiology, Hermeneutics, and Pneumatology," in *Experiences of the Spirit: Conference on Pentecostal and Charismatic Research in Europe at Utrecht University, 1989*, ed. Jan A. B. Jongeneel (Frankfurt: Peter Lang, 1991), 7–22.

53. These methodological claims are also found in Frank D. Macchia, "The Kingdom and the Power: Spirit Baptism in Pentecostal and Ecumenical Perspective," in *The Work of the Spirit: Pneumatology and Pentecostalism*, ed. Michael Welker (Grand Rapids, MI: Eerdmans, 2006), 109–25; Frank D. Macchia, "Baptized in the Spirit: A Reflection on the Future of Pentecostal Theology," in *The Future of Pentecostalism in the United States*, ed. Eric Patterson and Edmund Rybarczyk (Lanham, MD: Lexington Books, 2007), 15–25; Frank D. Macchia, "Pentecostal and Charismatic Theology," in *The Oxford Handbook of Eschatology*, ed. Jerry L. Walls (Oxford: Oxford University Press, 2008), 280–94; Frank D. Macchia, "Baptized in the Spirit: Towards a Global Pentecostal Theology," in *Defining Issues in Pentecostalism: Classical and Emergent*, ed. Steven M. Studebaker (Eugene, OR: Pickwick, 2008), 13–28.

54. Macchia, *Baptized in the Spirit*, 15–18. It should be noted that Macchia affirms the frequent pentecostal association of pneumatology in Luke-Acts with mission and charisma and association of Paul's pneumatology with soteriology, while maintaining the qualification that Luke-Acts at least *implies* soteriological dimensions.

55. For example, see *"Final Report* of the International Roman Catholic/Pentecostal Dialogue (1972–1976)," *PNEUMA: The Journal of the Society for Pentecostal Studies* 12, no. 2 (1990): 85–95. For a review of several Roman Catholic theological assessments of the relationship between charismatic experiences and conversion, as well as the use of the phrase "baptism in the Holy Spirit," see Ralph Del Colle, "Spirit Baptism: A Catholic Perspective," in *Perspectives on Spirit Baptism*, ed. Chad Owen Brand (Nashville, TN: Broadman and Holman, 2004), 241–89.

56. Macchia, *Baptized in the Spirit*, 62–63.

57. Macchia, *Baptized in the Spirit*, 86, 106, 153–54.

58. Macchia, *Baptized in the Spirit*, 157, 190–92. The dialectic between church and kingdom is driven by the Spirit, whom Macchia refers to as "the great dialectician in relation to the church" (190). He adopts this description of the Spirit from Jan Milič Lochman, "Kirche," in *Dogmatik im Dialog*, vol. 1, ed. F. Buri et al. (Gütersloh: Gütersloher Verlaghaus Gerd Mohn, 1973), 135.

59. Macchia, *Baptized in the Spirit*, 205, 210.

60. Macchia, *Baptized in the Spirit*, 211, 222–23.

61. Macchia, *Baptized in the Spirit*, 227.

62. Macchia, *Baptized in the Spirit*, 227–29.

63. Macchia, *Baptized in the Spirit*, 232–35, 240.

64. Macchia, *Baptized in the Spirit*, 107–10. Macchia offers these observations in part to broaden Wolfhart Pannenberg's statement that the early church was led to affirm Jesus' preexistence in part due to his resurrection (Wolfhart Pannenberg, *Systematic Theology*, vol. 1 [Grand Rapids, MI: Eerdmans, 1991], 265). Macchia

wishes to add to this precisely the point that Jesus became the Spirit-baptizer by virtue of his resurrection, signaling further his divinity. Traces of these sentiments can be seen as early as Macchia's criticism of Jürgen Moltmann's *Spirit of Life* for its association of the impartation of the Spirit with Jesus' resurrection, thereby, diminishing Pentecost (Macchia, "North American Response," 32–33).

65. Macchia, *Baptized in the Spirit*, 107–11. Macchia notes Augustine's *De Trinitate* 15.46, where Augustine argues that the Son must be God if the Son imparts the Spirit.

66. Macchia, *Baptized in the Spirit*, 178–90. Macchia states that the failure to recognize Jesus as the unique Spirit-baptizer, and thus as the one who inaugurates a unique kingdom, is the precise error that John Hick makes in developing his vision of religious pluralism in *The Metaphor of God Incarnate* (London: SCM Press, 1993).

67. For Macchia's own assessments of how the Blumhardts' thought functions within his theology, see Frank D. Macchia, "*Dominus Iesus*: A Pentecostal Perspective," *PNEUMA: The Journal of the Society for Pentecostal Studies* 22, no. 2 (2000): 170; Macchia, *Baptized in the Spirit*, 279–80. On Lochman, see Frank D. Macchia, "Discerning the Spirit in Life: A Review of *God the Spirit* by Michael Welker," *Journal of Pentecostal Theology* 10 (1997): 10; Frank D. Macchia, "Jan Milič Lochman: A Tribute to My *Doktorvater*," *PNEUMA: The Journal of the Society for Pentecostal Studies* 29, no. 1 (2007): 1–3.

68. For some candid reflections on his immersion in Barth's theology, see Frank D. Macchia (with Amos Yong, Dale T. Irvin, and Ralph Del Colle), "Christ and Spirit: Dogma, Discernment, and Dialogical Theology in a Religiously Plural World," *Journal of Pentecostal Theology* 12, no. 1 (2003): 15–83. Macchia writes, "There is no question that Reformed theology has been the dominant influence on me, especially by way of Barth. During my second year at Basel, it was the centennial of Barth's birthday. Every faculty member in the divinity school offered coursework on Barth. I had four seminars that year—the early Barth, Barth's ethics, Barth as Old Testament interpreter, Barth as New Testament interpreter! I read hundreds of pages from Barth in German. At the end of the year, there was a three-day conference in which theologians . . . gathered to give lectures on Barth. . . . Barth became the major dialogue partner for me. Others have been important too, but not quite on that level. I do not deny that Catholic and Orthodox theology have been important for me. . . . But I found in Barth a kind of Reformed theology different than the sterile, ecumenically closed, and dead theology found here among some Evangelicals in the US" (63). This does not indicate, however, that Macchia is incapable of criticizing Barth. See, for example, Frank D. Macchia, "The Spirit of God and the Spirit of Life: An Evangelical Response to Karl Barth's Pneumatology," in *Karl Barth in Evangelical Theology: Convergences and Divergences*, ed. Sung Wook Chung (Grand Rapids, MI: Baker Academic Press, 2006), 149–71. Macchia states, "I, as a Pentecostal, find that [Barth] could have placed more stress on the experiential and contextual elements of the life of the Spirit, as well as on the human capacity ultimately and finally to reject God's claim on us" (170).

69. See, for example, Macchia, "Sighs Too Deep for Words," 61–64; Macchia, "Tongues as a Sign," 71–72; Macchia, "A North American Response," 25–28; Macchia, "Discerning the Spirit in Life," 13–14; Macchia, "Groans Too Deep for Words," 154–56.

70. Moltmann, *Spirit of Life*, especially 31–38.

71. Macchia, "North American Response," 26.

72. Macchia, "North American Response," 26–28. For Moltmann's reply to Macchia on immanence and transcendence, see Jürgen Moltmann, "A Response to My Pentecostal Dialogue Partners," *Journal of Pentecostal Theology* 4 (1994): 64–66. For additional clarification of Macchia's criticisms of Moltmann on immanence and transcendence, see Macchia, "The Spirit and Life," 121–27.

73. Macchia, *Baptized in the Spirit*, 6.

74. See, for example, Macchia, *Baptized in the Spirit*, 60, 89, 91, 112, 129. Creation as God's dwelling place is also a prominent theme in Jürgen Moltmann, *God in Creation* (London: SCM Press, 1985). By 2011, Macchia is able to make the first sentence of *Justified in the Spirit* a quotation from Moltmann's *God in Creation*. See Macchia, *Justified in the Spirit*, 3.

75. There is further continuity between Moltmann's *The Spirit of Life* and Macchia's *Baptized in the Spirit* in terms of the close association between justification and social justice (Moltmann, *Spirit of Life*, 123–43; Macchia, *Baptized in the Spirit*, 129–40) and the treatment of the soteriological *loci* of justification, regeneration, sanctification, and charismatic gifts under the larger metaphor of "life in the Spirit" (Moltmann, *Spirit of Life*, 83–213; Macchia, *Baptized in the Spirit*, 64–72, 129–54). For Moltmann's observation that Christoph Blumhardt is "a common source of theological inspiration" for Moltmann and Macchia, see Moltmann, "On the Abundance of the Holy Spirit," 13.

76. Paul Tillich, *Systematic Theology*, vol. 3 (Chicago, IL: University of Chicago Press, 1951–63); Paul Tillich, *The Protestant Era* (Chicago, IL: University of Chicago Press, 1948).

77. Tillich, *Systematic Theology*, III:114–17.

78. Tillich, *Protestant Era*, 109.

79. Macchia, "Sighs Too Deep for Words," 61–62.

80. Macchia's acknowledgment of Tillich's influence in relation to justification is also insightful. He writes, "Tillich taught me more than anyone else that justification is the embrace of ambiguous life by God's indwelling presence. This is a stunning insight that has shone for me like a beacon amidst the confusion that plagues soteriology in the West" (Macchia, *Justified in the Spirit*, 71).

81. Macchia states that pentecostals have never actually based initial evidence on an "inductive method of biblical interpretation" but rather on "a creative interaction with the book of Acts in the context of Pentecostal worship." He writes further, "The charge that Pentecostals arrive at a full-blown doctrine of initial evidence from a simplistic interpretation of isolated texts in Acts is itself simplistic" (Macchia, "Tongues as a Sign," 65, 67). While I agree that initial evidence is not *in fact* based solely on biblical interpretation, it is more difficult to argue that no pentecostal has ever *believed* that it was based solely on this. A defense of the doctrine based on an inductive study of relevant passages in Acts is clearly present in all three of the figures I discuss in chapter 1. See Myer Pearlman, *Knowing the Doctrines of the Bible* (Springfield, MO: Gospel Publishing House, 1937), 313; E. S. Williams, *Systematic Theology*, vol. 3 (Springfield, MO: Gospel Publishing House, 1953), 48–49. Although he writes after Macchia, see also French L. Arrington, *Christian Doctrine: A Pentecostal Perspective*, vol. 3 (Cleveland, TN: Pathway Press, 1994), 62–65. Pearlman, whose comments are representative, writes, "We grant that in every case mentioned in the book of Acts, the results of the impartation [of the Holy Spirit] are not recorded; but where the results are described there is always an immediate, supernatural, outward expression, convincing not only the receiver but the people listening to him, that a divine power is controlling the

person; and in every case there is an ecstatic speaking in a language that the person has never learned" (Pearlman, *Knowing the Doctrines*, 313).

82. The significance of this achievement can hardly be overstated in light of the general unwillingness of pentecostal denominations to grant official support to formal ecumenical dialogues and their occasional disciplinary actions against members for their participation in them. For brief introductions to and examples of these points, see Robeck and Sandidge, "Dialogue, Catholic and Pentecostal," 576–82; Russell P. Spittler, "Du Plessis, David Johannes," in *The New International Dictionary of Pentecostal and Charismatic Movements*, revised and expanded edition, ed. Stanley M. Burgess and Eduard M. van der Maas (Grand Rapids, MI: Zondervan, 2003), 589–93; Cecil M. Robeck, Jr., "National Association of Evangelicals," in *The New International Dictionary of Pentecostal and Charismatic Movements*, revised and expanded edition, ed. Stanley M. Burgess and Eduard M. van der Maas (Grand Rapids, MI: Zondervan, 2003), 922–25; Cecil M. Robeck, Jr., and Jerry L. Sandidge, "World Council of Churches," in *The New International Dictionary of Pentecostal and Charismatic Movements*, revised and expanded edition, ed. Stanley M. Burgess and Eduard M. van der Maas (Grand Rapids, MI: Zondervan, 2003), 1213–17.

83. Macchia, "Tongues as a Sign," 68–71. Macchia reinforces his desire for a theology of glossolalia to bear ecumenical fruit with the concluding words of this article: "The term 'sacrament,' if defined carefully, can shed new light on the heart of Pentecostal spirituality and open the door for fruitful ecumenical dialogue with other Church traditions. Veni, Spiritus unitatis!" (76).

84. See "Word and Spirit, Church and World" (on Word and sacrament; Macchia, *Baptized in the Spirit*, 149); "*Final Report* of the International Roman Catholic/Pentecostal Dialogue (1972–1976)" (on Christ's presence in the eucharist; Macchia, *Baptized in the Spirit*, 255); "*Perspectives on Koinonia*: Final Report of the International Roman Catholic/Pentecostal Dialogue (1985–1989)," *PNEUMA: The Journal of the Society for Pentecostal Studies* 12, no. 2 (1990): 117–42 (on *koinonia*; Macchia, *Baptized in the Spirit*, 163).

85. Macchia, *Baptized in the Spirit*, 61–62.

86. Macchia, *Baptized in the Spirit*, 22–26.

87. Macchia, *Baptized in the Spirit*, 62. For an example of this tendency, see "*Final Report* of the International Roman Catholic/Pentecostal Dialogue (1972–1976)."

88. On Macchia's concern for "realized eschatology," see Macchia, "Sighs Too Deep for Words," 49; Macchia, "Tongues and Prophecy," 65; Macchia, *Baptized in the Spirit*, 157, 190–91.

89. These are my translations. II Cor 5:4b–6 reads: ἵνα καταποθῇ τὸ θνητὸν ὑπὸ τῆς ζωῆς. ὁ δὲ κατεργασάμενος ἡμᾶς εἰς αὐτὸ τοῦτο θεός, ὁ δοὺς ἡμῖν τὸν ἀρραβῶνα τοῦ πνεύματος. θαρροῦντες οὖν πάντοτε καὶ εἰδότες ὅτι ἐνδημοῦντες ἐν τῷ σώματι ἐκδημοῦμεν ἀπὸ τοῦ κυρίου. *Novum Testamentum Graece*, Nestle-Aland, 27th ed., Deutsche Bibelgesesellschaft, 1993.

90. By no means, however, is Macchia's theology devoid of Spirit-christology (see, for example, Macchia, *Baptized in the Spirit*, 135–36). I refer rather to a point of emphasis, subsequently acknowledged in Macchia, "Baptized in the Spirit: Reflections," 17–18. For a more recent account of Jesus as bearer of the Spirit, see Macchia, *Justified in the Spirit*, 146–55.

91. Frank D. Macchia, "Theology, Pentecostal," in *The New International Dictionary of Pentecostal and Charismatic Movements*, revised and expanded edition, ed. Stanley M. Burgess and Eduard M. van der Maas (Grand Rapids, MI: Zondervan, 2003), 1124.

92. On Spirit-christology and the fivefold gospel, see also my assessment of Steven J. Land at the end of chapter 2.

93. After the famous words in which Karl Barth reflects on the possibility of a theology "predominantly and decisively of the Holy Spirit"—with which Macchia prefaces *Baptized in the Spirit* (6)—Barth continues by asking, "Might not even the christology which dominates everything be illuminated on this basis (*conceptus de Spiritu Sancto!*)?" See Karl Barth, "Concluding Unscientific Postscript on Schleiermacher," in *The Theology of Schleiermacher* (Grand Rapids, MI: Eerdmans, 1982), 278.

94. Especially as articulated in Simon Chan, *Pentecostal Theology and the Christian Spiritual Tradition* (Sheffield: Sheffield Academic Press, 2000). Chan himself alludes to these tensions in his review of *Baptized in the Spirit* in *PNEUMA: The Journal of the Society for Pentecostal Studies* 30, no. 2 (2008): 325–26. See my discussion of Chan's ecclesiology in chapter 2.

95. Especially Hans Küng, *The Church* (New York, NY: Sheed and Ward, 1967). See Macchia, *Baptized in the Spirit*, 155–256.

96. Macchia makes only passing mention of this elsewhere in the book (Macchia, *Baptized in the Spirit*, 127–28, 221). See especially Amos Yong, *Discerning the Spirit(s): A Pentecostal-Charismatic Contribution to Christian Theology of Religions* (Sheffield: Sheffield Academic Press, 2000); Amos Yong, *Beyond the Impasse: Toward a Pneumatological Theology of Religions* (Grand Rapids, MI: Baker Academic, 2003). See my discussion of Yong's theology of religions in chapter 4.

97. To Chan and Yong could be added the example of Veli-Matti Kärkkäinen, who questions the very notion that a pneumatological theology might be a worthwhile project on the basis that an additional hermeneutical strategy, that is, pneumatology, simply adds to the further fragmentation of the universal church. See Veli-Matti Kärkkäinen, "David's Sling: The Promise and the Problem of Pentecostal Theology Today: A Response to D. Lyle Dabney," *PNEUMA: The Journal of the Society for Pentecostal Studies* 23, no. 1 (2001): 151–52.

98. While pneumatology is not prominent in the brief constructive portion of *Spirituality and Social Liberation*, it becomes a primary object of concern in the early 1990s in Macchia's first articles (on glossolalia).

99. There are, of course, elements of both the kingdom of God and pneumatology in Macchia's work on justification, but they do not reach the degree of integration achieved in *Baptized in the Spirit*.

CHAPTER 4

1. See also Tony Richie, *Speaking by the Spirit: A Pentecostal Model for Interreligious Dialogue* (Lexington, KY: Emeth Press, 2011). Richie advances on a number of fronts from Yong's work and suggests that testimony should find a legitimate place within interreligious dialogue.

2. For an autobiographical sketch, see Amos Yong, "Between the Local and the Global: Autobiographical Reflections on the Emergence of the Global Theological Mind," in *Shaping a Global Theological Mind*, ed. Darren C. Marks (Burlington, VT: Ashgate, 2008), 187–94.

3. Amos Yong, *Discerning the Spirit(s): A Pentecostal-Charismatic Contribution to Christian Theology of Religions* (Sheffield: Sheffield Academic Press, 2000); Amos Yong, *Beyond the Impasse: Toward a Pneumatological Theology of Religions* (Grand Rapids,

MI: Baker Academic, 2003); Amos Yong, *Spirit-Word-Community: Theological Hermeneutics in Trinitarian Perspective* (Burlington, VT: Ashgate, 2002); Amos Yong, *The Spirit Poured Out on All Flesh: Pentecostalism and the Possibility of Global Theology* (Grand Rapids, MI: Baker Academic, 2005); Amos Yong, *Theology and Down Syndrome: Reimagining Disability in Late Modernity* (Waco, TX: Baylor University Press, 2007); Amos Yong, *The Bible, Disability, and the Church: A New Vision of the People of God* (Grand Rapids, MI: Eerdmans, 2011); Amos Yong, *Hospitality and the Other: Pentecost, Christian Practices, and the Neighbor* (Maryknoll, NY: Orbis Books, 2008); Amos Yong, *In the Days of Caesar: Pentecostalism and Political Theology* (Grand Rapids, MI: Eerdmans, 2010); Amos Yong, *The Spirit of Creation: Modern Science and Divine Action in the Pentecostal-Charismatic Imagination* (Grand Rapids, MI: Eerdmans, 2011); Amos Yong, *Pneumatology and the Christian-Buddhist Dialogue: Does the Spirit Blow through the Middle Way?* (Leiden: E. J. Brill, 2012); Amos Yong, *The Cosmic Breath: Spirit and Nature in the Christianity-Buddhism-Science Trialogue* (Leiden: E. J. Brill, 2012); Amos Yong, *Spirit of Love: A Trinitarian Theology of Grace* (Waco, TX: Baylor University Press, 2012).

4. For a brief discussion of Yong vis-à-vis the exclusivist tendencies of evangelical theologians, see Veli-Matti Kärkkäinen, "Evangelical Theology and the Religions," in *The Cambridge Companion to Evangelical Theology*, ed. Timothy Larsen and Daniel J. Treier (Cambridge: Cambridge University Press, 2007), 205.

5. See also Amos Yong, "The Hermeneutical Trialectic: Notes toward a Consensual Hermeneutic and Theological Method," *Heythrop Journal* 45, no. 1 (2004): 22–39.

6. See also Amos Yong, "The Inviting Spirit: Pentecostal Beliefs and Practices Regarding the Religions Today," in *Defining Issues in Pentecostalism: Classical and Emergent*, ed. Steven M. Studebaker (Eugene, OR: Pickwick, 2008), 29–45.

7. For a discussion of Yong in relation to the problems and possibilities of metaphysics in conversation with Gadamer, Levinas, and Marion, see Skip Horton-Parker, "Tracking the Theological 'Turn': The Pneumatological Imagination and the Renewal of Metaphysics and Theology in the 21st Century," *PentecoStudies* 6, no. 1 (2007): 47–75.

8. On philosophical and fundamental theology, see Thomas P. Flint and Michael C. Rea, "Introduction," in *The Oxford Handbook of Philosophical Theology*, ed. Thomas P. Flint and Michael C. Rea (Oxford: Oxford University Press, 2009), 1–7; Gerald O'Collins, *Fundamental Theology* (New York, NY: Paulist Press, 1981), 5–31; Francis Schüssler Fiorenza, *Foundational Theology: Jesus and the Church* (New York, NY: Crossroad Publishing, 1984), 5–28.

9. For the phrase "pneumatology of quest," see Amos Yong, "On Divine Presence and Divine Agency: Toward a Foundational Pneumatology," *Asian Journal of Pentecostal Studies* 3, no. 2 (2000): 179; Amos Yong, *Discerning the Spirit(s)*, 32, 314–15, 323–24; idem, *Spirit-Word-Community*, 21–24.

10. Yong, "On Divine Presence," 175. For Yong, a "pneumatological" perspective is ultimately tantamount to a "trinitarian" one. Yong neither orients theology exclusively to pneumatology nor subordinates christology to pneumatology. Rather, he makes pneumatology the entry point for a robustly trinitarian theology.

11. Yong, *Discerning the Spirit(s)*, 99.

12. For example, Yong writes, "The public for a foundational pneumatology is therefore the universal *humanum*, and properly includes any and all who are interested in the subject matter. Correlatively, the truth of the matter in foundational pneumatology cannot be parochial by virtue of the universal experiences of the Spirit . . . and the universal scope of the public to which it is addressed. What is

true of the Holy Spirit in a foundational pneumatology cannot be true only for Christians, but has to be both relevant and compelling for all" (Yong, "On Divine Presence," 172–73).

13. Yong, "On Divine Presence," 178–80. Elsewhere, Yong states that "ecclesial pneumatology is, ultimately, concerned with explicating the presence and activity of God among the elect, while foundational pneumatology attempts to correlate ecclesiological pneumatology with the most general features of this same presence and activity in the world" (Yong, *Spirit-Word-Community*, 134–35).

14. Yong refers to the differences between "systematic coherence" and "referential correspondence" in terms of the differences between "meaning" and "truth," respectively (Yong, "On Divine Presence," 178). For the argument that truth claims should satisfy certain criteria associated with coherence, correspondence, and pragmatism, as well as a nuanced account of their relationships to the categories of "meaning" and "truth," see Yong, *Spirit-Word-Community*, 164–75.

15. Yong, "On Divine Presence," 175. The reasons that Yong sees this optimism as "chastened" will become clear in my discussion of the "pneumatological imagination."

16. Yong, *Spirit-Word-Community*, 100. Elsewhere, Yong writes that foundational pneumatology rejects "strong Cartesian foundationalism that bases all beliefs ultimately on self-evident intuitions" and maintains instead that "all knowledge is provisional, relative to the question posed by the community of inquirers, and subject to the ongoing process of conversation and discovery" (Yong, "On Divine Presence," 168).

17. Yong's doctrine of the Trinity is part of the basis of his triadic metaphysic, which follows C. S. Peirce's notions of Firstness (a thing's pure potentiality), Secondness (a thing's resistant capacity vis-à-vis other things), and Thirdness (the real, relational mediation between Firstness and Secondness) (Yong, *Spirit-Word-Community*, 91–96). Yong's triadic metaphysic is offered in explicit distinction from dialectical thinking that ultimately privileges one pole over the other or combines the two poles into a third term. For a criticism of Hegel on the latter point, see Yong, *Spirit-Word-Community*, 105–09, 117–18; Amos Yong, "A Theology of the Third Article? Hegel and the Contemporary Enterprise in First Philosophy and First Theology," in Semper Reformandum: *Studies in Honour of Clark H. Pinnock*, ed. Stanley E. Porter and Anthony R. Cross (Carlisle: Paternoster Press, 2003), 208–31.

18. Yong prefers to reverse the traditional order of "Word and Spirit" to "Spirit and Word" in order to underscore the pneumatological entry point into the doctrine of the Trinity as part of the mode of operation within a foundational pneumatology (50).

19. Yong, *Spirit-Word-Community*, 49–81. For the criticism that the notion of the Spirit as the bond of love between Father and Son is insufficiently developed in *Discerning the Spirit(s)*, see Ralph Del Colle, "Amos Yong's *Discerning the Spirit(s)*: A Catholic Theological Commentary," *Proceedings of the 31st Annual Meeting of the Society for Pentecostal Studies*, 10–11, Lakeland, FL, 2002. While *Discerning the Spirit(s)* trades almost exclusively on the two-hands model, the Spirit as the bond of love between Father and Son receives extensive treatment in *Spirit-Word-Community*.

20. For the biblical exegesis that sustains the claim that the Holy Spirit is the principle of relationality, see Yong, *Spirit-Word-Community*, 28–34.

21. Yong, *Spirit-Word-Community*, 52–59.

22. Yong's account of the Augustinian model draws heavily on David Coffey's "return model" of the Trinity, which emphasizes both the Father's bestowal of love on the

Son and the Son's return of that love to the Father. See David Coffey, *Grace: The Gift of the Holy Spirit* (Sydney: Faith and Culture, 1979); David Coffey, Deus Trinitas: *The Doctrine of the Triune God* (Oxford: Oxford University Press, 1999). In the former work, Coffey employs the term "bestowal model" to describe what in the latter work he calls the "return model."

23. Yong, *Spirit-Word-Community*, 67–72. The prominence that Yong gives to relationality should not be taken as indication of an uncritical or wholesale adoption of a social doctrine of the Trinity. For Yong's suspicion that social trinitarianism may not be able to avoid tritheism, see Yong, *Spirit-Word-Community*, 80.

24. Yong, *Discerning the Spirit(s)*, 116–17. Yong writes further, "Each determination of being is what it is by virtue of the presence and activity of the Logos within the force fields set in motion by the Spirit, the supreme field of force. The Logos is the concrete form or pattern of each thing even as the Spirit is the power of its actualization and instantiation" (118).

25. Yong, *Spirit-Word-Community*, 69–70.

26. Yong, *Spirit-Word-Community*, 84–86. For a discussion of the Spirit as the mutual love between Father and Son in conversation with Thomas Aquinas, see Yong, *Spirit of Love*, 9–14.

27. Yong, *Spirit-Word-Community*, 58–59. Yong adapts the metaphor "symbiotic relationality" from Jerry H. Gill, *Mediated Transcendence: A Postmodern Reflection* (Macon, GA: Mercer University Press, 1989).

28. For the criticism that Yong's trinitarian formulations, specifically in *Beyond the Impasse*, contain "a decidedly Western metaphysical commitment" to the neglect of Eastern Orthodox trinitarian theology, see Dale T. Irvin, "A Review of Amos Yong's *Beyond the Impasse*," *Journal of Pentecostal Theology* 12, no. 2 (2004): 279. Yong replies that privileging either Eastern or Western trinitarian models seems to have its own set of problems and that part of the motivation for his trinitarian-based triadic metaphysic is "to go beyond . . . this impasse in the theological tradition." See Amos Yong, "Beyond *Beyond the Impasse*? Responding to Dale Irvin," *Journal of Pentecostal Theology* 12, no. 2 (2004): 282–83.

29. Yong, *Spirit-Word-Community*, 35–41.

30. Yong, *Spirit-Word-Community*, 43–48.

31. Yong, *Spirit-Word-Community*, 88–91. For criticism of Whitehead's concept of "person," see Amos Yong, "Personal Selfhood (?) and Human Experience in Whitehead's Philosophy of Organism," *Paideia Project: Proceedings of the 20th World Congress of Philosophy* (1998), www.bu.edu/wcp/MainPPer.htm.

32. Yong describes his realist position with the following terminology: "committed metaphysical realis[m]" (Yong, "On Divine Presence," 179), "critical realism" (Yong, *Spirit-Word-Community*, 79), "metaphysical realism" (83, 101), and "relational, critical, and communal realism" (99–100). For a description of Yong's position as "hermeneutical realism," see L. William Oliverio, Jr., "An Interpretive Review Essay on Amos Yong's *Spirit-Word-Community: Theological Hermeneutics in Trinitarian Perspective*," *Journal of Pentecostal Theology* 18, no. 2 (2009): 301–11. For the suggestion that Yong's program may be compatible with "perspective realism" (as defined by Evander McGilvary), see Frederick L. Ware, "Review Article on Amos Yong's *The Spirit Poured Out on All Flesh: Pentecostalism and the Possibility of Global Theology*," *Journal of the European Pentecostal Theological Association* 28, no. 1 (2008): 82. See also Amos Yong, "Extending the Conversation: A Response to Frederick L. Ware," *Journal of the European Pentecostal Theological Association* 28, no. 1 (2008): 84–93.

33. Yong, *Spirit-Word-Community*, 123.
34. Yong, *Spirit-Word-Community*, 133–35. Yong adopts the notion of "root metaphors" from Stephen Pepper, *World Hypotheses* (Berkley: University of California Press, 1942).
35. In *Spirit-Word-Community*, Yong correlates foundational pneumatology's categories of relationality, rationality, and dynamism with the pneumatological imagination's categories of truth as coherence, correspondence, and pragmatic, respectively.
36. Yong, *Spirit-Word-Community*, 164–75. Elsewhere, Yong writes, "Truth . . . is an interpretive activity deriving from the triadic relationship wherein knower and known are connected by signs. As correspondence, truth is therefore the correlation between what is propositionally expressed via a potentially indefinite succession of signs and the reality they point to. As coherence, truth is the interconnectedness of all signs without express contradiction. As pragmatic, truth is not only what guides our engagement with the world correctly, but also that which is able to predict the behavior or habits of things" (Yong, *Discerning the Spirit(s)*, 217).
37. Yong, *Spirit-Word-Community*, 176–83.
38. Yong, "On Divine Presence," 175.
39. Yong, *Spirit-Word-Community*, 184.
40. For the argument that a turn to hermeneutics goes hand in hand with the demise of epistemology understood as a comprehensive theory of human knowing, see Richard Rorty, *Philosophy and the Mirror of Nature* (Princeton, NJ: Princeton University Press, 1979), 315–56.
41. In addition to fallibilism, ongoing interpretation is required also by Yong's modified process ontology, for objects of interpretation constantly undergo transformation.
42. Yong, *Spirit-Word-Community*, 275–76.
43. Yong, *Spirit-Word-Community*, 303–04. Yong illustrates this point by stating succinctly some of the diverse interpretive communities in which he has been simultaneously situated (303).
44. In addition to *Discerning the Spirit(s)*, *Beyond the Impasse*, and *Hospitality and the Other*, see Amos Yong, "Discerning the Spirit(s) in the World of Religions: Toward a Pneumatological Theology of Religions," in *No Other Gods before Me? Evangelicals and the Challenge of World Religion*, ed. John G. Stackhouse, Jr. (Grand Rapids, MI: Baker Academic, 2001), 37–61; Amos Yong, "Spiritual Discernment: A Biblical-Theological Reconsideration," in *The Spirit and Spirituality: Essays in Honour of Russell P. Spittler*, ed. Wonsuk Ma and Robert P. Menzies (London: T & T Clark, 2004), 83–107; Amos Yong, "'Not Knowing Where the Wind Blows . . .': On Envisioning a Pentecostal-Charismatic Theology of Religions," *Journal of Pentecostal Theology* 14 (1999): 81–112; Amos Yong, "The Turn to Pneumatology in Christian Theology of Religions: Conduit or Detour?" *Journal of Ecumenical Studies* 35, nos. 3–4 (1998): 437–54.
45. Yong states that his foundational pneumatology is motivated in part by the problem of "how Word and Spirit are related and yet sufficiently distinct so as to enable a theology of religions to develop within a pneumatological framework" (Yong, *Discerning the Spirit(s)*, 133).
46. On the question of whether it is possible to discern the Spirit's presence without also discerning Christ's presence (or to develop a pneumatological imagination without also developing a christological one), see Del Colle, "Amos Yong's *Discerning the Spirit(s)*," 2–4. Yong subsequently states that in his determination to distinguish

between the Spirit's and Word's respective missions he "consciously erred . . . in order to purchase theological space for understanding the distinctiveness of the mission of the Spirit" (Yong, *Spirit Poured Out on All Flesh*, 111, n. 81).

47. See Yong's statement that "a pneumatological theology of religions that validates the distinction between the economy of the Word and Spirit holds the christological problem in abeyance" (Yong, *Discerning the Spirit(s)*, 70). See also Yong, *Beyond the Impasse*, 86–91.

48. It should be underscored that Yong wishes only to delay rather than to remove christological criteria from interreligious dialogue. He writes, "Surely, there is no doubt that the christological question would be merely postponed, not entirely dismissed. Eventually, Christology and pneumatology must be understood within a broader trinitarian framework. . . . Yet it would be intriguing to explore in that light how the Word and Spirit accomplish and mediate the salvific gift of the Father, both separately, if discernible, and in tandem" (Yong, *Discerning the Spirit(s)*, 58). Similarly, he states, "For heuristic purposes . . . we will seek to investigate the religious dimensions of the Spirit's economy with the intention that the christological issues will not be discarded forever" (70). Yong's temporary suspension of explicitly christological criteria from interreligious dialogue has been misunderstood as being "sub-Christian," involving "de-Christianization," and requiring Christians to "betray their faith commitments" in order to participate in interreligious dialogue. All of these opinions are expressed with reference to *Beyond the Impasse* in James R. A. Merrick, "The Spirit of Truth as Agent in False Religions? A Critique of Amos Yong's Pneumatological Theology of Religions with Reference to Current Trends," *Trinity Journal* 29, no. 1 (2008): 107–25. See also Tony Richie, "'The Spirit of Truth as Guide into All Truth: A Response to James R. A. Merrick, 'The Spirit of Truth as Agent in False Religions? A Critique of Amos Yong's Pneumatological Theology of Religions with Reference to Current Trends,'" *Cyberjournal for Pentecostal-Charismatic Research* 19 (2010): 1–24.

49. Yong, *Discerning the Spirit(s)*, 133.

50. Yong, *Discerning the Spirit(s)*, 136; Yong, *Beyond the Impasse*, 164–67. For an engagement with Yong's notions of the demonic in light of his larger theological program, see David Bradnick, "Demonology and Anthropology in Conversation: Applying the Theological Method of Amos Yong Towards a Demonology for the Twenty-First Century," *Proceedings of the 38th Annual Meeting of the Society for Pentecostal Studies*, 1–26, Eugene, OR, 2009.

51. Yong, *Discerning the Spirit(s)*, 137.

52. Yong, *Discerning the Spirit(s)*, 141–44; Yong, *Beyond the Impasse*, 174–83.

53. Yong, *Discerning the Spirit(s)*, 250–55.

54. In light of Yong's determination not to cease discernment at the phenomenological level, the (pejorative) description of Yong's theology of discernment as "phenomenologically . . . driven" is a dismissive label that overlooks the sophistication of both his theology of discernment and his larger theological method and hermeneutic. This description (of *Beyond the Impasse*) is found in John A. Studebaker, Jr., *The Lord Is the Spirit: The Authority of the Holy Spirit in Contemporary Theology and Church Practice* (Eugene, OR: Pickwick, 2008), 368–89.

55. According to Yong, this characteristic distinguishes his pneumatological theology of religions from his predecessors. He writes, "What needs to occur at this point, then, is what has been neglected by previous pneumatological approaches to the religions. Whereas others have remained contented with more or less general theological affirmations about the Spirit's presence and activity in the

non-Christian world, I propose a detailed empirical investigation that tests the adequacy of the proposed categories and the perspicuity of the [theology of discernment]" (Yong, *Discerning the Spirit(s)*, 255).

56. See also his comparative considerations of Christianity and Islam on the idea of "spirit" in Yong, *Spirit Poured Out on All Flesh*, 257–66. For an account of Christian-Muslim relations in Nigeria, see Yong, *Hospitality and the Other*, 15–29. Yong's trinitarian hermeneutic is placed in conversation with Islam in John P. Spaulding, "Qur'anic Interpretation in Trinitarian Perspective: Testing Amos Yong's Hermeneutics and Theology of Religions" (ThM Thesis, Luther Seminary, 2005).

57. Yong, *Discerning the Spirit(s)*, 256–309.

58. Yong, *Discerning the Spirit(s)*, 258–64.

59. Yong, *Discerning the Spirit(s)*, 264–72.

60. Yong, *Discerning the Spirit(s)*, 272–80.

61. Yong illustrates this ambiguity with respect to Umbandist understanding of "Exú," spirits that have to be placated by mediums. He writes, "Yet the ambiguity of Exú is itself a stumbling-block in the process of discernment. What kind of spirit or reality is Exú? Is Exú evil, or evil and yet capable of good? Or is Exú an arm or attribute of divinity? Going further, is Exú just an elemental force in nature? Or, perhaps, is Exú no more than a symbol projected from the human psyche? This ambiguity is pervasive throughout the Umbandist cosmos" (Yong, *Discerning the Spirit(s)*, 286).

62. Yong writes, "Herewith lies the importance and, indeed, indispensability of the ongoing interreligious dialogue. Discernment is always of concrete situations, and can never be in general. What is discerned as the Holy Spirit or some other spirit in this or that particular situation today, may be decidedly reversed or no longer applicable when the situation is examined tomorrow. Such may be part and parcel of life in the Spirit, and if so, then the dialogue always commences *in via* and should never be prematurely terminated" (Yong, *Discerning the Spirit(s)*, 287).

63. Yong, *Discerning the Spirit(s)*, 288–309.

64. For the evaluation that in spite of the case study of Umbanda Yong's pneumatological theology of religions remains too abstract, see Veli-Matti Kärkkäinen, "Toward a Pneumatological Theology of Religions: A Pentecostal-Charismatic Inquiry," *International Review of Mission* 91, no. 361 (2002): 193; Veli-Matti Kärkkäinen, *An Introduction to the Theology of Religions: Biblical, Historical and Contemporary Perspectives* (Downers Grove, IL: InterVarsity Press, 2003), 281. This claim is debatable with respect to *Discerning the Spirit(s)*, and it certainly does not maintain in light of Yong's subsequent work on Christian-Buddhist dialogue.

65. Amos Yong, "The Holy Spirit and the World Religions: On the Christian Discernment of Spirit(s) 'after' Buddhism," *Buddhist-Christian Studies* 24 (2004): 191–207. On competing truth claims among religions, see also Amos Yong, "The Spirit Bears Witness: Pneumatology Truth, and the Religions," *Scottish Journal of Theology* 57, no. 1 (2004): 14–38.

66. Yong, *Pneumatology and the Christian-Buddhist Dialogue*, 101–77; Amos Yong, "Technologies of Liberation: A Comparative Soteriology of Eastern Orthodoxy and Theravada Buddhism," *Dharma Deepika* 7, no. 1 (2003): 17–60. Yong's comparison is based primarily on Orthodoxy's *Philokalia* and Theravada Buddhism's *Visuddhimagga*.

67. Yong, *Pneumatology and the Christian-Buddhist Dialogue*, 159–77; Yong, "Technologies of Liberation," 42–50.

68. Yong, "Technologies of Liberation," 43–44.
69. Yong, "Technologies of Liberation," 46–48.
70. Yong summarizes the significant theological divergences as follows: "We are already aware that the differences between Orthodox Christianity and Theravada Buddhism are most striking when theological and ultimate questions are posed. Here, the phenomenological, practical, psychological and epistemic categories break down since the notion of divinity is itself foreign to Theravada Buddhism. Thus the Orthodox goal of theosis and Theravadin quest for Nibbana summarize the radical divergence between these two spiritual paths. To be created in the image of God as seen in the incarnation of the Son is foreign to Buddhist sensibilities even while final salvation understood as liberation from the cycle of rebirth is incomprehensible to the Christian" (Yong, "Technologies of Liberation," 48).
71. Yong, *Pneumatology and the Christian-Buddhist Dialogue*, 171–73; Yong, "Technologies of Liberation," 48.
72. Yong, *Pneumatology and the Christian-Buddhist Dialogue*, 172; Yong, "Technologies of Liberation," 49–50.
73. Yong, "Holy Spirit and the World Religions," 205.
74. Yong, "Holy Spirit and World Religions," 191. Elsewhere, Yong writes, "But it is also important to emphasize that my theological interests put to one side the question of whether or not Buddhists can be saved in the Christian sense. Rather, I want to explore the meaning of liberation and salvation as Buddhists conceive it in order [to] achieve a Christian theological vision more conducive to the global and interreligious context of theological reflection in the twenty-first century" ("Technologies of Liberation," 18).
75. For Yong's survey of Christian shifts from exclusivism to inclusivism to pluralism, see Yong, *Discerning the Spirit(s)*, 35–58; Yong, *Beyond the Impasse*, 22–29. For his discussion of whether exclusivism, inclusivism, and pluralism are the only three logical possibilities available for answering questions about the soteriological status of non-Christian religions, see Yong, *Hospitality and the Other*, 66–67. See also Amos Yong, "Whither Theological Inclusivism? The Development and Critique of an Evangelical Theology of Religions," *Evangelical Quarterly* 71, no. 4 (1999): 327–48.

    For the description of Yong as an inclusivist, see Todd L. Miles, *A God of Many Understandings? The Gospel and a Theology of Religions* (Nashville, TN: Broadman and Holman, 2010). While labeling Yong an inclusivist may have legitimate bases, it overlooks the fact that his theology of religions is concerned primarily with discerning the Spirit's presence, activity, and absence within world religions, not with the ultimate salvation of their practitioners. Miles observes this point but applies the label to him nonetheless. The failure to acknowledge that Yong's interests are not primarily soteriological also plagues Keith E. Johnson, *Rethinking the Trinity and Religious Pluralism: An Augustinian Assessment* (Downers Grove, IL: IVP Academic, 2011), 93–140.
76. Hence, Yong's title *The Spirit Poured Out on All Flesh: Pentecostalism and the Possibility of Global Theology*. See also Amos Yong, "Poured Out on All Flesh: The Spirit, World Pentecostalism, and the Renewal of Theology and Praxis in the 21st Century," *PentecoStudies* 6, no. 1 (2007): 16–45.
77. Yong, *Spirit Poured Out on All Flesh*, 18. For the observation that Yong's use of the phrases "global theology" and "global pentecostal theology" is ambiguous, see Allan Anderson, "A Global Pentecostal Theology? Amos Yong's *The Spirit Poured Out on All Flesh*," *Journal of Pentecostal Theology* 16, no. 1 (2007): 98–99. Anderson's

observation seems to overlook the fact that it is precisely the global spread of pentecostalism that raises the question of the possibility of a global theology for Yong. That is, pentecostalism's profound growth suggests that any theology that is truly global is likely to be pentecostal de facto. See also Amos Yong, "Beyond the Liberal-Conservative Divide: An Appreciative Rejoinder to Allan Anderson," *Journal of Pentecostal Theology* 16, no. 1 (2007): 103–11.

78. See Yong, *Spirit Poured Out on All Flesh*. For an interpretation of this book situated within the trajectories proposed in D. Lyle Dabney, "Saul's Armor: The Problem and the Promise of Pentecostal Theology Today," *PNEUMA: The Journal of the Society for Pentecostal Studies* 23, no. 1 (2001): 115–46, see Wolfgang Vondey, "Pentecostalism and the Possibility of Global Theology: Implications of the Theology of Amos Yong," *PNEUMA: The Journal of the Society for Pentecostal Studies* 28, no. 2 (2006): 289–312. See also Amos Yong, "Performing Global Pentecostal Theology: A Response to Wolfgang Vondey," *PNEUMA: The Journal of the Society for Pentecostal Studies* 28, no. 2 (2006): 313–21.

79. See Yong, *Theology and Down Syndrome*, 151–295.

80. Yong writes, "This volume is intended as a modest pentecostal contribution to the contemporary discussion in pneumatological theology. More precisely, my wager is that this pneumatological orientation and dynamic open up space for the Spirit of God to redeem the perspectives and contributions of all flesh . . . including those engaged in ecumenical, multifaith, and religion-science dialogues—in order to orchestrate this plurality of voices and to hasten the coming reign of God" (Yong, *Spirit Poured Out on All Flesh*, 28).

81. Yong, *Spirit Poured Out on All Flesh*, 31–80.

82. The primacy that Yong gives to a pneumatologically oriented soteriology within pentecostal systematic theology presupposes that pentecostal experience of the Spirit consists of both charismatic and soteriological elements. Concerning John the Baptist's statement that Jesus would baptize with the Holy Spirit, Yong writes, "I suggest that this baptism of (or in) the Holy Spirit relates to neither merely the classical pentecostal emphasis of the endowment for power to witness (although it includes this as well) nor merely the idea of Christian initiation into the body of Christ (although, again, it includes this also). Rather, I propose that we retrieve this metaphor of baptism of the Holy Spirit to capture the dynamic and full experience of Christian salvation not only in terms of dying with Christ but also in terms of being raised with him to do the things that he did. In this way, the baptism of the Holy Spirit denotes Christian salvation, broadly considered, as nothing less than the gift of Jesus Christ himself to us in the totality of his Spirit-anointed life, death, and resurrection" (Yong, *Spirit Poured Out on All Flesh*, 101).

83. Yong, *Spirit Poured Out on All Flesh*, 91–98.

84. Yong, *Spirit Poured Out on All Flesh*, 91. On the fivefold gospel and pentecostal theology, see my discussion of Steven J. Land in chapter 2.

85. Yong, *Spirit Poured Out on All Flesh*, 120. In *In the Days of Caesar*, Yong employs the fivefold gospel as a heuristic device for structuring pentecostal political theology.

86. Yong, *Spirit Poured Out on All Flesh*, 99–109.

87. On the early church's expectations surrounding Christian initiation and charismatic demonstrations, Yong follows Kilian McDonnell and George T. Montague, *Christian Initiation and Baptism in the Holy Spirit: Evidence from the First Eight Centuries*, 2nd revised edition (Collegeville, MN: Liturgical Press, 1994).

88. On the pneumatological dimensions of justification, Yong follows Frank D. Macchia, "Justification and the Spirit: A Pentecostal Reflection on the Doctrine by

Which the Church Stands or Falls," *PNEUMA: The Journal of the Society for Pentecostal Studies* 22, no. 1 (2000): 3–21; Veli-Matti Kärkkäinen, "The Holy Spirit and Justification: The Ecumenical Significance of Luther's Doctrine of Salvation," *PNEUMA: The Journal of the Society for Pentecostal Studies* 24, no. 1 (2002): 26–39.

89. On the idea that John Wesley's soteriology is described better by the phrase *via salutis*, Yong follows Randy Maddox, *Responsible Grace: John Wesley's Practical Theology* (Nashville, TN: Kingswood, 1994).

90. On the expanded senses of conversion, Yong follows Donald L. Gelpi, *The Conversion Experience: A Reflective Process for RCIA Participants and Others* (New York, NY: Paulist Press, 1998); Donald L. Gelpi, *The Firstborn of Many: A Christology for Converting Christians*, 3 vols. (Milwaukee, WI: Marquette University Press, 2001). Gelpi's own understanding of Christian conversion is informed by Bernard Lonergan, *Method in Theology* (New York, NY: Seabury Press, 1972).

91. Yong, *Spirit Poured Out on All Flesh*, 112–16.

92. Yong, *Spirit Poured Out on All Flesh*, 121–22, 127.

93. Yong, *Spirit Poured Out on All Flesh*, 127–31.

94. With respect to the New Testament witness, Yong refers specifically to Acts 2:38, "And Peter said to them, 'Repent and be baptized every one of you in the name of Jesus Christ for the forgiveness of your sins; and you shall receive the gift of the Holy Spirit'" (RSV). See Yong, *Spirit Poured Out on All Flesh*, 157.

95. For a brief discussion of the significance of invoking the Holy Spirit as a point of continuity between the pentecostal and Roman Catholic traditions, see Ralph Del Colle, "Whither Pentecostal Theology? Why a Catholic Is Interested," *PNEUMA: The Journal of the Society for Pentecostal Studies* 31, no. 1 (2009): 36–37.

96. In this context, Yong writes, "By 'enacts' and 'represents,' I wish to find a way beyond the impasse of saying either 'baptism saves/gives the Spirit' or 'baptism merely symbolizes'" (Yong, *Spirit Poured Out on All Flesh*, 159, n. 78).

97. Yong, *Spirit Poured Out on All Flesh*, 156–60.

98. This belief is based in part on I Peter 2:24, "He himself bore our sins in his body on the tree, that we might die to sin and live to righteousness. By his wounds you have been healed" (RSV).

99. Yong, *Spirit Poured Out on All Flesh*, 163.

100. Yong, *Spirit Poured Out on All Flesh*, 160–66.

101. On baptism and eucharist, also see Amos Yong, "Ordinances and Sacraments," in *Encyclopedia of Pentecostal and Charismatic Christianity*, ed. Stanley M. Burgess (New York, NY: Routledge, 2006), 345–48.

102. See also Amos Yong, "Disability, the Human Condition, and the Spirit of the Eschatological Long Run: Toward a Pneumatological Theology of Disability," *Journal of Religion, Disability and Health* 11, no. 1 (2007): 5–25.

103. Yong, *Theology and Down Syndrome*, 10–14.

104. Yong, *Theology and Down Syndrome*, 157–65.

105. According to Yong, the functional view can be compatible with a theology of disabilities if properly formulated. He writes, "But if we understand this gift (and responsibility) of God that empowers human dominion less as the power to rule *over* and more as the power to rule *with* others, then that opens up space for us to see people with disabilities as manifesting the divine image precisely in their solidarity with others who are more actively engaged in exercising dominion in the world" (Yong, *Theology and Down Syndrome*, 173).

106. Yong, *Theology and Down Syndrome*, 169–74.

107. Yong writes, "My thesis is that the *imago Dei* is less about some constitutive element of the human person and more about God's revelation in Christ and in the faces of our neighbors; yet the life of Jesus provides a normative account for what it means to be human, and the Holy Spirit creatively enables and empowers our full humanity in relationship to ourselves, others, and God, even in the most ambiguous of situations" (Yong, *Theology and Down Syndrome*, 180–81).

108. Yong, *Theology and Down Syndrome*, 181–91.

109. Yong, *Theology and Down Syndrome*, 190.

110. For Yong's historical survey of traditional beliefs about resurrection as the restoration of Edenic perfection, see Yong, *Theology and Down Syndrome*, 261–67.

111. Yong, *Theology and Down Syndrome*, 271–92.

112. Yong, *Spirit-Word-Community*, 306.

113. Yong, *Spirit of Creation*, 27–29.

114. Yong, *Spirit of Creation*, 34–47, 102–32.

115. Yong, *Spirit of Creation*, 25–33.

116. Yong, *Pneumatology and the Christian-Buddhist Dialogue*, 43–51.

117. Yong, *Pneumatology and the Christian-Buddhist Dialogue*, 67–74.

118. Yong, *Spirit of Love*, 21–38.

119. See especially *Collected Papers of Charles Sanders Peirce*, ed. Charles Hartshorne and Paul Weiss (Cambridge, MA: Belknap Press, 1974), vol. 1, 141–80, and vol. 5, 29–131. See also Amos Yong, "The Demise of Foundationalism and the Retention of Truth: What Evangelicals Can Learn from C. S. Peirce," *Christian Scholars Review* 29, no. 3 (2000): 563–88.

120. Donald L. Gelpi, *The Divine Mother: A Trinitarian Theology of the Holy Spirit* (Lanham, MD: University Press of America, 1984).

121. For his explicit interactions with Gelpi, see Yong, *Discerning the Spirit(s)*, 99–104; Yong, *Beyond the Impasse*, 58–63; Yong, "On Divine Presence," 167–74. For important qualifications to his analysis of the place of Christian conversion in Gelpi's foundational pneumatology, see Yong, *Spirit Poured Out on All Flesh*, 106–09. See also Amos Yong, "In Search of Foundations: The *Oeuvre* of Donald L. Gelpi, SJ, and Its Significance for Pentecostal Theology and Philosophy," *Journal of Pentecostal Theology* 11, no. 1 (2002): 3–26.

122. David Tracy, *The Analogical Imagination: Christian Theology and the Culture of Pluralism* (New York, NY: Crossroad Publishing, 1981), 47–98.

123. Tracy, *Analogical Imagination*, 56–57.

124. Yong, *Spirit-Word-Community*, 275–310.

125. Yong, *Spirit Poured Out on All Flesh*, 27.

126. Cf. his method of biblical interpretation in Yong, *Spirit-Word-Community*, 27–48. Here, his interpretation seems to be driven more by philosophical and theological categories (relationality, rationality, and dynamism) than by any single canonical lens. Either way, the point remains that Yong's biblical interpretation allows certain biblical texts to move to the foreground while others recede to the background.

127. One of the most notable exceptions to this among evangelicals is Kevin J. Vanhoozer, *Is There a Meaning in This Text? The Bible, the Reader, and the Morality of Literary Knowledge* (Grand Rapids, MI: Zondervan, 1998); Kevin J. Vanhoozer, *First Theology: God, Scripture, and Hermeneutics* (Downers Grove, IL: InterVarsity Press, 2002); Kevin J. Vanhoozer, *The Drama of Doctrine: A Canonical-Linguistic Approach to Christian Theology* (Louisville, KY: Westminster/John Knox Press, 2005).

128. For Yong's own account of this trend among pentecostal scholars, see Amos Yong, "Pentecostalism and the Theological Academy," *Theology Today* 64 (2007): 244–50.

For a consideration of this trend in the broader context of the history of pentecostal theology, see Christopher A. Stephenson, "Pentecostal Theology: Retrospect
and Prospect," *Religion Compass* 5, no. 9 (2011): 490–500.

129. The only noteworthy shift in Yong's thought is the extent to which he engages in
speculative reasoning about God's inner life. In *Discerning the Spirit(s)*, Yong is
reluctant to say much about the immanent Trinity (105–11); yet, in *Spirit-Word-
Community*, Yong develops a detailed account of the immanent Trinity (49–81).
This is not to say, however, that Yong speculates about the immanent Trinity
without basis. Following the logic of David Coffey's procedure of reflecting on the
"biblical Trinity" before the immanent Trinity (Coffey, Deus Trinitas, 33–45),
Yong moves from his framework of the Spirit as relational, rational, and
dynamic—which is thoroughly informed by scripture—to this framework's implications for the doctrine of the Trinity. Further, Yong does not speculate about the
immanent Trinity for its own sake. Rather, the immanent Trinity serves as part of
the theological basis for his triadic metaphysic.

The following statement from *Discerning the Spirit(s)* is illustrative of Yong's earlier hesitancy to speak about the immanent Trinity: "[I]t is noteworthy to mention
here that there are important Pentecostal reasons for adhering to a trinitarian
metaphysics of creation *ex nihilo*. To begin with, there is a general anti-intellectualist attitude inherent in Pentecostalism which eschews the speculative moment in
the process of cognition. This disposition has not motivated many Pentecostals to
extensive consideration of the trinitarian mystery. The result is that trinitarian
Pentecostals have more or less adopted the classical Nicene and Reformation theological formulas without critical reflection. In spite of this acceptance, Pentecostals
generally prefer to retain biblical terminology and metaphors in their theologizing.
This results in much more of an emphasis among Pentecostals on 'God for us' than
on God in Godself. This view of God as essentially indeterminate except as creator
of all things *ex nihilo* is, I suggest, in line with the intuitive Pentecostal distrust of
speculating on the divine life *ad intra*" (109). See also Amos Yong, "Oneness and
Trinity: The Theological and Ecumenical Implications of Creation *Ex Nihilo* for an
Intra-Pentecostal Dispute," *PNEUMA: The Journal of the Society for Pentecostal Studies* 19, no. 1 (1997): 81–107.

130. For example, Yong, *Spirit-Word-Community*, 16, 53–59, 74–75, 79–80, 93–94, 116–
17, 177–78, 243.

131. One option preferred by several contemporary theologians for reworking a notion
like *perichoresis* apart from substance metaphysics is a form of the social doctrine
of the Trinity, but Yong's ambivalence about social trinitarianism's ability to avoid
tritheism suggests that such is not likely to be a viable reformulation for him. See
Yong, *Spirit-Word-Community*, 80.

132. Yong makes this contention throughout *Discerning the Spirit(s)* and *Spirit-Word-
Community*, as well as other places.

CHAPTER 5

1. Studebaker argues specifically that pentecostals have unintentionally subordinated pneumatology to christology in their soteriologies. See Steven M. Studebaker, "Pentecostal Soteriology and Pneumatology," *Journal of Pentecostal Theology*
11, no. 2 (2003): 248–70.

2. In addition to these, the fivefold gospel and the doctrine of the Trinity have been proposed as orienting points for pentecostal theology. For the fivefold gospel, see John Christopher Thomas, "Pentecostal Theology in the Twenty-First Century," *PNEUMA: The Journal of the Society for Pentecostal Studies* 20, no. 1 (1998): 3–19. For the doctrine of the Trinity, see Terry L. Cross, "Can There be a Pentecostal Systematic Theology? An Essay on Theological Method in a Postmodern World," *Proceedings of the 30th Annual Meeting of the Society for Pentecostal Studies*, 145–66, Tulsa, OK, 2001; Terry L. Cross, "A Response to Clark Pinnock's 'Church in the Power of the Holy Spirit,'" *Journal of Pentecostal Theology* 14, no. 2 (2006): 175–82.

3. Chan and Macchia suggest but do not significantly developed a role for *lex orandi, lex credendi* in pentecostal theology. See Simon Chan, "The Church and the Development of Doctrine," *Journal of Pentecostal Theology* 13, no. 1 (2004): 66; Simon Chan, *Liturgical Theology* (Downers Grove, IL: InterVarsity Press, 2006), 48–52; Macchia, *Baptized in the Spirit*, 54. In addition to his brief comments in Amos Yong, *The Spirit Poured Out on All Flesh: Pentecostalism and the Possibility of Global Theology* (Grand Rapids, MI: Baker Academic, 2005), 29, see Yong's more extensive reflections on *lex orandi, lex credendi* from the perspective of speech-act theory in Amos Yong, *Hospitality and the Other: Pentecost, Christian Practices, and the Neighbor* (Maryknoll, NY: Orbis Books, 2008), 38–64. My desire to incorporate *lex orandi, lex credendi* into pentecostal theological method has some structural similarities with Yong's own, especially concerning the integration of beliefs and practices. However, my attempt is offered neither within the context of a theology of religions nor with primary emphasis on the practice of hospitality. For my initial attempt at integration, see Christopher A. Stephenson, "The Rule of Spirituality and the Rule of Doctrine: A Necessary Relationship in Theological Method," *Journal of Pentecostal Theology* 15, no. 1 (2006): 83–105.

4. I choose the Lord's supper in part because I believe that pentecostal participation in formal ecumenical dialogue is critical to the health of pentecostal communities and to the progress of ecumenism. The Lord's supper is one of the most divisive theological issues among Christians. If pentecostals are to engage other Christian traditions adequately on this important ecumenical front, then they must first articulate a more comprehensive theology of the Lord's supper that is intelligible and coherent within the contexts of their own faith communities.

   While my suggestions about the Lord's supper could be improperly exploited to bring further division from other Christian traditions on this issue, the ability to represent the theological commitments of one's tradition is a sine qua non of formal ecumenical dialogue. Therefore, at this stage, I am more concerned with articulating a doctrine of the Lord's supper that pentecostals could begin to take to the dialogue table as representative of their theological concerns than with whether members of other Christian traditions will find my conclusions about the supper to be compatible with their own. In George Hunsinger, *The Eucharist and Ecumenism: Let Us Keep the Feast* (Cambridge: Cambridge University Press, 2008), Hunsinger wisely acknowledges that any ecumenical proposals on the Lord's supper that lead to "insuperable barriers" with pentecostal and charismatic churches are "self-defeating." He also understandably states that he is "at a loss" concerning how to coordinate his own proposals with those churches (11, 313–14). I hope that my suggestions can be a small step toward an intelligible theology of the Lord's supper that pentecostals can take to the dialogue table and that other traditions can engage when making their own proposals in conversation with pentecostals.

5. For now, let me state generally the most explicit similarities of their theologies with both my methodological proposal and case study. These are only the aspects of their theologies most directly related to my methodological proposal, not the only ones for which I have sympathy. For my further assessments of each of these theologians, see the concluding portions of chapters 1–4.

   First, I affirm the prominent place that Pearlman, Williams, and Arrington give to scripture in theology, although with the qualification that biblical interpretation alone never exhausts the work that systematic theology requires. Among these three theologians, I see as most compatible with my concerns Arrington's steps toward a perspectival hermeneutic, aside from a number of qualifications of his categorical use of "pentecostal experience" to explain certain dynamics of biblical interpretation.

   Second, I affirm with Land and Chan that pentecostals must thoroughly integrate spirituality into systematic theology. With Land, I affirm that pentecostal spirituality should have an eschatological and pneumatological tenor, and with Chan, I affirm the need for an ordered liturgy that gives a prominent place to the Lord's supper in pentecostal worship.

   Third, I affirm Macchia's desire to avoid "realized eschatology" by making sufficient distinction between the church and the fullness of the kingdom without dichotomizing the two or failing to acknowledge that the inauguration of the kingdom is the church itself.

   Fourth, I affirm Yong's insistence that human knowing is nonfoundational and his accompanying refusal of attempting to construct any theology based on a single principle, whether the Holy Spirit, scripture, or tradition. I also affirm Yong's insistence that human knowing is fallible and extend this principle explicitly to Christian doctrine.

   The need to acknowledge the fallibility of human knowing is one reason that the "Bible doctrines" method may hinder constructive theology among pentecostals. Since most pentecostals are uncomfortable with the statement that the Bible is fallible, they will be unable to accept the fact that Christian doctrine is fallible as long as they fail to understand that Christian doctrine is not found in the Bible as such but is derived from it. Only once important conceptual space is established between the Bible and Christian doctrine will pentecostal theologians be able to speak freely about the fallibility of doctrine without necessarily making the same claim about the Bible.

6. Simon Chan, *Pentecostal Theology and the Christian Spiritual Tradition* (Sheffield: Sheffield Academic Press, 2000), 12.

7. See, for example, Geoffrey Wainwright, "Lex Orandi, Lex Credendi," in *Dictionary of the Ecumenical Movement*, 2nd ed., ed. Nicholas Lossky et al. (Geneva: WCC Publications, 2002), 679–83; W. Taylor Stevenson, "Lex Orandi-Lex Credendi," in *The Study of Anglicanism*, ed. Stephen Sykes, John Booty, and Jonathan Knight (Minneapolis, MN: Fortress Press, 1998), 174–88; Paul L. Gavrilyuk, "Canonical Liturgies: The Dialectic of *Lex Orandi* and *Lex Credendi*," in *Canonical Theism: A Proposal for Theology and the Church*, ed. William J. Abraham, Jason E. Vickers, Natalie B. Van Kirk (Grand Rapids, MI: Eerdmans, 2008), 61–72; Michael Downey, "Lex Orandi, Lex Credendi: Taking It Seriously in Systematic Theology," in *Promise of Presence*, ed. Michael Downey and Richard N. Fragomeni (Washington, DC: Pastoral Press, 1992), 3–25; Duncan B. Forrester, "Lex Orandi, Lex Credendi," in *Theology and Practice*, ed. Duncan B. Forrester (London: Epworth Press, 1990), 71–80; Charles R. Hohenstein, "'Lex Orandi, Lex Credendi': Cautionary Notes," *Wesleyan Theological*

Journal 32, no. 2 (1997): 140–57; Mary M. Schaefer, "Lex Orandi, Lex Credendi: Faith, Doctrine, and Theology in Dialogue," *Studies in Religion/Sciences Religieuses* 26, no. 4 (1997): 467–79; Kenneth Stevenson, "Lex Orandi, Lex Credendi—Strange Bed-Fellows? Some Reflections on Worship and Doctrine," *Scottish Journal of Theology* 39, no. 2 (1986): 225–41; Julia Upton, "A Feminist Perspective: Lex Orandi, Lex Credendi," *Liturgical Ministry* 1 (1992): 137–39; Teresa Berger, "Prayers and Practices of Women: Lex Orandi Reconfigured," *Yearbook of the European Society of Women in Theological Research* 9 (2001): 63–77; Orlando O. Espín, "Whose *Lex Orandi*? Whose *Lex Credendi*? Latino/a Catholicism as a Theological Challenge for Liturgy," paper presented at the annual meeting of the North American Academy of Liturgy, San Diego, CA, 2006, 53–71; Robert E. Cushman, "Lex Orandi, Lex Credendi," *Journal of Religious Thought* 18, no. 2 (1961): 113–19; Paul V. Marshall, "Reconsidering 'Liturgical Theology': Is There a *Lex Orandi* for All Christians?" *Studia Liturgica* 25, no. 2 (1995): 129–50.

8. Prosper of Aquitaine, *De gratia Dei et libero voluntatis arbitrio*, Patrologia Latina, 51:209. For a brief history of Prosper's use of the phrase (*ut legem credendi lex statuat supplicandi*) and of the later use of its derivative (*lex orandi, lex credendi*), see Paul De Clerck, "'Lex orandi, lex credendi': Sens originel et avatars historiques d'un adage équivoque," *Questions Liturgiques/Studies in Liturgy* 59, no. 4 (1978): 193–212.

9. Geoffrey Wainwright, *Doxology: The Praise of God in Worship, Doctrine, and Life* (New York, NY: Oxford University Press, 1980). Wainwright devotes a chapter to *lex orandi* (218–50) and a chapter to *lex credendi* (251–83).

10. Wainwright, *Doxology*, 218, 251. See also James F. Kay, "The *Lex Orandi* in Recent Protestant Theology," in *Ecumenical Theology in Worship, Doctrine, and Life: Essays Presented to Geoffrey Wainwright on His Sixtieth Birthday*, ed. David S. Cunningham et al. (New York, NY: Oxford University Press, 1999), 11–21.

11. Wainwright, *Doxology*, 251–52.

12. Wainwright, *Doxology*, 219.

13. Maurice Wiles, *The Making of Christian Doctrine: A Study in the Principles of Early Doctrinal Development* (Cambridge: Cambridge University Press, 1967).

14. For a discussion of the complications of speaking of the "development" of doctrine, see Maurice Wiles, *The Remaking of Christian Doctrine* (Philadelphia, PA: Westminster Press, 1978), 5–19.

15. Wiles, *Making of Christian Doctrine*, 87–88.

16. Wiles, *Making of Christian Doctrine*, 89.

17. Wiles, *Making of Christian Doctrine*, 93.

18. For a brief argument of this point with some examples, see Anthea Butler, "Pentecostal Traditions We Should Pass On: The Good, the Bad, and the Ugly," *PNEUMA: The Journal of the Society for Pentecostal Studies* 27, no. 2 (2005): 343–53.

19. It is beyond the scope of this book to give a comprehensive account of the category "experience." More research that is philosophically and anthropologically informed from pentecostal perspectives is needed in this area. Some of the standard questions on this matter include the following: Are there such things as "religious experiences," that is, experiences whose content is inherently religious? Or is it more proper simply to speak of experiences that are "experienced religiously," that is, experiences that are not inherently religious but whose significances are legitimately interpreted from religious perspectives? Answers to these questions will have important implications for pentecostal spirituality inasmuch as speaking of "experiences of the Spirit" seems to assume that some experiences have an

inherently pneumatological character and some do not. On the hermeneutical nature of experience, see Yong, *Spirit-Word-Community*, 245–53. On experience and its relation to pentecostal theology, see Terry L. Cross, "The Divine-Human Encounter: Towards a Pentecostal Theology of Experience," *PNEUMA: The Journal of the Society for Pentecostal Studies* 31, no. 1 (2009): 3–34; Peter Althouse, "Toward a Theological Understanding of the Pentecostal Appeal to Experience," *Journal of Ecumenical Studies* 38, no. 4 (2001): 399–411. Althouse builds on George P. Schner, "The Appeal to Experience," *Theological Studies* 53, no. 1 (1992): 40–59. For a discussion of experience in connection with modern notions of human subjectivity, see Philip Rossi, "The Authority of Experience: What *Counts as* Experience," in *Religious Experience and Contemporary Theological Epistemology*, ed. Lieven Boeve, Yves De Maeseneer, and Stijn Van den Bossche (Leuven: Leuven University Press, 2005), 269–84.

20. Walter Principe, "Spirituality, Christian," in *The New Dictionary of Catholic Spirituality*, ed. Michael Downey (Collegeville, MN: Liturgical Press, 1993), 932.

21. For a definition of doctrine as a church's official teaching, see Chan, "Development of Doctrine."

22. However, for the suggestion that the Assemblies of God has sometimes been guided by a quasi magisterium, see Cecil M. Robeck, Jr., "An Emerging Magisterium? The Case of the Assemblies of God," in *The Spirit and Spirituality: Essays in Honour of Russell P. Spittler*, ed. Wonsuk Ma and Robert P. Menzies (London: T & T Clark, 2004), 212–52.

23. One of the most prominent examples in the history of the pentecostal tradition of simultaneously antagonistic beliefs and practices is the historic pentecostal belief in dispensationalism, which is usually accompanied by cessationism among non-pentecostals, and the pentecostal practice of charismatic spiritual gifts. This kind of antagonism is precisely what I wish to avoid. On pentecostals and dispensationalism, see Gerald T. Sheppard, "Pentecostals and the Hermeneutics of Dispensationalism: The Anatomy of an Uneasy Relationship," *PNEUMA: The Journal of the Society for Pentecostal Studies* 6, no. 2 (1984): 5–33.

24. For an introduction to the theological and cultural diversity of pentecostalism, see the opening articles devoted to a global survey of the pentecostal tradition in *The New International Dictionary of Pentecostal and Charismatic Movements*, revised and expanded edition, ed. Stanley M. Burgess and Eduard M. van der Maas (Grand Rapids, MI: Zondervan, 2003), 1–302. See also Walter J. Hollenweger, *The Pentecostals: The Charismatic Movement in the Churches* (London: SCM Press, 1972); Allan Anderson, *An Introduction to Pentecostalism: Global Charismatic Christianity* (Cambridge: Cambridge University Press, 2004); Keith Warrington, *Pentecostal Theology: A Theology of Encounter* (London: T & T Clark, 2008).

25. This reciprocal relationship between *lex orandi* and *lex credendi* in which neither term is "a norm that is not normed" is compatible with Yong's theological method and hermeneutic because each resists any attempt to found one term solely upon the other in denial of a mutually influential relationship.

26. "O foolish Galatians! Who has bewitched you, before whose eyes Jesus Christ was publicly portrayed as crucified. Let me ask you only this: Did you receive the Spirit by works of the law, or by hearing with faith? Are you so foolish? Having begun with the Spirit, are you now ending with the flesh? Did you experience so many things in vain?—if it really is in vain. Does he who supplies the Spirit to you and works miracles among you do so by works of the law, or by hearing with faith?" (RSV).

27. Basil of Caesarea, *On the Holy Spirit*, trans. David Anderson (Crestwood, NY: St. Vladimir's Seminary Press, 1980); Sources Chrétiennes, vol. 17.
28. Basil, *On the Holy Spirit*, 1.3.
29. Basil, *On the Holy Spirit*, 10.24. (εἰς ὄνομα Πατρὸς καὶ Υἱοῦ καὶ ἁγίου Πνεύματος).
30. Basil, *On the Holy Spirit*, 10.26.
31. Gustavo Gutiérrez, *We Drink from Our Own Wells: The Spiritual Journey of a People* (Maryknoll, NY: Orbis Books, 1984).
32. In this respect, I support the initiatives to construct pentecostal theology in conversation with the Christian spiritual tradition (Chan), with contemporary ecumenical theology (Macchia), and with world religions (Yong).
33. For example, Edmund J. Rybarczyk, *Beyond Salvation: Eastern Orthodoxy and Classical Pentecostalism on Becoming like Christ* (Waynesboro, GA: Paternoster, 2004). For an argument by a pentecostal for the soteriological gains of *theosis*, see Veli-Matti Kärkkäinen, *One with God: Salvation as Deification and Justification* (Collegeville, MN: Liturgical Press, 2004); Veli-Matti Kärkkäinen, "Grace and the Ecumenical Potential of *Theosis*," in *Toward a Pneumatological Theology: Pentecostal and Ecumenical Perspectives on Ecclesiology, Soteriology, and Theology of Mission*, ed. Amos Yong (Lanham, MA: University Press of America, 2002), 149–65.
34. For example, Mark J. Cartledge, *Testimony in the Spirit: Rescripting Ordinary Pentecostal Theology* (Burlington, VT: Ashgate, 2010); Mark J. Cartledge, *Practical Theology: Charismatic and Empirical Perspectives* (Waynesboro, GA: Paternoster Press, 2003); Mark J. Cartledge, *Charismatic Glossolalia: An Empirical-Theological Study* (Burlington, VT: Ashgate, 2002).
35. See D. William Faupel, *The Everlasting Gospel: The Significance of Eschatology in the Development of Pentecostal Thought* (Sheffield: Sheffield Academic Press, 1996).
36. Some pentecostals are beginning to articulate detailed theologies of the Lord's supper. For a brief discussion (in conversation with Tom F. Driver) of the Lord's supper as a ritual performance, see Macchia, *Baptized in the Spirit*, 252–56. For the Lord's supper as physical, ecclesial, political, and eschatological act, see Yong, *Spirit Poured Out on All Flesh*, 162–66. For the Lord's supper as an indispensable part of normative Christian liturgy, see Simon Chan, *Liturgical Theology*, 62–84. For a correlation of each point of the fivefold gospel with a sacrament, see Thomas, "Pentecostal Theology," 17–19. (Thomas connects the Lord's supper with "Jesus as soon coming king.") For an expansion of Thomas's proposal, see Kenneth J. Archer, "Nourishment for Our Journey: The Pentecostal *Via Salutis* and Sacramental Ordinances," *Journal of Pentecostal Theology* 13, no. 1 (2004): 94–95. For an account of the Lord's supper focusing on *anamnesis* and *epiclesis*, see Veli-Matti Kärkkäinen, "The Spirit and the Lord's Supper," in *Toward a Pneumatological Theology: Pentecostal and Ecumenical Perspectives on Ecclesiology, Soteriology, and the Theology of Mission*, ed. Amos Yong (Lanham, MD: University Press of America, 2002), 135–46. For the claim that pentecostal practice of the Lord's supper is part of an implicit liturgical ethic, see Katy Attanasi, "Toward a Pentecostal Liturgical Ethic: Lord's Supper, Prayers for Healing, and Spirit Baptism," *Proceedings of the 35th Annual Meeting of the Society for Pentecostal Studies*, 1–8, Pasadena, CA, 2006. For the argument that pentecostals should interpret the Lord's supper as a divine-human encounter that mediates grace through symbols, see Wesley Scott Biddy, "Re-envisioning the Pentecostal understanding of the Eucharist: An Ecumenical Proposal," *PNEUMA: The Journal of the Society for Pentecostal Studies* 28, no. 2 (2006): 228–51. For a consideration of Paul's theology of the Lord's supper in conversation with

the communal nature of African cultures, see J. Ayodeji Adewuya, "Revisiting 1 Corinthians 11.27–34: Paul's Discussion of the Lord's Supper and African Meals," *Journal for the Study of the New Testament* 30, no. 1 (2007): 95–112. For a discussion of the Lord's supper in the context of an ecclesiology centered on the imagery of bread, see Wolfgang Vondey, *People of Bread: Rediscovering Ecclesiology* (New York, NY: Paulist Press, 2008), 141–94. See also Wolfgang Vondey, *Beyond Pentecostalism: The Crisis of Global Christianity and the Renewal of the Theological Agenda* (Grand Rapids, MI: Eerdmans, 2010), 109–40; Wolfgang Vondey, "Pentecostal Ecclesiology and Eucharistic Hospitality: Toward a Systematic and Ecumenical Account of the Church," *PNEUMA: The Journal of the Society for Pentecostal Studies* 32, no. 1 (2010): 41–55; Wolfgang Vondey and Chris W. Green, "Between This and That: Reality and Sacramentality in the Pentecostal Worldview," *Journal of Pentecostal Theology* 19, no. 2 (2010): 243–64.

37. For some exceptions, see Hollenweger, *Pentecostals*, 385–89.

38. Also consider John 6:25–59 and Acts 2:42, 46.

39. The text-critical issues surrounding the longer and shorter readings of Luke's Last Supper account have no bearing on my concerns here. Even if the longer reading, which contains ἀνάμνησις, is followed instead of the shorter reading, which does not, the point remains that we are given no elaboration on precisely how ἀνάμνησις is to be understood. For a discussion of the text-critical issues of Luke 22:17–20, see Bruce M. Metzger, *A Textual Commentary on the New Testament*, 2nd ed. (Stuttgart: German Bible Society, 1994), 148–50; Joachim Jeremias, *The Eucharistic Words of Jesus* (Oxford: Blackwell, 1955), 87–106.

   For the claim that ἀνάμνησις evokes a so-called biblical view of memory, see Kärkkäinen, "Spirit and the Lord's Supper," 137–38.

40. Wiles, *Making of Christian Doctrine*, 89.

41. D. Lyle Dabney, "Saul's Armor: The Problem and the Promise of Pentecostal Theology Today," *PNEUMA: The Journal of the Society for Pentecostal Studies* 23, no. 1 (2001): 130. In this article, Dabney encourages pentecostals to take up the challenge of constructing a pneumatological theology. For Dabney's additional works on pneumatological theology, see D. Lyle Dabney, "Otherwise Engaged in the Spirit: A First Theology for a Twenty-First Century," in *The Future of Theology: Essays in Honor of Jürgen Moltmann*, ed. Miroslav Volf, Carmen Krieg, Thomas Kucharz (Grand Rapids, MI: Eerdmans, 1996), 154–63; D. Lyle Dabney, "*Pneumatologia Crucis*: Reclaiming *Theologia Crucis* for a Theology of the Spirit Today," *Scottish Journal of Theology* 53, no. 4 (2000): 511–24; D. Lyle Dabney, "'Justified by the Spirit': Soteriological Reflections on the Resurrection," *International Journal of Systematic Theology* 3, no. 1 (2001): 46–68; D. Lyle Dabney, "Starting with the Spirit: Why the Last Should Now Be First," in *Starting with the Spirit*, ed. Gordon Preece and Stephen Pickard (Adelaide, Australia: Openbook Publishers, 2001), 3–27; D. Lyle Dabney, "(Re)Turning to the Spirit: Theology in a World Post-Christendom," *Quarterly Review* 21, no. 2 (2001): 117–29; D. Lyle Dabney, "The Nature of the Spirit: Creation as a Premonition of God," in *The Work of the Spirit: Pneumatology and Pentecostalism*, ed. Michael Welker (Grand Rapids, MI: Eerdmans, 2006), 71–86.

42. Paschasius Radbertus, *De corpore et sanguine Domini*, Patrologia Latina, 120: 1267–1350; Ratramnus, *De corpore et sanguine Domini*, Patrologia Latina, 121: 125–70.

43. Luke 5:33–35: "And they said to him, 'The disciples of John fast often and offer prayers, and so do the disciples of the Pharisees, but yours eat and drink.' And

Jesus said to them, 'Can you make wedding guests fast while the bridegroom is with them? The days will come, when the bridegroom is taken away from them, and then they will fast in those days'" (RSV).

44. Concerning the idea of Jesus' absence, specifically in Mark, see Werner H. Kelber, *The Kingdom in Mark: A New Place and a New Time* (Philadelphia, PA: Fortress Press, 1974), 20, 123. Cf. Joel Marcus, *Mark 1–8: A New Translation with Introduction and Commentary* (New York, NY: Doubleday, 2000), 236–38.

45. "The cup of blessing that we bless—is it not a common share (κοινωνία) of the blood of Christ? The bread that we break—is it not a common share (κοινωνία) of the body of Christ" (my translation).

46. "What do I imply then? That food offered to idols is anything, or that an idol is anything? No, I imply that what pagans sacrifice they offer to demons and not to God" (RSV).

47. "Therefore, my beloved, shun the worship of idols" (RSV). Richard Hays rightly underscores the unity between Paul's warnings form Israel's history of idolatry in 10:1–13 with Paul's reflections on the Lord's supper in 10:14–22. See Richard B. Hays, *First Corinthians* (Louisville, KY: John Knox Press, 1997), 159–71.

48. Wendel Lee Willis, *Idol Meat in Corinth: The Pauline Argument in 1 Corinthians 8 and 10* (Chico, CA: Scholars Press, 1985), 205–09.

49. "Do you not know that all of us who have been baptized into Christ Jesus were baptized into his death? We were buried with him by baptism into death, so that as Christ was raised from the dead by the glory of the Father, we too might walk in newness of life. For if we have been united with him in a death like his, we shall certainly be united with him in a resurrection like his" (RSV).

50. "Indeed I count everything as loss because of the surpassing worth of knowing Christ Jesus my Lord. For his sake I have suffered the loss of all things, and count them as refuse, in order that I may gain Christ and be found in him, not having a righteousness of my own, based on the law, but that which is through faith in Christ, the righteousness from God that depends on faith; that I may know him and the power of his resurrection, and may share his sufferings, becoming like him in his death, that if possible I may attain to the resurrection from the dead" (RSV).

51. "Because there is one bread, we who are many are one body, for we all partake of the one bread" (RSV).

52. C. K. Barrett, *The First Epistle to the Corinthians* (New York, NY: Harper and Row, 1968), 231–32.

53. "So then, my brethren, when you come together to eat, wait for one another—if any one is hungry, let him eat at home—lest you come together to be condemned" (RSV).

54. Yong, *Spirit Poured Out on All Flesh*. Yong leaves open the possibility that pentecostals might be able to affirm that the presence of Christ is somehow mediated through the elements of the supper by the power of the Spirit, although he states that this presence should be understood in "interpersonal and intersubjective" terms rather than in "physicalist or consubstantive" terms (163–64).

55. Cf. Kärkkäinen, "Spirit and the Lord's Supper," 145; Thomas, "Pentecostal Theology," 19.

56. See Hays, *First Corinthians*. Concerning I Cor 11:24–26, he writes, "The word 'remembrance' . . . is sometimes thought to suggest the actual making-present of the Lord through the representation of his body and blood in the eucharistic elements. Whatever value such a eucharistic theology may possess on other grounds,

it is far removed from Paul's concerns here in the argument of I Corinthians. Indeed, according to verse 26, the Lord's Supper expresses precisely the opposite of
the 'real presence' of the Lord. It expresses, instead, the community's memory of
his death in the interval between cross and *parousia*. . . . Thus, the meal acknowledges the *absence* of the Lord and mingles memory and hope, recalling his death
and awaiting his coming again" (199).

57. For example, the Church of God (Cleveland, TN), which recognizes three levels of
ministerial credentialing, does not grant its "exhorters" (the entry level credentialed position) the authority to "[a]dminister Holy Sacraments" (although they
can baptize "[i]n cases of emergency"). The implication is that the supper cannot
be administered unless a member of one of the other two credentialed positions
("ordained minister" and "ordained bishop") is present. One can conclude only
that if the supper cannot be administered it cannot be celebrated. See *Minutes
2010: Church of God Book of Discipline, Church Order, and Governance* (Cleveland,
TN: Church of God Publishing House, 2010), 146–53.

58. This seems to be the logic of vv. 27–29. Paul says that the one who eats and drinks
unworthily shows contempt or hostility toward the body and blood of the Lord
(v. 27). Therefore, each of them should examine himself or herself (v. 28), appar-
ently to make sure that he or she properly discerns the body (v. 29).

59. Here, I follow the shorter reading of 11:29, which excludes τοῦ κυρίου (and
ἀναξίως).

60. Larry W. Hurtado, "Jesus' Death as Paradigmatic in the New Testament," *Scottish
Journal of Theology* 57, no. 4 (2004): 420.

61. See Kenneth Grayston, *Dying, We Live: A New Enquiry into the Death of Christ in the
New Testament* (London: Darton, Longman, and Todd, 1990). Concerning this statement from Mark 10:45, Grayston writes, "The saying is intended as a model of
behaviour for his followers, that is to say, in order to serve others, he . . . throws
himself on God's compassion and surrenders his life. Others should do likewise. It
is taken for granted that God will respond, and there is no need of theological
calculation about how and why. The only thing is that Christ's self-giving is a
model of Christian service" (359).

62. William T. Cavanaugh, *Torture and Eucharist: Theology, Politics, and the Body of
Christ* (Oxford: Blackwell, 1998), 279. See also William T. Cavanaugh, *Theopolitical
Imagination: Discovering the Liturgy as a Political Act in an Age of Consumerism* (Lon-
don: T & T Clark, 2002).

63. Walter Brueggemann, *The Prophetic Imagination*, 2nd ed. (Minneapolis, MN: Fortress Press, 2001), xx.

64. Of course, a pneumatological entry point does not preclude pentecostals from
considering if and how Christ is present in the supper. It simply gives priority to
questions of the Spirit's presence. If pentecostals turn to such christological questions, they would do well to develop differentiated senses of understanding
Christ's presence. At very least, the distinctions between the omnipresence of
Christ's divine nature and a unique eucharistic presence would need to be main-
tained.

65. *Book of Common Prayer*, Holy Eucharist, Rite II.

66. Walter Hollenweger's comment that the Lord's supper is already "the central point
[*der Mittelpunkt*] of Pentecostal worship" (Hollenweger, *Pentecostals*, 385) is a gross
exaggeration that does not reflect actual pentecostal practice. For the German, see
Walter Hollenweger, *Enthusiastisches Christentum: Die Pfingstbewegung in Geschichte und Gegenwart* (Wuppertal: Theologischer Verlag, 1969), 432. Similarly,

Keith Warrington's claim that pentecostals celebrate the Lord's supper every Sunday is too generalized, even if accurate about a minority of pentecostals (Warrington, *Pentecostal Theology*, 165). Although, for the observation that practitioners of some British pentecostal churches do celebrate it every Sunday, see Richard Bicknell, "The Ordinances: The Marginalised Aspects of Pentecostalism," in *Pentecostal Perspectives*, ed. Keith Warrington (Carlisle: Paternoster Publishing, 1998), 204–22.

67. See Murray W. Dempster, "Christian Social Concern in Pentecostal Perspective: Reformulating Pentecostal Eschatology," *Journal of Pentecostal Theology* 2 (1993): 51–64.

68. For an argument that evangelicals, including pentecostals, should celebrate the Lord's supper more frequently than they tend to do so, see Chan, *Liturgical Theology*, 64–66.

69. *Institutes of the Christian Religion* (1559), 4.14.4.

CONCLUSION

1. For example, D. Lyle Dabney, "Saul's Armor: The Problem and the Promise of Pentecostal Theology Today," *PNEUMA: The Journal of the Society for Pentecostal Studies* 23, no. 1 (2001): 115–46; Cheryl Bridges Johns, *Pentecostal Formation: A Pedagogy among the Oppressed* (Sheffield: Sheffield Academic Press, 1993), 7–9.

2. Neither does Dabney nor Johns think this.

3. See I Sam 16:14–23.

BIBLIOGRAPHY

Adewuya, J. Ayodeji. "Revisiting 1 Corinthians 11.27–34: Paul's Discussion of the Lord's Supper and African Meals." *Journal for the Study of the New Testament* 30, no. 1 (2007): 95–112.

Albrecht, Daniel E. *Rites in the Spirit: A Ritual Approach to Pentecostal/Charismatic Spirituality*. Sheffield: Sheffield Academic Press, 1999.

Alexander, Estrelda. *Limited Liberty: The Legacy of Four Pentecostal Women*. Cleveland, OH: Pilgrim Press, 2008.

———. *The Women of Azusa Street*. Cleveland, OH: Pilgrim Press, 2005.

Alexander, Paul. *Peace to War: Shifting Allegiances in the Assemblies of God*. Telford, PA: Cascadia Publishing House, 2009.

Althouse, Peter. *Spirit of the Last Days: Pentecostal Eschatology in Conversation with Jürgen Moltmann*. London: T & T Clark, 2003.

———. "Toward a Theological Understanding of the Pentecostal Appeal to Experience." *Journal of Ecumenical Studies* 38, no. 4 (2001): 399–411.

Anderson, Allan. "A Global Pentecostal Theology? Amos Yong's The Spirit Poured Out on All Flesh." *Journal of Pentecostal Theology* 16, no. 1 (2007): 97–102.

———. *An Introduction to Pentecostalism: Global Charismatic Christianity*. Cambridge: Cambridge University Press, 2004.

Anderson, Robert Mapes. *Vision of the Disinherited: The Making of American Pentecostalism*. New York, NY: Oxford University Press, 1979.

Archer, Kenneth J. "Nourishment for Our Journey: The Pentecostal *Via Salutis* and Sacramental Ordinances." *Journal of Pentecostal Theology* 13 (2004): 79–96.

———. *A Pentecostal Hermeneutic for the Twenty-First Century: Spirit, Scripture and Community*. London: T & T Clark, 2004.

Arrington, French L. *The Spirit-Anointed Jesus: A Study of the Gospel of Luke*. Cleveland, TN: Pathway Press, 2008.

———. *Unconditional Eternal Security: Myth or Truth?* Cleveland, TN: Pathway Press, 2005.

———. *Encountering the Holy Spirit: Paths of Christian Growth and Service*. Cleveland, TN: Pathway Press, 2003.

———. *Exploring the Declaration of Faith*. Cleveland, TN: Pathway Press, 2003.

———. "The Use of the Bible by Pentecostals." *PNEUMA: The Journal of the Society for Pentecostal Studies* 16, no. 1 (1994): 101–7.

———. *Christian Doctrine: A Pentecostal Perspective*. 3 vols. Cleveland, TN: Pathway Press, 1992–94.

———. *The Acts of the Apostles: An Introduction and Commentary*. Peabody, MA: Hendrickson, 1988.

———. "Hermeneutics, Historical Perspectives on Pentecostal and Charismatic." In *Dictionary of Pentecostal and Charismatic Movements*. Edited by Stanley Burgess and Gary B. McGee. Grand Rapids, MI: Zondervan, 1988, 376–89.

———. *The Ministry of Reconciliation: A Study of 2 Corinthians*. Grand Rapids, MI: Baker Book House, 1980.

———. *Paul's Aeon Theology in I Corinthians*. Washington, DC: University Press of America, 1978.

Attanasi, Katy. "Toward a Pentecostal Liturgical Ethic: Lord's Supper, Prayers for Healing, and Spirit Baptism." *Proceedings of the 35th Annual Meeting of the Society for Pentecostal Studies*, 1–8. Pasadena, CA, 2006.

Augustine. "Sermon 227." In *The Works of Saint Augustine*, III/6. Edited by John E. Rotelle and translated by Edmund Hill. New York, NY: New City Press, 1993, 254–56.

Aumann, Jordan. *Spiritual Theology*. London: Continuum, 2006; 1980.

Baptism, Eucharist and Ministry. Geneva: World Council of Churches, 1982.

Barnes, Michel René. *The Power of God: Δύναμις in Gregory of Nyssa's Trinitarian Theology*. Washington, DC: Catholic University of America Press, 2001.

Barr, James. *The Concept of Biblical Theology: An Old Testament Perspective*. Minneapolis, MN: Fortress Press, 1999.

Barrett, C. K. *The First Epistle to the Corinthians*. New York, NY: Harper and Row, 1968.

Barth, Karl. "Concluding Unscientific Postscript on Schleiermacher." In *The Theology of Schleiermacher*. Grand Rapids, MI: Eerdmans, 1982, 261–79.

———. *Evangelical Theology: An Introduction*. Translated by Grover Foley. Grand Rapids, MI: Eerdmans, 1963.

———. *Church Dogmatics*. 4 vols. Translated by Geoffrey W. Bromiley et al. Edinburgh: T & T Clark, 1936–68.

Basil of Caesarea. *On the Holy Spirit*. Translated by David Anderson. Crestwood, NY: St. Vladimir's Seminary Press, 1980.

Bavinck, Herman. *Reformed Dogmatics*. 4 vols. Grand Rapids, MI: Baker Academic, 2003–08.

Bebbington, David. *Evangelicalism in Modern Britain: A History from the 1730s to the 1980s*. London: Unwin Hyman, 1989.

Berger, Teresa. "Prayers and Practices of Women: Lex Orandi Reconfigured." *Yearbook of the European Society of Women in Theological Research* 9 (2001): 63–77.

Berkhof, Louis. *Systematic Theology*, 4th ed. Grand Rapids, MI: Eerdmans, 1941.

Bernard, David K. *The Oneness of God*, revised edition. Hazelwood, MO: Word Aflame Press, 2001.

Bicknell, Richard. "The Ordinances: The Marginalised Aspects of Pentecostalism." In *Pentecostal Perspectives*. Edited by Keith Warrington. Carlisle: Paternoster Publishing, 1998, 204–22.

Biddy, Wesley Scott. "Re-envisioning the Pentecostal understanding of the Eucharist: An Ecumenical Proposal." *PNEUMA: The Journal of the Society for Pentecostal Studies* 28, no. 2 (2006): 228–51.

Bishop, David S. "The Sacraments in Worship." In *Pentecostal Worship*. Edited by Cecil B. Knight. Cleveland, TN: Pathway Press, 1974, 101–20.

Bloch-Hoell, Nils. *The Pentecostal Movement: Its Origin, Development, and Distinctive Character*. Oslo: Universitetsforlaget, 1964.

Bloesch, Donald. *The Church: Sacraments, Worship, Ministry, Mission*. Downers Grove, IL: InterVarsity Press, 2002.

Blumhofer, Edith L. *The Assemblies of God: A Chapter in the Story of American Pentecostalism*. 2 vols. Springfield, MO: Gospel Publishing House, 1989.

Bradnick, David. "Demonology and Anthropology in Conversation: Applying the Theological Method of Amos Yong Towards a Demonology for the Twenty-First Century." *Proceedings of the 38th Annual Meeting of the Society for Pentecostal Studies*, 1–26. Eugene, OR, 2009.

Brueggemann, Walter. *The Prophetic Imagination*, 2nd ed. Minneapolis, MN: Fortress Press, 2001.

———. "Canonization and Contextualization." In *Interpretation and Obedience: From Faithful Reading to Faithful Living*. Philadelphia, PA: Fortress Press, 1991, 119–42.

Bruner, Frederick Dale. *A Theology of the Holy Spirit: The Pentecostal Experience and the New Testament Witness*. Grand Rapids, MI: Eerdmans, 1970.

Buckley, James J., and David S. Yeago, eds. *Knowing the Triune God: The Work of the Spirit in the Practices of the Church*. Grand Rapids, MI: Eerdmans, 2001.

Bundy, David. "The Genre of Systematic Theology in Pentecostalism." *PNEUMA: The Journal of the Society for Pentecostal Studies* 15, no. 1 (1993): 89–107.

Butler, Anthea D. *Women in the Church of God in Christ: Making a Sanctified World*. Chapel Hill, NC: University of North Carolina Press, 2007.

———. "Pentecostal Traditions We Should Pass On: The Good, the Bad, and the Ugly." *PNEUMA: The Journal of the Society for Pentecostal Studies* 27, no. 2 (2005): 343–53.

Caird, G. B. *New Testament Theology*. Completed and edited by L. D. Hurst. Oxford: Oxford University Press, 1994.

Cartledge, Mark J. *Testimony in the Spirit: Rescripting Ordinary Pentecostal Theology*. Burlington, VT: Ashgate, 2010.

———, ed. *Speaking in Tongues: Multi-Disciplinary Perspectives*. Waynesboro, GA: Paternoster Press, 2006.

———. *Practical Theology: Charismatic and Empirical Perspectives*. Waynesboro, GA: Paternoster Press, 2003.

———. *Charismatic Glossolalia: An Empirical-Theological Study*. Burlington, VT: Ashgate, 2002.

Cavanaugh, William T. *Theopolitical Imagination*. London: T & T Clark, 2002.

———. *Torture and Eucharist: Theology, Politics, and the Body of Christ*. Oxford: Blackwell, 1998.

Chan, Simon. "Future of the Liturgy: A Pentecostal Contribution." In *The Great Tradition—A Great Labor: Studies in Ancient-Future Faith*. Edited by Philip Harrold and D. H. Williams. Eugene, OR: Cascade Books, 2011, 55–69.

———. *Pentecostal Ecclesiology: An Essay on the Development of Doctrine*. Blandford Forum: Deo, 2011.

———. "Folk Christianity and Primal Spirituality: Prospects for Theological Development." In *Christian Movements in Southeast Asia: A Theological Exploration*. Edited by Michael Nai-Chiu Poon. Singapore: Trinity Theological College, 2010, 1–17.

———. "Jesus as Spirit-Baptizer: Its Significance for Pentecostal Ecclesiology." In *Toward a Pentecostal Ecclesiology: The Church and the Fivefold Gospel*. Edited by John Christopher Thomas. Cleveland, TN: CPT Press, 2010, 139–56.

———. "The Liturgy as the Work of the Spirit: A Theological Perspective." In *The Spirit in Worship—Worship in the Spirit*. Edited by Teresa Berger and Bryan D. Spinks. Collegeville, MN: Liturgical Press, 2009, 41–57.

———. "New Directions in Evangelical Spirituality." *Journal of Spiritual Formation and Soul Care* 2, no. 2 (2009): 219–37.

———. "Evangelical Theology in Asian Contexts." In *The Cambridge Companion to Evangelical Theology*. Edited by Timothy Larsen and Daniel J. Treier. Cambridge: Cambridge University Press, 2007, 225–40.

———. "The Mission of the Trinity." *Christianity Today* 51, no. 6 (2007): 48–51.

———. "Communion Spirituality and Its Implications for Holistic Living in a Fragmented World." *Church and Society in Asia Today* 9, no. 2 (2006): 91–108.

———. *Liturgical Theology: The Church as Worshipping Community.* Downers Grove, IL: InterVarsity Press, 2006.

———. "Whither Pentecostalism?" In *Asian and Pentecostal: The Charismatic Face of Christianity in Asia.* Edited by Allan Anderson and Edmond Tang. London: Regnum International: Asia Pacific Theological Seminary Press, 2005, 575–86.

———. "The Church and the Development of Doctrine." *Journal of Pentecostal Theology* 13 (2004): 57–77.

———. "The Mystery of the Liturgy: Towards a Theology of Ecclesial Practices." *Trinity Theological Journal* 12 (2004): 93–110.

———. "Introduction." In *Truth to Proclaim: The Gospel in Church and Society.* Edited by Simon Chan. Singapore: Trinity Theological College, 2002, v–x.

———. "Mother Church: Toward a Pentecostal Ecclesiology." *PNEUMA: The Journal of the Society for Pentecostal Studies* 22, no. 2 (Fall 2000): 177–208.

———. *Pentecostal Theology and the Christian Spiritual Tradition.* Sheffield: Sheffield Academic Press, 2000.

———. "Problem and Possibility of an Asian Theological Hermeneutic." *Trinity Theological Journal* 9 (2000): 47–59.

———. "Evidential Glossolalia and the Doctrine of Subsequence." *Asian Journal of Pentecostal Studies* 2, no. 2 (1999): 195–211.

———. "A Hollowed-Out Spirituality: Spirituality without Theology as Illustrated in the Contemporary Worship Phenomenon." *Church and Society* 2, no. 3 (1999): 56–62.

———. "The Language Game of Eternal Security." *Church and Society* 2, no. 1 (1999): 23–28.

———. "The Problem of Transcendence and Immanence in Asian Contextual Theology." *Trinity Theological Journal* 8 (1999): 5–18.

———. "A Response to Max Turner." *Asian Journal of Pentecostal Studies* 2, no. 2 (1999): 279–81.

———. "Homosexuality: A Theological Perspective." *Church and Society* 1, no. 3 (1998): 79–87.

———. *Spiritual Theology: A Systematic Study of the Christian Life.* Downers Grove, IL: InterVarsity Press, 1998.

———. "The Language Game of Glossolalia, or Making Sense of 'Initial Evidence.'" In *Pentecostalism in Context: Essays in Honor of William W. Menzies.* Edited by Wonsuk Ma and Robert P. Menzies. Sheffield: Sheffield Academic Press, 1997, 80–95.

———. "The Logic of Hell: A Response to Annihilationism." *Evangelical Review of Theology* 18, no. 1 (1994): 20–32.

———. "Sharing the Trinitarian Life: John 17:20–26, I John 1:1–4." In *On the Way to Fuller* Koinonia. Edited by Thomas F. Best and Günther Gassmann. Geneva: World Council of Churches Publications, 1994, 85–90.

———. "Theological Education and Spirituality." *AETEI Journal* 3, no. 1 (1990): 23–27.

———. "Protestantism and Mysticism." *Trinity Theological Journal* 2 (1990): 55–76.

———. "Church and Society: A Historical Perspective." In *Church and Society: Singapore Context.* Edited by Bobby E. K. Sng. Singapore: Graduates Christian Fellowship, 1989, 38–46.

———. "Hush Your Heart to Listen." *Impact* (June–July 1989): 17–20.

———. "The Puritan Meditative Tradition, 1599–1691: A Study of Ascetical Piety." PhD diss., Cambridge University, 1986.

———. "Second Thoughts on Contextualization." *Evangelical Review of Theology* 9, no. 1 (1985): 50–54.

Childs, Brevard S. *Biblical Theology: A Proposal*. Minneapolis, MN: Fortress, Press, 2002.

———. *Biblical Theology of the Old and New Testaments: Theological Reflection on the Christian Bible*. London: SCM Press, 1992.

Chopp, Rebecca, and Mark Taylor, eds. *Reconstructing Christian Theology*. Minneapolis, MN: Fortress Press, 1994.

Clapper, Gregory S. *John Wesley on Religious Affections: His Views on Experience and Emotion and Their Role in the Christian Life and Theology*. Metuchen, NJ: Scarecrow Press, 1989.

Clark, Matthew S. "Pentecostalism's Anabaptist Roots: Hermeneutical Implications." In *The Spirit and Spirituality: Essays in Honour of Russell P. Spittler*. Edited by Wonsuk Ma and Robert P. Menzies. London: T & T Clark, 2004, 194–211.

———, and Henry I. Lederle. *What Is Distinctive about Pentecostal Theology?* Pretoria: University of South Africa, 1983.

Coffey, David Michael. *"Did You Receive the Holy Spirit When You Believed?" Some Basic Questions for Pneumatology*. Milwaukee, WI: Marquette University Press, 2005.

———. Deus Trinitas: *The Doctrine of the Triune God*. New York, NY: Oxford University Press, 1999.

———. *Grace: The Gift of the Holy Spirit*. Sydney: Faith and Culture, 1979.

Collins, John J. *The Apocalyptic Imagination: An Introduction to Jewish Apocalyptic Literature*, 2nd ed. Grand Rapids, MI: Eerdmans, 1998.

———, ed. *Apocalypse: The Morphology of a Genre*. Missoula, MT: Scholars Press, 1979. *Semeia* 14.

Congar, Yves. *I Believe in the Holy Spirit*. 3 vols. New York, NY: Seabury Press, 1983.

Conn, Charles W. *Like a Mighty Army: A History of the Church of God, Definitive Edition*. Cleveland, TN: Pathway Press, 1996.

Conyers, A. J. *God, Hope, and History: Jürgen Moltmann and the Christian Concept of History*. Macon, GA: Mercer University Press, 1988.

Coulter, Dale M. "The Development of Ecclesiology in the Church of God (Cleveland, TN): A Forgotten Contribution?" *PNEUMA: The Journal of the Society for Pentecostal Studies* 29, no. 1 (2007): 59–85.

Cox, Harvey. *Fire from Heaven: The Rise of Pentecostal Spirituality and the Reshaping of Religion in the Twenty-First Century*. Reading, MA: Addison-Wesley, 1995.

———. "A Review of *Pentecostal Spirituality: A Passion for the Kingdom* by Steven J. Land." *Journal of Pentecostal Theology* 5 (1994): 3–12.

———. *The Secular City: Secularization and Urbanization in Theological Perspective*. New York, NY: Macmillan, 1965.

Cross, Terry L. "The Divine-Human Encounter: Towards a Pentecostal Theology of Experience. *PNEUMA: The Journal of the Society for Pentecostal Studies* 31, no. 1 (2009): 3–34.

———. "A Response to Clark Pinnock's 'Church in the Power of the Holy Spirit.'" *Journal of Pentecostal Theology* 14, no. 2 (2006): 175–82.

———. "Can There Be a Pentecostal Systematic Theology? An Essay on Theological Method in a Postmodern World." *Proceedings of the 30th Annual Meeting of the Society for Pentecostal Studies*, 145–66. Tulsa, OK, 2001.

———. "Toward a Theology of the Word and the Spirit: A Review of J. Rodman Williams's *Renewal Theology*." *Journal of Pentecostal Theology* 3 (1993): 113–35.

Cushman, Robert E. "Lex Orandi, Lex Credendi." *Journal of Religious Thought* 18, no. 2 (1961): 113–19.

Dabney, D. Lyle. "The Justification of the Spirit: Soteriological Reflections on the Resurrection." In *Starting with the Spirit*. Edited by Gordon Preece and Stephen Pickard. Hindmarsh, S. Aust.: Australian Theological Forum, 2001, 59–82.

———. "'Justified by the Spirit': Soteriological Reflections on the Resurrection." *International Journal of Systematic Theology* 3, no. 1 (2001): 46–68.

———. "Naming the Spirit: Towards a Pneumatology of the Cross." In *Starting with the Spirit*. Edited by Gordon Preece and Stephen Pickard. Hindmarsh, S. Aust.: Australian Theological Forum, 2001, 28–58.

———. "The Nature of the Spirit: Creation as a Premonition of God." In *Starting with the Spirit*. Edited by Gordon Preece and Stephen Pickard. Hindmarsh, S. Aust.: Australian Theological Forum, 2001, 83–112.

———. "(Re)Turning to the Spirit: Theology in a World Post-Christendom." *Quarterly Review* 21, no. 2 (2001): 117–29.

———. "Saul's Armor: The Problem and the Promise of Pentecostal Theology Today." *PNEUMA: The Journal of the Society for Pentecostal Studies* 23, no. 1 (2001): 115–46.

———. "Starting with the Spirit: Why the Last Should Now Be First." In *Starting with the Spirit*. Edited by Gordon Preece and Stephen Pickard. Hindmarsh, S. Aust.: Australian Theological Forum, 2001, 3–27.

———. "*Pneumatologia Crucis*: Reclaiming *Theologia Crucis* for a Theology of the Spirit Today." *Scottish Journal of Theology* 53, no. 4 (2000): 511–24.

———. *Die Kenosis des Geistes: Kontinuität Zwischen Schöpfung und Erlösung im Werk des Heiligen Geistes*. Neukirchen-Vluyn: Neukirchener Verlag, 1997.

———. "Otherwise Engaged in the Spirit: A First Theology for a Twenty-First Century." In *The Future of Theology: Essays in Honor of Jürgen Moltmann*. Edited by Miroslav Volf, Carmen Krieg, and Thomas Kucharz. Grand Rapids, MI: Eerdmans, 1996, 154–63.

Daffe, Jerald J. "An Introduction to Worship for Bible College Ministerial Students." DMin diss., Western Conservative Baptist Seminary, 1983.

Dayton, Donald W. "Yet Another Layer of the Onion: Or Opening the Ecumenical Door to Let the Riffraff In." *The Ecumenical Review* 40, no. 1 (1988): 87–110.

———. *Theological Roots of Pentecostalism*. Metuchen, NJ: Scarecrow Press, 1987.

De Clerck, Paul. "'Lex orandi, lex credendi': Sens originel et avatars historiques d'un adage equivoque." *Questions Liturgiques/Studies in Liturgy* 59, no. 4 (1978): 193–212.

DeHart, Paul J. *The Trial of the Witnesses: The Rise and Decline of Postliberal Theology*. Malden, MA: Blackwell, 2006.

Del Colle, Ralph. Frank's *Justified in the Spirit*: The Spirit as the Substance of Justification—'A Bridge too Far.'" *Proceedings of the 40th Annual Meeting of the Society for Pentecostal Studies*, 1–22. Memphis, TN, 2011.

———. "Whither Pentecostal Theology? Why a Catholic Is Interested." *PNEUMA: The Journal of the Society for Pentecostal Studies* 31, no. 1 (2009): 35–46.

———. "Spirit Baptism: A Catholic Perspective." In *Perspectives on Spirit Baptism*. Edited by Chad Owen Brand. Nashville, TN: Broadman and Holman, 2004, 241–89.

———. "Pentecostalism and Apocalyptic Passion: A Review of Steve Land's *Pentecostal Spirituality: A Passion for the Kingdom*: A Roman Catholic Response." *Proceedings of the 25th Annual Meeting of the Society for Pentecostal Studies*, 1–17. Toronto, 1996.

———. *Christ and the Spirit: Spirit-Christology in Trinitarian Perspective*. Oxford: Oxford University Press, 1994.

Dempster, Murray W. "Christian Social Concern in Pentecostal Perspective: Reformulating Pentecostal Eschatology." *Journal of Pentecostal Theology* 2 (1993): 51–64.

Dieter, Melvin E. "The Development of Nineteenth Century Holiness Theology." *Wesleyan Theological Journal* 20, no. 1 (1985): 61–77.

Downey, Michael. "Lex Orandi, Lex Credendi: Taking It Seriously in Systematic Theology." In *Promise of Presence.* Edited by Michael Downey and Richard N. Fragomeni. Washington, DC: Pastoral Press, 1992, 3–25.

Driver, Tom F. *The Magic of Ritual: Our Need for Liberating Rites that Transform Our Lives and Our Communities.* New York, NY: Harper Collins, 1991.

Duffield, Guy P., and Nathaniel M. Van Cleave. *Foundations of Pentecostal Theology.* Los Angeles, CA: L.I.F.E Bible College, 1983.

Dunn, James D. G. *Baptism in the Holy Spirit: A Re-examination of the New Testament Teaching on the Gift of the Spirit in Relation to Pentecostalism Today.* Naperville, IL: A. R. Allenson, 1970.

England, John C. et al., eds. *Asian Christian Theologies: A Research Guide to Authors, Movements, Sources.* 3 vols. Delhi: Claretian Publishers, 2003.

Espín, Orlando O. "Whose *Lex Orandi*? Whose *Lex Credendi*? Latino/a Catholicism as a Theological Challenge for Liturgy." Paper presented at the Annual Meeting of the North American Academy of Liturgy, San Diego, CA, 2006, 53–71.

"Evangelism, Proselytism and Common Witness: The Report from the Fourth Phase of the International Dialogue (1990–1997) between the Roman Catholic Church and Some Classical Pentecostal Churches and Leaders." *PNEUMA: The Journal of the Society for Pentecostal Studies* 21, no. 1 (1999): 11–51.

Farley, Edward. Theologia: *The Fragmentation and Unity of Theological Education.* Philadelphia, PA: Fortress Press, 1983.

Faupel, D. William. *The Everlasting Gospel: The Significance of Eschatology in the Development of Pentecostal Thought.* Sheffield: Sheffield Academic Press, 1996.

——. "The Everlasting Gospel: The Significance of Eschatology in the Development of Pentecostal Thought." PhD diss., University of Birmingham, 1989.

——. "The American Pentecostal Movement: A Bibliographic Essay." In *The Higher Christian Life.* Edited by Donald W. Dayton. London: Garland, 1985, 109–38.

——. "The Function of 'Models' in the Interpretation of Pentecostal Thought." *PNEUMA: The Journal of the Society for Pentecostal Studies* 2, no. 1 (1980): 51–71.

Fee, Gordon D. *God's Empowering Presence: The Holy Spirit in the Letters of Paul.* Peabody, MA: Hendrickson, 1994.

"*Final Report* of the International Roman Catholic/Pentecostal Dialogue (1972–1976)." *PNEUMA: The Journal of the Society for Pentecostal Studies* 12, no. 2 (1990): 85–95.

"*Final Report* of the International Roman Catholic/Pentecostal Dialogue (1977–1982)." *PNEUMA: The Journal of the Society for Pentecostal Studies* 12, no. 2 (1990): 97–115.

Fiorenza, Francis Schüssler. *Foundational Theology: Jesus and the Church.* New York, NY: Crossroad, 1984.

Flint, Thomas P., and Michael C. Rea. "Introduction." In *Oxford Handbook of Philosophical Theology.* Edited by Thomas P. Flint and Michael C. Rea. Oxford: Oxford University Press, 2009, 1–7.

Forrester, Duncan B. "Lex Orandi, Lex Credendi." In *Theology and Practice.* Edited by Duncan B. Forrester. London: Epworth Press, 1990, 71–80.

Franklin, Robert M. *Crisis in the Village: Restoring Hope in African American Communities.* Minneapolis, MN: Fortress Press, 2007.

Frei, Hans W. *Types of Christian Theology.* Edited by George Hunsinger and William C. Placher. New Haven, CT: Yale University Press, 1992.

———. *The Identity of Jesus Christ: The Hermeneutical Bases of Dogmatic Theology*. Philadelphia, PA: Fortress Press, 1975.

———. *The Eclipse of Biblical Narrative: A Study in Eighteenth and Nineteenth Century Hermeneutics*. New Haven, CT: Yale University Press, 1974.

Garrigou-Lagrange, Reginald. *The Three Ages of the Interior Life: Prelude of Eternal Life*. 2 vols. Translated by M. Timothea Doyle. Rockford, IL: TAN Books, 1989.

Gavrilyuk, Paul L. "Canonical Liturgies: The Dialectic of *Lex Orandi* and *Lex Credendi*." In *Canonical Theism: A Proposal for Theology and the Church*. Edited by William J. Abraham, Jason E. Vickers, and Natalie B. Van Kirk. Grand Rapids, MI: Eerdmans, 2008, 61–72.

Gelpi, Donald L. *The Firstborn of Many: A Christology for Converting Christians*. 3 vols. Milwaukee, WI: Marquette University Press, 2001.

———. *The Conversion Experience: A Reflection Process for RCIA Participants and Others*. New York, NY: Paulist Press, 1998.

———. *The Divine Mother: A Trinitarian Theology of the Holy Spirit*. Lanham, MD: University Press of America, 1984.

Gill, Jerry H. *Mediated Transcendence: A Postmodern Reflection*. Macon, GA: Mercer University Press, 1989.

Gohr, G. W. "Pearlman, Myer." In *The New International Dictionary of Pentecostal and Charismatic Movements*, revised and expanded edition. Edited by Stanley M. Burgess and Eduard M. van der Maas. Grand Rapids, MI: Zondervan, 2003, 959.

Grayston, Kenneth. *Dying, We Live: A New Enquiry into the Death of Christ in the New Testament*. London: Darton, Longman, and Todd, 1990.

Gregory of Nyssa. *The Lord's Prayer, The Beatitudes*. Translated by Hilda C. Graef. Ancient Christian Writers, 18. New York, NY: Ramsey Press, 1954.

Grenz, Stanley J. *Renewing the Center: Evangelical Theology in a Post-theological Era*. Grand Rapids, MI: Baker Academic, 2000.

———. *Revisioning Evangelical Theology: A Fresh Agenda for the Twenty-first Century*. Downers Grove, IL: InterVarsity Press, 1993.

Gruits, Patricia D. *Understanding God: A Catechism of Christian Doctrine*. Detroit, MI: Evangel Press, 1962.

Gunton, Colin E. *The Promise of Trinitarian Theology*, 2nd ed. Edinburgh: T & T Clark, 1997.

Gutiérrez, Gustavo. *We Drink from Our Own Wells: The Spiritual Journey of a People*. Translated by Matthew J. O'Connell. Maryknoll, NY: Orbis Books, 1984.

Hanson, Paul D. *The Dawn of Apocalyptic: The Historical and Sociological Roots of Jewish Apocalyptic Eschatology*. Philadelphia, PA: Fortress Press, 1975.

Hauerwas, Stanley. *Resident Aliens: Life in the Christian Colony*. Nashville, TN: Abingdon Press, 1989.

———. *A Community of Character: Toward a Constructive Christian Social Ethic*. Notre Dame, IN: University of Notre Dame Press, 1981.

———, and L. Gregory Jones, eds. *Why Narrative? Readings in Narrative Theology*. Grand Rapids, MI: Eerdmans, 1989.

Hays, Richard B. *First Corinthians*. Louisville, KY: John Knox Press, 1997.

Healy, Nicholas M. "Practices and the New Ecclesiology: Misplaced Concreteness?" *International Journal of Systematic Theology* 5, no. 3 (2003): 287–308.

———. *Church, World, and the Christian Life: Practical-Prophetic Ecclesiology*. Cambridge: Cambridge University Press, 2000.

Hick, John. *The Metaphor of God Incarnate*. London: SCM Press, 1993.

Higgins, John R., Michael L. Dusing, and Frank D. Tallman. *An Introduction to Theology: A Classical Pentecostal Perspective*, 2nd ed. Dubuque, IA: Kendall/Hunt, 1994.

Hittenberger, Jeff, and Martin William Mittelstadt. "Power and Powerlessness in Pentecostal Theology: A Review Essay on Amos Yong's *Theology and Down Syndrome: Reimagining Disability in Late Modernity.*" PNEUMA: *The Journal of the Society for Pentecostal Studies* 30, no. 1 (2008): 137–45.

Hocken, Peter D. "Church, Theology of the." In *The New International Dictionary of Pentecostal and Charismatic Movements*, revised and expanded edition. Edited by Stanley M. Burgess and Eduard M. van der Maas. Grand Rapids, MI: Zondervan, 2003, 544–51.

Hodge, Charles. *Systematic Theology.* 3 vols. Grand Rapids, MI: Eerdmans, 1982.

Hohenstein, Charles R. "'Lex Orandi, Lex Credendi': Cautionary Notes." *Wesleyan Theological Journal* 32, no. 2 (1997): 140–57.

Holifield, E. Brooks. *Theology in America: Christian Thought from the Age of the Puritans to the Civil War.* New Haven, CT: Yale University Press, 2003.

Hollenweger, Walter. "The Critical Tradition of Pentecostalism." *Journal of Pentecostal Theology* 1 (1992): 7–17.

———. "Priorities in Pentecostal Research: Historiography, Missiology, Hermeneutics, and Pneumatology." In *Experiences of the Spirit: Conference on Pentecostal and Charismatic Research in Europe at Utrecht University, 1989.* Edited by Jan A. B. Jongeneel. Frankfurt: Peter Lang, 1991, 7–22.

———. "After Twenty Years' Research on Pentecostalism." *International Review of Mission* 75, no. 297 (1986): 3–12.

———. "Pentecostals and the Charismatic Movement." In *The Study of Spirituality.* Edited by Cheslyn Jones, et al. Oxford: Oxford University Press, 1986, 549–54.

———. *The Pentecostals: The Charismatic Movement in the Churches.* London: SCM Press, 1972.

———. "The Black Pentecostal Concept: Interpretations and Variations." *Concept* 30 (1970): 1–70.

———. *Enthusiastisches Christentum: Die Pfingsterbewegung in Geschichte und Gegenwart.* Wuppertal: Theologischer Verlag, 1969.

Horton-Parker, Skip. "Tracking the Theological 'Turn': The Pneumatological Imagination and the Renewal of Metaphysics and Theology in the 21st Century." *PentecoStudies* 6, no. 1 (2007): 47–75.

Hunsinger, George. *The Eucharist and Ecumenism: Let Us Keep the Feast.* Cambridge: Cambridge University Press, 2008.

———. "Postliberal Theology." In *The Cambridge Companion to Postmodern Theology.* Edited by Kevin J. Vanhoozer. Cambridge: Cambridge University Press, 2003, 42–57.

Hunter, Harold D. "Ordinances, Pentecostal." In *The New International Dictionary of Pentecostal and Charismatic Movements*, revised and expanded edition. Edited by Stanley M. Burgess and Eduard M. van der Maas. Grand Rapids, MI: Zondervan, 2003, 947–49.

Hurtado, Larry W. "Jesus' Death as Paradigmatic in the New Testament." *Scottish Journal of Theology* 57, no. 4 (2004): 413–33.

Hütter, Reinhard. *Suffering Divine Things: Theology as Church Practice.* Grand Rapids, MI: Eerdmans, 2000.

Irvin, Dale T. "A Review of Amos Yong's *Beyond the Impasse.*" *Journal of Pentecostal Theology* 12, no. 2 (2004): 277–80.

Jacobsen, Douglas G. *Thinking in the Spirit: Theologies of the Early Pentecostal Movement.* Bloomington, IN: Indiana University Press, 2003.

———. "Knowing the Doctrines of Pentecostals: The Scholastic Theology of the Assemblies of God, 1930–55." In *Pentecostal Currents in American Protestantism.* Edited by Edith L. Blumhofer, Russell P. Spittler, and Grant Wacker. Chicago, IL: University of Illinois Press, 1999, 90–107.

Jenson, Robert. "Justification as a Triune Act." *Modern Theology* 11, no. 4 (1995): 421–27.

Jeremias, Joachim. *The Eucharistic Words of Jesus*. Oxford: Blackwell, 1955.

Johns, Cheryl Bridges. "Partners in Scandal: Wesleyan and Pentecostal Scholarship." *PNEUMA: The Journal of the Society for Pentecostal Studies* 21, no. 2 (1999): 183–97.

———. *Pentecostal Formation: A Pedagogy among the Oppressed*. Sheffield: Sheffield Academic Press, 1993.

Johnson, Keith E. *Rethinking the Trinity and Religious Pluralism: An Augustinian Assessment*. Downers Grove, IL: IVP Academic, 2011.

Jones, Serene, and Paul Lakeland, eds. *Constructive Theology: A Contemporary Approach to Classical Themes*. Minneapolis, MN: Fortress Press, 2005.

Kärkkäinen, Veli-Matti. "Evangelical Theology and the Religions." In *The Cambridge Companion to Evangelical Theology*. Edited by Timothy Larsen and Daniel J. Treier. Cambridge: Cambridge University Press, 2007, 199–212.

———. *One with God: Salvation as Deification and Justification*. Collegeville, MN: Liturgical Press, 2004.

———. "Grace and the Ecumenical Potential of *Theosis*." In *Toward a Pneumatological Theology: Pentecostal and Ecumenical Perspectives on Ecclesiology, Soteriology, and Theology of Mission*. Edited by Amos Yong. Lanham, MD: University Press of America, 2002, 149–65.

———. "The Holy Spirit and Justification: The Ecumenical Significance of Luther's Doctrine of Salvation." *PNEUMA: The Journal of the Society for Pentecostal Studies* 24, no. 1 (2002): 26–39.

———. "The Spirit and the Lord's Supper." In *Toward a Pneumatological Theology: Pentecostal and Ecumenical Perspectives on Ecclesiology, Soteriology, and Theology of Mission*. Edited by Amos Yong. Lanham, MD: University Press of America, 2002, 135–46.

———. "Toward a Pneumatological Theology of Religions: A Pentecostal-Charismatic Inquiry." *International Review of Mission* 91, no. 361 (2002): 187–98.

———. "David's Sling: The Promise and the Problem of Pentecostal Theology Today: A Response to D. Lyle Dabney." *PNEUMA: The Journal of the Society for Pentecostal Studies* 23, no. 1 (2001): 147–52.

———. *Ad Ultimum Terrae: Evangelization, Proselytism, and Common Witness in the Roman Catholic-Pentecostal Dialogue (1990–1997)*. New York, NY: Peter Lang, 1999.

———. *Spiritus Ubi Vult Spirat: Pneumatology in Roman Catholic-Pentecostal Dialogue (1972–1989)*. Helsinki: Luther-Agricola, 1998.

Käsemann, Ernst. "The Beginnings of Christian Theology." In *New Testament Questions of Today*. Translated by W. J. Montague. London: SCM Press, 1969, 82–107.

———. "On the Subject of Primitive Christian Apocalyptic." In *New Testament Questions of Today*. Translated by W. J. Montague. London: SCM Press, 1969, 108–37.

———. "Zum Thema der urchristlichen Apokalyptik." *Zeitschrift für Theologie und Kirche* 59 (1962): 257–84.

———. "Die Anfänge christlicher Theologie." *Zeitschrift für Theologie und Kirche* 57 (1960): 162–85.

Kay, James F. "The *Lex Orandi* in Recent Protestant Theology." In *Ecumenical Theology in Worship, Doctrine, and Life: Essays Presented to Geoffrey Wainwright on His Sixtieth Birthday*. Edited by David S. Cunningham et al. New York, NY: Oxford University Press, 1999, 11–23.

Kay, William K. *Pentecostalism: A Very Short Introduction*. Oxford: Oxford University Press, 2011.

Kelber, Werner H. *The Kingdom in Mark: A New Place and a New Time*. Philadelphia, PA: Fortress Press, 1974.

Kirsch, Elmer E. "Systematic Theology II, III, IV by Ernest S. Williams, 1959." Pearlman Memorial Library. Central Bible College. Springfield, MO.

Klaus, Byron D. "Review of *Pentecostal Spirituality: A Passion for the Kingdom*." *Paraclete* 29, no. 3 (1995): 46–47.

———, et al., eds. *The Globalization of Pentecostalism*. Irvine, CA: Regnum, 1999.

Knight, Henry H. III. "Reflections on Frank Macchia's *Baptized in the Spirit*." *Journal of Pentecostal Theology* 16, no. 1 (2008): 5–8.

———. *The Presence of God in the Christian Life*. Metuchen, NJ: Scarecrow Press, 1992.

Kovach, Stephen D. "Review of *Spiritual Theology*." *Faith and Mission* 15, no. 2 (1998): 99–101.

Küng, Hans. *The Church*. New York, NY: Sheed and Ward, 1967.

Land, Steven J. "The Triune Center: Wesleyans and Pentecostals Together in Mission." *PNEUMA: The Journal of the Society for Pentecostal Studies* 21, no. 2 (1999): 199–214; *Wesleyan Theological Journal* 34, no. 1(1999): 83–100.

———. "Praying in the Spirit: A Pentecostal Perspective." In *Pentecostal Movements as an Ecumenical Challenge*. Edited by Jürgen Moltmann and Karl-Josef Kuschel. London: SCM Press, 1996, 85–93.

———. "Response to Professor Harvey Cox." *Journal of Pentecostal Theology*, 5 (1994): 13–16.

———. *Pentecostal Spirituality: A Passion for the Kingdom*. Sheffield: Sheffield Academic Press, 1993.

———. "A Passion for the Kingdom: Revisioning Pentecostal Spirituality." *Journal of Pentecostal Theology* 1 (1992): 19–46.

———. "Pentecostal Spirituality: Living in the Spirit." In *Christian Spirituality: Post-Reformation and Modern*. Edited by Louis Dupré and Don E. Saliers. New York, NY: Crossroad, 1989, 479–99.

———. "A Stewardship Manifesto for a Discipling Church." In *The Promise and the Power: Essays on the Motivations, Developments, and Prospects of the Ministries of the Church of God*. Edited by Donald N. Bowdle. Cleveland, TN: Pathway Press, 1980, 287–317.

———, and R. Lamar Vest. *Reclaiming Your Testimony: Your Story and the Christian Story*. Cleveland, TN: Pathway Press, 2002.

Lederle, Henry I. *Treasures Old and New: Interpretations of "Spirit-Baptism" in the Charismatic Renewal Movement*. Peabody, MA: Hendrickson, 1988.

Lindbeck, George A. *The Nature of Doctrine: Religion and Theology in a Postliberal Age*. Philadelphia, PA: Westminster Press, 1984.

Ling, Tan May. "A Response to Frank Macchia's 'Groans Too Deep for Words: Towards a Theology of Tongues As Initial Evidence.'" *Asian Journal of Pentecostal Studies* 1, no. 2 (1998): 175–83.

Lochman, Jan Milič. "Kirche." In *Dogmatik im Dialog*, Vol. 1. Edited by F. Buri et al. Gütersloh: Gütersloher Verlaghaus Gerd Mohn, 1973, 134–38.

Lodahl, Michael L. *The Story of God: Wesleyan Theology and Biblical Narrative*. Kansas City, MO: Beacon Hill Press, 1994.

Lombard, John A., Jr., and Jerald J. Daffe. *Speaking in Tongues: Initial Evidence of Spirit Baptism?* Cleveland, TN: Pathway Press, 2005.

Lonergan, Bernard. *Method in Theology*. New York, NY: Herder and Herder, 1972.

Macchia, Frank D. "The Spirit of Life and the Spirit of Immortality: An Appreciative Review of Levison's *Filled with the Spirit*." *PNEUMA: The Journal of the Society for Pentecostal Studies* 33, no. 1 (2011): 69–78.

———. *Justified in the Spirit: Creation, Redemption, and the Triune God*. Grand Rapids, MI: Eerdmans, 2010.

———. "The Oneness-Trinitarian Pentecostal Dialogue: Exploring the Diversity of Apostolic Faith." *Harvard Theological Review* 103, no. 3 (2010): 329–49.

———. *The Trinity, Practically Speaking*. Colorado Springs, CO: Biblica, 2010.

———. "Towards Individual Renewal: Reflections on Luke's Theology of Conversion." *Ex Auditu* 25 (2009): 92–105.

———. "A Parting Word of Gratitude." *PNEUMA: The Journal of the Society for Pentecostal Studies* 31, no. 2 (2009): 165–66.

———. "Pentecostal Theology: A Time of Ferment." *PNEUMA: The Journal of the Society for Pentecostal Studies* 31, no. 1 (2009): 1–2.

———. "The Oneness-Trinitarian Pentecostal Doctrine: Introductory Musings of an Editor." *PNEUMA: The Journal of the Society for Pentecostal Studies* 30, no. 2 (2008): 197–202.

———. "Pentecost as the Power of the Cross: The Witness of Seymour and Durham." *PNEUMA: The Journal of the Society for Pentecostal Studies* 30, no. 1 (2008): 1–3.

———. "The Book of Revelation and the Hermeneutics of the Spirit: A Response to Robby Waddell." *Journal of Pentecostal Theology* 17, no. 1 (2008): 19–21.

———. "Baptized in the Spirit: Reflections in Response to My Reviewers." *Journal of Pentecostal Theology* 16, no. 1 (2008): 14–20.

———. "Baptized in the Spirit: Towards a Global Pentecostal Theology." In *Defining Issues in Pentecostalism: Classical and Emergent*. Edited by Steven M. Studebaker. Eugene, OR: Pickwick, 2008, 13–28.

———. "Pentecostal and Charismatic Theology." In *The Oxford Handbook of Eschatology*. Edited by Jerry L. Walls. Oxford: Oxford University Press, 2008, 280–94.

———. "Baptized in the Spirit: A Reflection on the Future of Pentecostal Theology." In *The Future of Pentecostalism in the United States*. Edited by Eric Patterson and Edmund Rybarczyk. Lanham, MD: Lexington Books, 2007, 15–25.

———. "*Finitum Capax Infiniti*: A Pentecostal Distinctive?" *PNEUMA: The Journal of the Society for Pentecostal Studies* 29, no. 2 (2007): 185–87.

———. "Jan Milič Lochman: A Tribute to My *Doktorvater*." *PNEUMA: The Journal of the Society for Pentecostal Studies* 29, no. 1 (2007): 1–3.

———. *Baptized in the Spirit: A Global Pentecostal Theology*. Grand Rapids, MI: Zondervan, 2006.

———. "Pinnock's Pneumatology: A Pentecostal Appreciation." *Journal of Pentecostal Theology* 14, no. 2 (2006): 167–73.

———. "Babel and the Tongues of Pentecost: Reversal or Fulfillment?" In *Speaking in Tongues: Multi-Disciplinary Perspectives*. Edited by Mark J. Cartledge. Waynesboro, GA: Paternoster Press, 2006, 34–51.

———. "The Kingdom and the Power: Spirit Baptism in Pentecostal and Ecumenical Perspective." In *The Work of the Spirit: Pneumatology and Pentecostalism*. Edited by Michael Welker. Grand Rapids, MI: Eerdmans, 2006, 109–25.

———. "The Spirit of God and the Spirit of Life: An Evangelical Response to Karl Barth's Pneumatology." In *Karl Barth and Evangelical Theology: Convergences and Divergences*. Edited by Sung Wook Chung. Grand Rapids, MI: Baker Academic Press, 2006, 149–71.

———. "My Chance Meeting with Heinrich Ott." *PNEUMA: The Journal of the Society for Pentecostal Studies* 28, no. 2 (2006): 185–87.

———. "Intelligent Design: Bad Science?" *PNEUMA: The Journal of the Society for Pentecostal Studies* 28, no. 1 (2006): 1–3.

———. "Covenant of the Lamb's Bride: A Subversive Paradigm." *The Living Pulpit* 14, no. 3 (2005): 14–15.

———. "Unity and Otherness: Lessons from Babel and Pentecost." *The Living Pulpit* 13, no. 4 (2004): 5–7.

———. "Terrorists, Security, and the Risk of Peace: Toward a Moral Vision." *PNEUMA: The Journal of the Society for Pentecostal Studies* 26, no. 1 (2004): 1–3.

———. "Astonished by Faithfulness to God: A Reflection on Karl Barth's Understanding of Spirit Baptism." In *The Spirit and Spirituality: Essays in Honour of Russell P. Spittler*. Edited by Wonsuk Ma and Robert P. Menzies. London: T & T Clark, 2004, 164–76.

———. "Justification and the Spirit of Life: A Pentecostal Response to the Joint Declaration." *In Justification and the Future of the Ecumenical Movement: The Joint Declaration on the Doctrine of Justification*. Edited by William G. Rusch. Collegeville, MN: Liturgical Press, 2003, 133–49.

———. "'I Belong to Christ': A Pentecostal Reflection on Paul's Passion for Unity." *PNEUMA: The Journal of the Society for Pentecostal Studies* 25, no. 1 (2003): 1–6.

———. "Theology, Pentecostal." In *The New International Dictionary of Pentecostal and Charismatic Movements*, revised and expanded edition. Edited by Stanley M. Burgess and Eduard M. van der Maas. Grand Rapids, MI: Zondervan, 2003, 1120–41.

———. "Dialogue, Reformed—Pentecostal." In *The New International Dictionary of Pentecostal and Charismatic Movements*, revised and expanded edition. Edited by Stanley M. Burgess and Eduard M. van der Maas. Grand Rapids, MI: Zondervan, 2003, 575–76.

———. "The Time Is Near! Or, Is It? Dare We Abandon Our Eschatological Expectation?" *PNEUMA: The Journal of the Society for Pentecostal Studies* 25, no. 2 (2003): 161–63.

———. "Spirit, Word, and Kingdom: Theological Reflections on the Reformed/Pentecostal Dialogue." In *Theology between East and West: A Radical Heritage*. Edited by Frank D. Macchia and Paul S. Chung. Eugene, OR: Wipf and Stock, 2002, 77–91.

———. "African Enacting Theology: A Rediscovery of an Ancient Tradition?" *PNEUMA: The Journal of the Society for Pentecostal Studies* 24, no. 2 (2002):105–09.

———. "Christian Experience and Authority in the World: A Pentecostal Viewpoint." *Ecumenical Trends* 31, no. 8 (2002): 122–26.

———. "Salvation and Spirit Baptism: Another Look at James Dunn's Classic." *PNEUMA: The Journal of the Society for Pentecostal Studies* 24, no. 1 (2002): 1–6.

———. "The Secular and the Religious under the Shadow of the Cross: Implications in Christoph Blumhardt's Kingdom Spirituality for a Christian Response to World Religions." In *Religion in a Secular City: Essays in Honor of Harvey Cox*. Edited by Arvind Sharma. Harrisburg, PA: Trinity Press International, 2001, 59–77.

———. "Justification through New Creation: The Holy Spirit and the Doctrine by which the Church Stands or Falls." *Theology Today* 58, no. 2 (2001): 202–17.

———. "Praying for the Terrorists." *PNEUMA: The Journal of the Society for Pentecostal Studies* 23, no. 2 (2001): 193–96.

———. "Spirit, Word, and Kingdom: Theological Reflections on the Reformed/Pentecostal Dialogue." *Ecumenical Trends* 30, no. 3 (2001): 33–39.

———. "Karl Barth Meets David du Plessis: A New Pentecost or a Theater of the Absurd?" *PNEUMA: The Journal of the Society for Pentecostal Studies* 23, no. 1 (2001): 5–8.

———. "A Response and Corresponding Request for Forgiveness." *Journal of Pentecostal Theology* 17 (2000): 22–23.

———. "A Reply to Rickie Moore." *Journal of Pentecostal Theology* 17 (2000): 15–19.

———. "*Dominus Iesus*: A Pentecostal Perspective." *PNEUMA: The Journal of the Society for Pentecostal Studies* 22, no. 2 (2000): 169–75.

———. "Rediscovering the Church's Charismatic Structure." *The Living Pulpit* 9, no. 4 (2000): 28–29.

———. "Response." *Ecumenical Trends* 29, no. 10 (2000): 160.

———. "Justification and the Spirit: A Pentecostal Reflection on the Doctrine by which the Church Stands or Falls." *PNEUMA: The Journal of the Society for Pentecostal Studies* 22, no. 1 (2000): 3–21.

———. "The Wrath of the Lamb: A Case of Cognitive Dissonance." *The Living Pulpit* 8, no. 1 (1999): 40–42.

———. "The Struggle for the Spirit in the Church: The Gifts of the Spirit and the Kingdom of God in Pentecostal Perspective." In *Spirit's Gifts—God's Reign*. Theology and Worship Occasional Paper No. 11. Presbyterian Church (U.S.A.). Louisville, KY: 1999, 4–35.

———. "The Tongues of Pentecost: A Pentecostal Perspective on the Promise and Challenge of Pentecostal/Roman Catholic Dialogue." *Journal of Ecumenical Studies* 35 (1998): 1–18.

———. "Tradition and the *Novum* of the Spirit: A Review of Clark Pinnock's *Flame of Love*." *Journal of Pentecostal Theology* 13 (1998): 31–48.

———. "Groans Too Deep for Words: Towards a Theology of Tongues as Initial Evidence." *Asian Journal of Pentecostal Studies* 1, no. 2 (1998): 149–73.

———. "Discerning the Truth of Tongues Speech: A Response to Amos Yong." *Journal of Pentecostal Theology* 12 (1998): 67–71.

———. "Is Footwashing the Neglected Sacrament? A Theological Response to John Christopher Thomas." *PNEUMA: The Journal of the Society for Pentecostal Studies* 19, no. 2 (1997): 239–49.

———. "Discerning the Spirit in Life: A Review of *God the Spirit* by Michael Welker." *Journal of Pentecostal Theology* 10 (1997): 3–28.

———. "The 'Toronto Blessing': No Laughing Matter." *Journal of Pentecostal Theology* 8 (1996): 3–6.

———. "A Pentecostal Perspective." In *Pentecostal Movements as an Ecumenical Challenge*. Edited by Jürgen Moltmann and Karl-Josef Kuschel. London: SCM Press, 1996, 63–69.

———. "God Present in a Confused Situation: The Mixed Influence of the Charismatic Movement on Classical Pentecostalism in the United States." *PNEUMA: The Journal of the Society for Pentecostal Studies* 17, no. 2 (1995): 203–18.

———. "From Azusa to Memphis: Evaluating the Racial Reconciliation Dialogue among Pentecostals." *PNEUMA: The Journal of the Society for Pentecostal Studies* 17, no. 2 (1995): 203–18.

———. "Created Spirit Beings." In *Systematic Theology*, revised edition. Edited by Stanley M. Horton. Springfield, MO: Logion Press, 1995, 194–213.

———. "The Spirit and Life: A Further Response to Jürgen Moltmann." *Journal of Pentecostal Theology* 5 (1994): 121–27.

———. "A North American Response." *Journal of Pentecostal Theology* 4 (1994): 25–33.

———. "Revitalizing Theological Categories: A Classical Pentecostal Response to J. Rodman Williams's *Renewal Theology*." *PNEUMA: The Journal of the Society for Pentecostal Studies* 16, no. 2 (1994): 293–304.

———. "The Spirit and Life: A Further Response to Jürgen Moltmann." *Journal of Pentecostal Theology* 5 (1994): 121–27.

———. "The Spirit and the Kingdom: Implications in the Message of the Blumhardts for a Pentecostal Social Spirituality." *Transformation* 11 (1994): 1–5, 32.

———. *Spirituality and Social Liberation: The Message of the Blumhardts in the Light of Wuerttemberg Pietism*. Metuchen, NJ: Scarecrow Press, 1993.

———. "Tongues as a Sign: Towards a Sacramental Understanding of Pentecostal Experience." *PNEUMA: The Journal of the Society for Pentecostal Studies* 15, no. 1 (1993): 61–76.

———. "The Question of Tongues as Initial Evidence: A Review of *Initial Evidence*, Edited by Gary B. McGee." *Journal of Pentecostal Theology* 2 (1993): 117–27.

———. "Sighs Too Deep for Words: Toward a Theology of Glossolalia." *Journal of Pentecostal Theology* 1 (1992): 47–73.

———. "Spirituality and Social Liberation: The Message of the Blumhardts in the Light of Württemberg Pietism, with Implications for Pentecostal Theology." In *Experiences of the Spirit: Conference on Pentecostal and Charismatic Research in Europe at Utrecht University, 1989*. Edited by Jan A. B. Jongeneel. Frankfurt: Peter Lang, 1991, 65–84.

———, Amos Yong, Dale T. Irvin, and Ralph Del Colle. "Christ and Spirit: Dogma, Discernment, and Dialogical Theology in a Religiously Plural World." *Journal of Pentecostal Theology* 12, no. 1 (2003): 15–83.

Maddox, Randy L. *Responsible Grace: John Wesley's Practical Theology*. Nashville, TN: Kingswood Books, 1994.

Marcus, Joel. *Mark 1–8: A New Translation with Introduction and Commentary*. New York, NY: Doubleday, 2000.

Marshall, Paul V. "Reconsidering 'Liturgical Theology': Is There a *Lex Orandi* for All Christians?" *Studia Liturgica* 25, no. 2 (1995): 129–50.

Marty, Martin E. *A Nation of Behavers*. Chicago, IL: University of Chicago Press, 1976.

———. "Pentecostalism in the Context of American Piety and Practice." In *Aspects of Pentecostal-Charismatic Origins*. Edited by Vinson Synan. Plainfield, NJ: Logos International, 1975, 193–233.

Massey, Richard. "Review of Pentecostal Spirituality: A Passion for the Kingdom." *EPTA Bulletin* 14 (1995): 112–13.

McDonnell, Kilian. *The Other Hand of God: The Holy Spirit as the Universal Touch and Goal*. Collegeville, MN: Liturgical Press, 2003.

———, and George T. Montague. *Christian Initiation and Baptism in the Holy Spirit: Evidence from the First Eight Centuries*, 2nd revised edition. Collegeville, MN: Liturgical Press, 1994.

McGee, Gary B. "Initial Evidence." In *The New International Dictionary of Pentecostal and Charismatic Movements*, revised and expanded edition. Edited by Stanley M. Burgess and Eduard M. van der Maas. Grand Rapids, MI: Zondervan, 2003, 784–91.

———. "Historical Background." In *Systematic Theology*. Edited by Stanley M. Horton. Springfield, MO: Logion Press, 1994.

———, ed. *Initial Evidence: Historical and Biblical Perspectives on the Pentecostal Doctrine of Spirit Baptism*. Peabody, MA: Hendrickson, 1991.

McGonigle, Thomas D. "Illumination, illuminative way." In *The New Dictionary of Catholic Spirituality*. Edited by Michael Downey. Collegeville, MN: Liturgical Press, 1993, 529–31.

———. "Purgation, purgative way." In *The New Dictionary of Catholic Spirituality*. Edited by Michael Downey. Collegeville, MN: Liturgical Press, 1993, 800–02.

———. "Three ways." In *The New Dictionary of Catholic Spirituality*. Edited by Michael Downey. Collegeville, MN: Liturgical Press, 1993, 963–65.

———. "Union, unitive way." In *The New Dictionary of Catholic Spirituality*. Edited by Michael Downey. Collegeville, MN: Liturgical Press, 1993, 987–88.

Menzies, William W. *Anointed to Serve: The Story of the Assemblies of God*. Springfield, MO: Gospel Publishing House, 1971.

Merrick, James R. A. "The Spirit of Truth as Agent in False Religions? A Critique of Amos Yong's Pneumatological Theology of Religions with Reference to Current Trends." *Trinity Journal* 29, no. 1 (2008): 107–25.

Metzger, Bruce M. *A Textual Commentary on the New Testament*, 2nd ed. Stuttgart: German Bible Society, 1994.

Miles, Todd L. *A God of Many Understandings? The Gospel and a Theology of Religions*. Nashville, TN: Broadman and Holman, 2010.

Minutes 2010: Church of God Book of Discipline, Church Order, and Governance. Cleveland, TN: Church of God Publishing House, 2010.

Moltmann, Jürgen. "On the Abundance of the Holy Spirit: Friendly Remarks for *Baptized in the Spirit* by Frank D. Macchia." *Journal of Pentecostal Theology* 16, no. 1 (2008): 9–13.

———. "Was heisst heute 'evangelisch'? Von der Rechtfertigungslehre zur Reich-Gottes-Theologie." *Evangelische Theologie* 57, no. 1 (1997): 41–46.

———. "A Response to My Pentecostal Dialogue Partners." *Journal of Pentecostal Theology* 4 (1994): 59–70.

———. *The Trinity and the Kingdom: The Doctrine of God*. Translated by Margaret Kohl. Minneapolis, MN: Fortress Press, 1993.

———. *The Spirit of Life: A Universal Affirmation*. Translated by Margaret Kohl. London: SCM Press, 1992.

———. *God in Creation*. Translated by Margaret Kohl. London: SCM Press, 1985.

———. "The Fellowship of the Holy Spirit—Trinitarian Pneumatology." *Scottish Journal of Theology* 37, no. 3 (1984): 287–300.

———. *The Church in the Power of the Spirit: A Contribution to Messianic Ecclesiology*. Translated by Margaret Kohl. New York, NY: Harper and Row, 1977.

Morse, Christopher. *Not Every Spirit: A Dogmatics of Christian Disbelief*, 2nd ed. London: Continuum, 2009.

Muyskens, J. David. "Review of *Spiritual Theology*." *Reformed Review* 53, no. 1 (1999): 84.

Nichols, David R. "The Search for a Pentecostal Structure in Systematic Theology." *PNEUMA: The Journal of the Society for Pentecostal Studies* 6, no. 2 (1984): 57–76.

Noll, Mark A. *America's God: From Jonathan Edwards to Abraham Lincoln*. Oxford: Oxford University Press, 2002.

———. *The Scandal of the Evangelical Mind*. Grand Rapids, MI: Eerdmans, 1994.

O'Collins, Gerald. *Fundamental Theology*. New York, NY: Paulist Press, 1981.

Oliverio, L. William, Jr. *Theological Hermeneutics in the Classical Pentecostal Tradition: A Typological Account*. Leiden: E. J. Brill, 2012.

———. "An Interpretive Review Essay on Amos Yong's *Spirit-Word-Community: Theological Hermeneutics in Trinitarian Perspective*." *Journal of Pentecostal Theology* 18, no. 2 (2009): 301–11.

"On Becoming a Christian: Insights from Scripture and the Patristic Writings with Some Contemporary Reflections: Report of the Fifth Phase of the International Dialogue between Some Classical Pentecostal Churches and Leaders and the Catholic Church (1998–2006)." www.vatican.va/roman_curia/pontifical_councils/chrstuni/eccl comm-docs/rc_pc_chrstuni_doc_20060101_becoming-a-christian_en.html.

Pannenberg, Wolfhart. *Systematic Theology*. 3 vols. Grand Rapids, MI: Eerdmans, 1991–98.

Paschasius Radbertus. *De corpore et sanguine Domini*. Patrologia Latina, 120.

Pearlman, Irene P. *Myer Pearlman and His Friends*. Springfield, MO: Irene P. Pearlman, 1953.

Pearlman, Myer. *Knowing the Doctrines of the Bible*. Springfield, MO: Gospel Publishing House, 1937.

———. *The Heavenly Gift: Studies in the Work of the Holy Spirit*. Springfield, MO: Gospel Publishing House, 1935.

———. *Through the Bible Book by Book*. 4 vols. Springfield, MO: Gospel Publishing House, 1935.

———. *Seeing the Story of the Bible*. Springfield, MO: Gospel Publishing House, 1930.

Peirce, Charles Sanders. *Collected Papers of Charles Sanders Peirce*. Edited by Charles Hartshorne and Paul Weiss. 8 vols. Cambridge, MA: Belknap Press, 1974.

Pepper, Stephen. *World Hypotheses*. Berkley, CA: University of California Press, 1942.

"*Perspectives on Koinonia*: Final Report of the International Roman Catholic/Pentecostal Dialogue (1985–1989)." *PNEUMA: The Journal of the Society for Pentecostal Studies* 12, no. 2 (1990): 117–42.

Petersen, Douglas. *Not by Might nor by Power: A Pentecostal Theology of Social Concern in Latin America*. Oxford: Regnum, 1996.

Pickstock, Catherine. *On the Liturgical Consummation of Philosophy*. Malden, MA: Blackwell, 1998.

Pinnock, Clark H. "Review of Frank D. Macchia's *Baptized in the Spirit: A Global Pentecostal Theology*." *Journal of Pentecostal Theology* 16, no. 1 (2008): 1–4.

———. *Flame of Love: A Theology of the Holy Spirit*. Downers Grove, IL: InterVarsity Press, 1996.

Placher, William C. "Postliberal Theology." In *The Modern Theologians: An Introduction to Christian Theology in the Twentieth Century*, 2nd ed. Edited by David F. Ford. Oxford: Blackwell, 1997, 343–56.

Poloma, Margaret M. *Charisma and Institutional Dilemmas*. Knoxville, TN: University of Tennessee Press, 1989.

Principe, Walter. "Spirituality, Christian." In *The New Dictionary of Catholic Spirituality*. Edited by Michael Downey. Collegeville, MN: Liturgical Press, 1993, 931–38.

Prosper of Aquitaine. *De gratia Dei et libero voluntatis arbitrio*. Patrologia Latina, 51.

Rahner, Karl. "The Theology of the Symbol." In *Theological Investigations*, Vol. 4. New York, NY: Seabury Press, 1966, 221–52.

Ramsey, Ian T. *Religious Language: An Empirical Placing of Theological Phrases*. London: SCM Press, 1957.

Rasmusson, Arne. *The Church as Polis: From Political Theology to Theological Politics as Exemplified by Jürgen Moltmann and Stanley Hauerwas*. Notre Dame, IN: University of Notre Dame Press, 1995.

Ratramnus. *De corpore et sanguine Domini*. Patrologia Latina, 121.

Richie, Tony. *Speaking by the Spirit: A Pentecostal Model for Interreligious Dialogue*. Lexington, KY: Emeth Press, 2011.

———. "The Spirit of Truth as Guide into All Truth: A Response to James R. A. Merrick, 'The Spirit of Truth as Agent in False Religions? A Critique of Amos Yong's Pneumatological Theology of Religions with Reference to Current Trends.'" *Cyberjournal for Pentecostal-Charismatic Research* 19 (2010): 1–24.

Ridge, John Hiski. "Dionysus or Apollo: Observations on the Need for a Redefined Pentecostal Epistemology." *Proceedings of the 29th Annual Meeting of the Society for Pentecostal Studies*, 1–25. Kirkland, WA, 2000.

Robeck, Cecil M., Jr. *The Azusa Street Mission and Revival: The Birth of the Global Pentecostal Movement*. Nashville, TN: Thomas Nelson, 2006.

——. "An Emerging Magisterium? The Case of the Assemblies of God." In *The Spirit and Spirituality: Essays in Honour of Russell P. Spittler*. Edited by Wonsuk Ma and Robert P. Menzies. London: T & T Clark, 2004, 212–52.

——. "National Association of Evangelicals." In *The New International Dictionary of Pentecostal and Charismatic Movements*, revised and expanded edition. Edited by Stanley M. Burgess and Eduard M. van der Maas. Grand Rapids, MI: Zondervan, 2003, 922–25.

——. "Williams, Ernest Swing." In *The New International Dictionary of Pentecostal and Charismatic Movements*, revised and expanded edition. Edited by Stanley M. Burgess and Eduard M. van der Maas. Grand Rapids, MI: Zondervan, 2003, 1197–98.

——, and Jerry L. Sandidge. "World Council of Churches." In *The New International Dictionary of Pentecostal and Charismatic Movements*, revised and expanded edition. Edited by Stanley M. Burgess and Eduard M. van der Maas. Grand Rapids, MI: Zondervan, 2003, 1213–17.

Roberts, Mark E., ed. *Commemorating Thirty Years of Annual Meetings, 1971–2001.* Society for Pentecostal Studies, 2001.

Rorty, Richard. *Philosophy and the Mirror of Nature*. Princeton, NJ: Princeton University Press, 1979.

Rosato, Philip J. *The Spirit as Lord: The Pneumatology of Karl Barth*. Edinburgh: T & T Clark, 1981.

Rossi, Philip. "The Authority of Experience: What *Counts as* Experience." In *Religious Experience and Contemporary Theological Epistemology*. Edited by Lieven Boeve, Yves De Maeseneer, and Stijn Van den Bossche. Leuven: Leuven University Press, 2005, 269–84.

Rowland, Christopher. *The Open Heaven: A Study of Apocalyptic in Judaism and Early Christianity*. New York, NY: Crossroads, 1982.

Runyon, Theodore H. "The Importance of Experience for Faith." In *Aldersgate Reconsidered*. Edited by Randy L. Maddox. Nashville, TN: Kingswood Books, 93–107.

Rybarczyk, Edmund J. *Beyond Salvation: Eastern Orthodoxy and Classical Pentecostalism on Becoming like Christ*. Carlisle: Paternoster Press, 2004.

Saliers, Don E. "Prayer and Theology in Karl Barth." In Karl Barth, *Prayer*. Edited by Don E. Saliers. Philadelphia, PA: Westminster Press, 1985, ix–xx.

——. *Worship and Spirituality*. Philadelphia, PA: Westminster Press, 1984.

——. *The Soul in Paraphrase*. New York, NY: Seabury Press, 1980.

Sandeen, Ernest R. *The Roots of Fundamentalism: British and American Millenarianism 1800–1930*. Chicago, IL: University of Chicago Press, 1970.

Sauls, Ned D. *Pentecostal Doctrines: A Wesleyan Approach*. Dunn, NC: Heritage Press, 1979.

Schaefer, Mary M. "Lex Orandi, Lex Credendi: Faith, Doctrine, and Theology in Dialogue." *Studies in Religion/Sciences Religieuses* 26, no. 4 (1997): 467–79.

Schillebeeckx, Edward. *Christ: The Experience of Jesus as Lord*. New York, NY: Seabury Press, 1980.

——. *Christ, the Sacrament of Encounter with God*. London: Sheed and Ward, 1965.

Schleiermacher, Friedrich. *The Christian Faith*. Edinburgh: T & T Clark, 1928.

Schner, George P. "The Appeal to Experience." *Theological Studies* 53, no. 1 (1992): 40–59.

Sheppard, Gerald T. "The Nicean Creed, Filioque, and Pentecostal Movements in the United States." *Greek Orthodox Theological Review* 31, nos. 3–4 (1986): 401–16.

———. "Pentecostals and the Hermeneutics of Dispensationalism: The Anatomy of an Uneasy Relationship." *PNEUMA: The Journal of the Society for Pentecostal Studies* 6, no. 2 (1984): 5–33.

———. "Canonization: Hearing the Voice of the Same God through Historically Dissimilar Traditions." *Interpretation: A Journal of Bible and Theology* 36 (1982): 21–33.

Smith, James K. A. *Thinking in Tongues: Pentecostal Contributions to Christian Philosophy.* Grand Rapids, MI: Eerdmans, 2010.

———. "Scandalizing Theology: A Pentecostal Response to Noll's *Scandal.*" *PNEUMA: The Journal of the Society for Pentecostal Studies* 19, no. 2 (1997): 225–38.

Solivan, Samuel. *The Spirit, Pathos and Liberation: Toward an Hispanic Pentecostal Theology.* Sheffield: Sheffield Academic Press, 1998.

Spaulding, John P. "Qur'anic Interpretation in Trinitarian Perspective: Testing Amos Yong's Hermeneutics and Theology of Religions." ThM Thesis, Luther Seminary, 2005.

Spinks, D. Christopher. "Response to Macchia." *Ex Auditu* 25 (2009): 106–09.

Spittler, Russell P. "Du Plessis, David Johannes." In *The New International Dictionary of Pentecostal and Charismatic Movements*, revised and expanded edition. Edited by Stanley M. Burgess and Eduard M. van der Maas. Grand Rapids, MI: Zondervan, 2003, 589–93.

———. "Are Pentecostals and Charismatics Fundamentalists? A Review of American Uses of These Categories." In *Charismatic Christianity as a Global Culture.* Edited by Karla Poewe. Columbia: University of South Carolina Press, 1994, 103–16.

———. "Theological Style among Pentecostals and Charismatics." In *Doing Theology in Today's World: Essays in Honor of Kenneth S. Kantzer.* Edited by John D. Woodbridge and Thomas Edward McComiskey. Grand Rapids, MI: Zondervan, 1991, 291–318.

Stephenson, Christopher A. "Pentecostal Theology: Retrospect and Prospect." *Religion Compass* 5, no. 9 (2011): 490–500.

———. "Symbol, Sacrament, and Spirit(s): Paul Tillich in Recent Pentecostal Theology." *Bulletin of the North American Paul Tillich Society* 35, no. 2 (2009): 25–29.

———. "The Rule of Spirituality and the Rule of Doctrine: A Necessary Relationship in Theological Method." *Journal of Pentecostal Theology* 15, no. 1 (2006): 83–105.

Stephenson, Lisa P. *Dismantling the Dualisms for American Pentecostal Women in Ministry: A Feminist-Pneumatological Approach.* Leiden: E. J. Brill, 2012.

Stevenson, Kenneth. "Lex Orandi, Lex Credendi—Strange Bed-Fellows? Some Reflections on Worship and Doctrine." *Scottish Journal of Theology* 39, no. 2 (1986): 225–41.

Stevenson, W. Taylor. "Lex Orandi-Lex Credendi." In *The Study of Anglicanism.* Edited by Stephen Sykes, John Booty, and Jonathan Knight. Minneapolis, MN: Fortress Press, 1998, 174–88.

Stewart, John W. "Introducing Charles Hodge to Postmoderns." In *Charles Hodge Revisited: A Critical Appraisal of His Life and Work.* Edited by John W. Stewart. Grand Rapids, MI: Eerdmans, 2002, 1–39.

Stott, John. "The Logic of Hell: A Brief Rejoinder." *Evangelical Review of Theology* 18, no. 1 (1994): 33–34.

Stout, B. M. "Boyd, Frank Matthews." In *Dictionary of Pentecostal and Charismatic Movements.* Edited by Stanley M. Burgess and Gary McGee. Grand Rapids, MI: Zondervan, 1988, 94–95.

Studebaker, John A., Jr. *The Lord Is the Spirit: The Authority of the Holy Spirit in Contemporary Theology and Church Practice.* Eugene, OR: Pickwick, 2008.

Studebaker, Steven M. "Beyond Tongues: A Pentecostal Theology of Grace." In *Defining Issues in Pentecostalism: Classical and Emergent*. Edited by Steven M. Studebaker. Eugene, OR: Pickwick, 2008, 46–68.

———. "Pentecostal Soteriology and Pneumatology." *Journal of Pentecostal Theology* 11, no. 2 (2003): 248–70.

Synan, Vinson. *The Holiness-Pentecostal Tradition: Charismatic Movements in the Twentieth Century*, 2nd ed. Grand Rapids, MI: Eerdmans, 1997.

Tanquerey, Adolphe. *The Spiritual Life: A Treatise on Ascetical and Mystical Theology*, 2nd ed. Translated by Herman Branderis. Belgium: Society of St. John the Evangelist, 1932.

Taylor, Charles. *Philosophical Arguments*. Cambridge, MA: Harvard University Press, 1995.

Thiessen, Henry. *Lectures in Systematic Theology*. Grand Rapids, MI: Eerdmans, 1979.

Thomas, John Christopher. "Pentecostal Theology in the Twenty-First Century." *PNEUMA: The Journal of the Society for Pentecostal Studies* 20, no. 1 (1998): 3–19.

Thorsen, Donald A. D. *The Wesleyan Quadrilateral: Scripture, Tradition, Reason, and Experience as a Model of Evangelical Theology*. Grand Rapids, MI: Asbury Press, 1990.

Tillich, Paul. *Systematic Theology*. 3 vols. Chicago, IL: University of Chicago Press, 1951–63.

———. *The Protestant Era*. Chicago, IL: University of Chicago Press, 1948.

Tinon, Stan. "Review of Pentecostal Spirituality: A Passion for the Kingdom." *Ashland Theological Journal* 27 (1995): 177–78.

Tracy, David. *The Analogical Imagination: Christian Theology and the Culture of Pluralism*. New York, NY: Crossroad, 1981.

———. *Blessed Rage for Order: The New Pluralism in Theology*. New York, NY: Seabury Press, 1975.

Turner, Max. "Interpreting the Samaritans of Acts 8: The Waterloo of Pentecostal Soteriology and Pneumatology?" *PNEUMA: The Journal of the Society for Pentecostal Studies* 23, no. 2 (2001): 265–86.

———. "The 'Spirit of Prophecy' As the Power of Israel's Restoration and Witness." In *Witness to the Gospel: The Theology of Acts*. Edited by I. Howard Marshall and David Peterson. Grand Rapids, MI: Eerdmans, 1998, 327–48.

———. "Tongues: An Experience for All in the Pauline Churches?" *Asian Journal of Pentecostal Studies* 1, no. 2 (1998): 231–53.

Upton, Julia. "A Feminist Perspective: Lex Orandi, Lex Credendi." *Liturgical Ministry* 1 (1992): 137–39.

Van Dyk, Leanne. "The Church in Evangelical Theology and Practice." In *The Cambridge Companion to Evangelical Theology*. Edited by Timothy Larsen and Daniel J. Treier. Cambridge: Cambridge University Press, 2007, 125–41.

Vanhoozer, Kevin J. *The Drama of Doctrine: A Canonical-Linguistic Approach to Christian Theology*. Louisville, KY: Westminster John Knox Press, 2005.

———. *First Theology: God, Scripture, and Hermeneutics*. Downers Grove, IL: InterVarsity Press, 2002.

———. *Is There a Meaning in This Text? The Bible, the Reader, and the Morality of Literary Knowledge*. Grand Rapids, MI: Zondervan, 1998.

Villafañe, Eldin. *The Liberating Spirit: Toward an Hispanic American Pentecostal Social Ethic*. Grand Rapids, MI: Eerdmans, 1993.

Volf, Miroslav. *After Our Likeness: The Church as the Image of the Trinity*. Grand Rapids, MI: Eerdmans, 1998.

———, and Dorothy C. Bass, eds. *Practicing Theology: Beliefs and Practices in Christian Life*. Grand Rapids, MI: Eerdmans, 2002.

Vondey, Wolfgang. *Beyond Pentecostalism: The Crisis of Global Christianity and the Renewal of the Theological Agenda*. Grand Rapids, MI: Eerdmans, 2010.

———. "Pentecostal Ecclesiology and Eucharistic Hospitality: Toward a Systematic and Ecumenical Account of the Church." *PNEUMA: The Journal of the Society for Pentecostal Studies* 32, no. 1 (2010): 41–55.

———. *People of Bread: Rediscovering Ecclesiology*. New York, NY: Paulist Press, 2008.

———. "Pentecostalism and the Possibility of Global Theology: Implications of the Theology of Amos Yong." *PNEUMA: The Journal of the Society for Pentecostal Studies* 28, no. 2 (2006): 289–312.

———, and Chris W. Green. "Between This and That: Reality and Sacramentality in the Pentecostal Worldview." *Journal of Pentecostal Theology* 19, no. 2 (2010): 243–64.

Wacker, Grant. *Heaven Below: Early Pentecostals and American Culture*. Cambridge, MA: Harvard University Press, 2001.

Waddell, Robby. "The Spirit of Reviews and Response." *PNEUMA: The Journal of the Society for Pentecostal Studies* 17, no. 1 (2008): 22–31.

Wainwright, Geoffrey. "Lex Orandi, Lex Credendi." In *Dictionary of the Ecumenical Movement*, 2nd ed. Edited by Nicholas Lossky, et al. Geneva: WCC Publications, 2002, 679–83.

———. *Doxology: The Praise of God in Worship, Doctrine, and Life*. New York, NY: Oxford University Press, 1980.

Wan, Yee Tham. "Review of Spiritual Theology." *Journal of Asian Mission* 4, no. 1 (2002): 141–43.

Ware, Frederick L. "Review Article on Amos Yong's *The Spirit Poured Out on All Flesh: Pentecostalism and the Possibility of Global Theology*." *Journal of the European Pentecostal Theological Association* 28, no. 1 (2008): 77–83.

Warfield, B. B. "Christianity and Revelation." In *Selected Shorter Writings of Benjamin B. Warfield*, Vol. 1. Edited by John E. Meeter. Phillipsburg, NJ: Presbyterian and Reformed Publishing House, 1973, 23–30.

———. "The Inerrancy of the Original Autographs." In *Selected Shorter Writings of Benjamin B. Warfield*, Vol. 2. Edited by John E. Meeter. Phillipsburg, NJ: Presbyterian and Reformed Publishing House, 1973, 580–87.

———. "Inspiration." In *Selected Shorter Writings of Benjamin B. Warfield*, Vol. 2. Edited by John E. Meeter. Phillipsburg, NJ: Presbyterian and Reformed Publishing House, 1973, 614–36.

———. "The Biblical Idea of Inspiration." In *The Inspiration and Authority of the Bible*. Edited by Samuel G. Craig. Phillipsburg, NJ: Presbyterian and Reformed Publishing House, 1948, 129–66.

Warrington, Keith. *Pentecostal Theology: A Theology of Encounter*. London: T & T Clark, 2008.

———. "Review of *Pentecostal Spirituality: A Passion for the Kingdom*." *Evangelical Quarterly* 68, no. 3 (1996): 271–73.

Wells, David F. *God in the Wasteland: The Reality of Truth in a World of Fading Dreams*. Grand Rapids, MI: Eerdmans, 1994.

———. *No Place for Truth*. Grand Rapids, MI: Eerdmans, 1993.

———. "Charles Hodge." In *The Princeton Theology*. Edited by David F. Wells. Grand Rapids, MI: Baker Book House, 1989, 37–62.

Westphal, Merold. "Hermeneutics and Holiness." In *Analytic Theology: New Essays in the Philosophy of Theology*. Edited by Oliver D. Crisp and Michael C. Rea. Oxford: Oxford University Press, 2009, 265–79.

Wiles, Maurice F. *The Remaking of Christian Doctrine*. Philadelphia, PA: Westminster Press, 1978.

———. *The Making of Christian Doctrine: A Study in the Principles of Early Doctrinal Development.* London: Cambridge University Press, 1967.

Williams, Ernest S. "The Life Story of Reverend Ernest S. Williams, 1979–80." Pearlman Memorial Library. Central Bible College. Springfield, MO.

———. "Pentecostal Origins." Interview by James S. Tinney. *Agora* 2, no. 3 (1979): 4–6.

———. *Systematic Theology.* 3 vols. Springfield, MO: Gospel Publishing House, 1953.

Williams, J. Rodman. *Renewal Theology: Systematic Theology from a Charismatic Perspective.* 3 vols. Grand Rapids, MI: Zondervan, 1988–92.

Willis, Wendel Lee. *Idol Meat in Corinth: The Pauline Argument in 1 Corinthians 8 and 10.* Chico, CA: Scholars Press, 1985.

"Word and Spirit, Church and World: The Final Report of the International Dialogue between Representatives of the World Alliance of Reformed Churches and Some Classical Pentecostal Churches and Leaders 1996–2000." *PNEUMA: The Journal of the Society for Pentecostal Studies* 23, no. 1 (2001): 9–43.

Yong, Amos. *Spirit of Love: A Trinitarian Theology of Grace.* Waco, TX: Baylor University Press, 2012.

———. *The Cosmic Breath: Spirit and Nature in the Christianity-Buddhism-Science Trialogue.* Leiden: E. J. Brill, 2012.

———. *Pneumatology and the Christian-Buddhist Dialogue: Does the Wind Blow through the Middle Way?* Leiden: E. J. Brill, 2012.

———. *Who Is the Holy Spirit? A Walk with the Apostles.* Brewster, MA: Paraclete Press, 2011.

———. *The Bible, Disability, and the Church: A New Vision of the People of God.* Grand Rapids, MI: Eerdmans, 2011.

———. *The Spirit of Creation: Modern Science and Divine Action in the Pentecostal Charismatic Imagination.* Grand Rapids, MI: Eerdmans, 2011.

———. "The Spirit of Science: Are Pentecostals Ready to Engage the Discussion?" *Cyberjournal for Pentecostal-Charismatic Research* 20 (2011).

———. "From Demonization to Kin-domization: The Witness of the Spirit and the Renewal of Missions in a Pluralistic World." In *Global Renewal, Religious Pluralism, and the Great Commission: Towards a Renewal Theology of Mission and Interreligious Encounter.* Edited by Amos Yong and Clifton Clarke. Lexington, KY: Emeth Press, 2011, 157–74.

———. "Science and Religion: Introducing the Issues, Entering the Debates—A Review Essay." *Christian Scholar's Review* 40, no. 2 (2011): 189–203.

———. "Sex, Drugs, Rock-n-Roll . . . , and Race!—Or Something to That Effect: Whither Pentecostal Studies?" *PNEUMA: The Journal of the Society for Pentecostal Studies* 33, no. 2 (2011): 171–73.

———. *In the Days of Caesar: Pentecostalism and Political Theology.* Grand Rapids, MI: Eerdmans, 2010.

———. "The Church and Mission Theology in a Post-Constantinian Era: Soundings from the Anglo-American Frontier." In *A New Day: Essays on World Christianity in Honor of Lamin Sanneh.* Edited by Akintunde E. Akinade. New York, NY: Peter Lang, 2010, 49–61.

———. "Pentecostalism and the Political—Trajectories in Its Second Century." *PNEUMA: The Journal of the Society for Pentecostal Studies* 32, no. 3 (2010): 333–36.

———. "Disability and the Gifts of the Spirit: Pentecost and the Renewal of the Church." *Journal of Pentecostal Theology* 19, no. 1 (2010): 76–93.

———. "The Trans/Formation of Dust: R. D. Hughes's Pneumatological Theology of the Spiritual Life in Pentecostal Perspective." *Sewanee Theological Review* 53, no. 3 (2010): 345–58.

————. "How Does God Do What God Does? Pentecostal-Charismatic Perspectives on Divine Action in Dialogue with Modern Science." In *Science and the Spirit: A Pentecostal Engagement with the Sciences*. Edited by James K. A. Smith and Amos Yong. Bloomington, IN: Indiana University Press, 2010, 50–71.

————. "The Missiology of Jamestown—1607–2007 and Beyond: Toward a Postcolonial Theology of Mission in North America." In *Remembering Jamestown: Hard Questions about Christian Mission*. Edited by Amos Yong and Barbara Brown Zikmund. Eugene, OR: Pickwick, 2010, 157–67.

————. "Charismatic and Pentecostal Movements in Asia." In *The Cambridge Dictionary of Christianity*. Edited by Daniel Patte. Cambridge: Cambridge University Press, 2010, 190–91.

————. "Towards a Pneumatological Theology of Religions." In *The Gospel among Religions: Christian Ministry, Theology, and Spirituality in a Multifaith World*. Edited by David R. Brockman and Ruben L. F. Habito. Maryknoll, NY: Orbis Books, 2010, 215–17.

————. "Many Tongues, Many Practices: Pentecost and Theology of Mission at 2010." In *Mission after Christendom: Emergent Themes in Contemporary Mission*. Edited by Ogbu U. Kalu et al. Louisville, KY: Westminster John Knox Press, 2010, 43–58.

————. "The Spirit at Work in the World: A Pentecostal-Charismatic Perspective on the Divine Action Project." *Theology and Science* 7, no. 2 (2009): 123–40.

————. "Poured Out on All Creation?! Searching for the Spirit in the Pentecostal Encounter with Science." In *The Spirit Renews the Face of the Earth: Pentecostal Forays in Science and Theology of Creation*. Edited by Amos Yong. Eugene, OR: Pickwick, 2009, xi–xxiii.

————. "Many Tongues, Many Senses: Pentecost, the Body Politic, and the Redemption of Dis/Ability." *PNEUMA: The Journal of the Society for Pentecostal Studies* 31, no. 2 (2009): 167–88.

————. "Disability and the Love of Wisdom: De-forming, Re-forming, and Per-forming Philosophy of Religion." *Ars Disputandi* 9 (2009): 54–71.

————. "The Spirit at Work in the World: A Pentecostal-Charismatic Perspective on the Divine Action Project." *Theology and Science* 7, no. 2 (2009): 123–40.

————. "Restoring, Reforming, Renewing: Accompaniments to *The Cambridge Companion to Evangelical Theology*." *Evangelical Review of Theology* 33, no. 2 (2009): 179–83.

————. "'The Light Shines in the Darkness': Johannine Dualism and the Challenge for Christian Theology of Religions Today." *Journal of Religion* 89, no. 1 (2009): 31–56.

————. "From Azusa Street to the Bo Tree and Back: Strange Babblings and Interreligious Interpretations in the Pentecostal Encounter with Buddhism." In *The Spirit in the World: Emerging Pentecostal Theologies in Global Contexts*. Edited by Veli-Matti Kärkkäinen. Grand Rapids, MI: Eerdmans, 2009, 203–26.

————. "Salvation, Society, and the Spirit: Pentecostal Contextualization and Political Theology from Cleveland to Birmingham, from Springfield to Seoul." *Pax Pneuma* 5, no. 2 (2009): 22–34.

————. *Hospitality and the Other: Pentecost, Christian Practices, and the Neighbor*. Maryknoll, NY: Orbis Books, 2008.

————. "Whither Asian American Evangelical Theology? What Asian, Which American, Whose *Evangelion*?" *Evangelical Review of Theology* 32, no. 1(2008): 22–37.

————. "Extending the Conversation: A Response to Frederick L. Ware." *Journal of the European Pentecostal Theological Association* 28, no. 1 (2008): 84–93.

————. "The Buddhist-Christian Encounter in the USA: Reflections on Christian Practices." In *Border Crossings: Explorations of an Interdisciplinary Historian: Festschrift for Irving Hexham*. Edited by Ulrich van der Heyden and Andreas Feldtkeller. Stuttgart: Franz Steiner Verlag, 2008, 457–72.

———. "Mind and Life, Religion and Science: His Holiness the Dalai Lama and the Buddhism-Christianity-Science Trialogue." *Buddhist-Christian Studies* 28 (2008): 43–63.

———. "Tibetan Buddhism Going Global? A Case Study of a Contemporary Buddhist Encounter with Science." *Journal of Global Buddhism* 9 (2008): 1–26.

———. "The Inviting Spirit: Pentecostal Beliefs and Practices Regarding the Religions Today." In *Defining Issues in Pentecostalism: Classical and Emergent*. Edited by Steven M. Studebaker. Eugene, OR: Pickwick, 2008, 29–45.

———. "Natural Laws and Divine Intervention: What Difference Does Being Pentecostal or Charismatic Make?" *Zygon* 43, no. 4 (2008): 961–89.

———. "Divining 'Divine Action' in Theology-and-Science: A Review Essay." *Zygon* 43, no. 1 (2008): 191–200.

———. "Between the Local and the Global: Autobiographical Reflections on the Emergence of the Global Theological Mind." In *Shaping a Global Theological Mind*. Edited by Darren C. Marks. Burlington, VT: Ashgate, 2008, 187–94.

———. *Theology and Down Syndrome: Reimagining Disability in Late Modernity*. Waco, TX: Baylor University Press, 2007.

———. "Radically Orthodox, Reformed, and Pentecostal: Rethinking the Intersection of Post/Modernity and the Religions in Conversation with James K. A. Smith." *Journal of Pentecostal Theology* 15, no. 2 (2007): 233–50.

———. "Trinh Thuan and the Intersection of Science and Buddhism." *Zygon* 42, no. 3 (2007): 677–84.

———. "The Future of Asian Pentecostal Theology: An Asian American Assessment." *Asian Journal of Pentecostal Studies* 10, no. 1 (2007): 22–41.

———. "Disability, the Human Condition, and the Spirit of the Eschatological Long Run: Toward a Pneumatological Theology of Disability." *Journal of Religion, Disability & Health* 11, no. 1 (2007): 5–25.

———. "Beyond the Liberal-Conservative Divide: An Appreciative Rejoinder to Allan Anderson." *Journal of Pentecostal Theology* 16, no. 1 (2007): 103–11.

———. "Poured Out on All Flesh: The Spirit, World Pentecostalism, and the Renewal of Theology and Praxis in the 21st Century." *PentecoStudies* 6, no. 1 (2007): 16–45.

———. "God and the Evangelical Laboratory: Recent Conservative Protestant Thinking about Theology and Science." *Theology and Science* 5, no. 2 (2007): 203–21.

———. "Pentecostalism and the Theological Academy." *Theology Today* 64 (2007): 244–50.

———. "The Spirit of Hospitality: Pentecostal Perspectives Toward a Performative Theology of Interreligious Encounter." *Missiology: An International Review* 35, no. 1 (2007): 55–73.

———. "Can We Get 'Beyond the Paradigm'?—A Response to Terry Muck's Proposal in Theology of Religions." *Interpretation* 61, no. 1 (2007): 28–32.

———. "Wesley and Fletcher—Dayton and Wood: Appreciating Wesleyan-Holiness Tongues, Essaying Pentecostal-Charismatic Interpretations." In *From the Margins: A Celebration of the Theological Work of Donald W. Dayton*. Edited by Christian T. Collins Winn. Eugene, OR: Pickwick, 2007, 179–90.

———. "Ordinances and Sacraments." In *Encyclopedia of Pentecostal and Charismatic Christianity*. Edited by Stanley M. Burgess. New York, NY: Routledge, 2006, 345–48.

———. "*Ruach*, the Primordial Chaos, and the Breath of Life: Emergence Theory and the Creation Narratives in Pneumatological Perspective." In *The Work of the Spirit: Pneumatology and Pentecostalism*. Edited by Michael Welker. Grand Rapids, MI: Eerdmans, 2006, 183–204.

———. "Whither Evangelical Theology? The Work of Veli-Matti Kärkkäinen as a Case Study of Contemporary Trajectories." *Evangelical Review of Theology* 30, no. 1 (2006): 60–85.

———. "Performing Global Pentecostal Theology: A Response to Wolfgang Vondey." *PNEUMA: The Journal of the Society for Pentecostal Studies* 28, no. 2 (2006): 313–21.

———. *The Spirit Poured Out on All Flesh: Pentecostalism and the Possibility of Global Theology*. Grand Rapids, MI: Baker Academic, 2005.

———. "Academic Glossolalia? Pentecostal Scholarship, Multi-disciplinarity, and the Science-Religion Conversation." *Journal of Pentecostal Theology* 14, no. 1 (2005): 63–82.

———. "A P(new)matological Paradigm for Christian Mission in a Religiously Plural World." *Missiology: An International Review* 33, no. 2 (2005): 175–91.

———. "Significant Turns in Contemporary Theology of Religions." *Theology News and Notes* 52, no. 1 (2005): 4–6, 22.

———. "The Demonic in Pentecostal-Charismatic Christianity and in the Religious Consciousness of Asia." In *Asian and Pentecostal: The Charismatic Face of Christianity in Asia*. Edited by Allan Anderson and Edmond Tang. London: Regnum International: Asia Pacific Theological Seminary Press, 2005, 93–127.

———. "From Quantum Mechanics to the Eucharistic Meal: John Polkinghorne's Vision of Science and Theology." *Metanexus Online Digest: Transdisciplinary Approaches to Foundational Questions* 5, no. 6 (2005). www.metanexus.net/metanexus_online/printer_friendly.asp?9285.

———. "Christian and Buddhist Perspectives on Neuropsychology and the Human Person: *Pneuma* and *Pratityasamutpada*." *Zygon* 40, no. 1 (2005): 143–65.

———. "The Spirit and Creation: Possibilities and Challenges for a Dialogue between Pentecostal Theology and the Sciences." *Journal of the European Pentecostal Theological Association* 25 (2005): 82–110.

———. "Discerning the Spirit(s) in the Natural World: Toward a Typology of 'Spirit' in the Religion and Science Conversation." *Theology and Science* 3, no. 3 (2005): 315–29.

———. "'The Spirit Hovers over the World': Toward a Typology of 'Spirit' in the Religion and Science Dialogue." *The Digest: Transdisciplinary Approaches to Foundational Questions* 4 (2004). www.metanexus.net/digest/2004_10_27.htm.

———. "The Spirit Bears Witness: Pneumatology, Truth and the Religions." *Scottish Journal of Theology* 57, no. 1 (2004): 14–38.

———. "Rapture." In *The Encyclopedia of Protestantism*, Vol. 3. Edited by Hans J. Hillerbrand. New York, NY: Routledge, 2004, 1590–91.

———. "The Hermeneutical Trialectic: Notes toward a Consensual Hermeneutic and Theological Method." *Heythrop Journal* 45, no. 1 (2004): 22–39.

———. "Beyond *Beyond the Impasse*: Responding to Dale Irvin." *Journal of Pentecostal Theology* 12 (2004): 281–85.

———. "The Holy Spirit and the World Religions: On the Christian Discernment of Spirit(s) 'After' Buddhism." *Buddhist-Christian Studies* 24 (2004): 191–207.

———. "Spiritual Discernment: A Biblical-Theological Reconsideration." In *The Spirit and Spirituality: Essays in Honour of Russell P. Spittler*. Edited by Wonsuk Ma and Robert P. Menzies. London: T & T Clark, 2004, 83–104.

———. "Spirit Possession, the Living, and the Dead: A Review Essay and Response from a Pentecostal Perspective." *Dharma Deepika: A South Asian Journal of Missiological Research* 8, no. 2 (2004): 77–88.

———. "Divine Knowledge and Relation to Time." In *Philosophy of Religion: Introductory Essays*. Edited by Thomas Jay Oord. Kansas City, MO: Beacon Hill Press/Nazarene Publishing House, 2003, 136–52.

———. "Technologies of Liberation: A Comparative Soteriology of Eastern Orthodoxy and Theravada Buddhism." *Dharma Deepika: A South Asian Journal of Missiological Research* 7, no. 1 (2003): 17–60.

———. "'As the Spirit Gives Utterance . . .': Pentecost, Intra-Christian Ecumenism, and the Wider *Oekumene.*" *International Review of Mission* 92 (July 2003): 299–314.

———. "A Theology of the Third Article? Hegel and the Contemporary Enterprise in First Philosophy and First Theology." In *Semper Reformandum: Studies in Honour of Clark H. Pinnock.* Edited by Stanley E. Porter and Anthony R. Cross. Carlisle: Paternoster Press, 2003, 208–31.

———. *Beyond the Impasse: Toward a Pneumatological Theology of Religions.* Grand Rapids, MI: Baker Academic, 2003.

———. "In Search of Foundations: The Oeuvre of Donald L. Gelpi, S. J., and Its Significance for Pentecostal Theology and Philosophy." *Journal of Pentecostal Theology* 11, no. 1 (2002): 3–26.

———. "The Marks of the Church: A Pentecostal Re-Reading." *Evangelical Review of Theology* 26, no. 1 (2002): 45–67.

———. *Spirit-Word-Community: Theological Hermeneutics in Trinitarian Perspective.* Burlington, VT: Ashgate, 2002.

———. "Going Where the Spirit Goes . . . : Engaging the Spirit(s) in J. C. Ma's Pneumatological Missiology." *Journal of Pentecostal Theology* 10 (2002): 110–28.

———. "Divine Omniscience and Future Contingents: Weighing the Presuppositional Issues in the Contemporary Debate." *Evangelical Review of Theology* 26, no. 3 (2002): 240–64.

———. "The 'Baptist Vision' of James William McClendon, Jr.: A Wesleyan-Pentecostal Response." *Wesleyan Theological Journal* 37, no. 2 (2002): 32–57.

———. "The Word and the Spirit, or the Spirit and the Word? Exploring the Boundaries of Evangelicalism in Relationship to Modern Pentecostalism." *Trinity Journal* 23, no. 2 (2002): 235–52.

———. "Pentecostalism and Ecumenism: Past, Present, and Future," part 5. *Pneuma Review* 5, no. 2 (2002): 29–38.

———. "Pentecostalism and Ecumenism: Past, Present, and Future," part 4. *Pneuma Review* 4, no. 4 (2001): 50–57.

———. "Pentecostalism and Ecumenism: Past, Present, and Future," part 3. *Pneuma Review* 4, no. 3 (2001): 16–27.

———. "Pentecostalism and Ecumenism: Past, Present, and Future," part 2. *Pneuma Review* 4, no. 2 (2001): 36–48.

———. "Pentecostalism and Ecumenism: Past, Present, and Future," part 1. *Pneuma Review* 4, no. 1 (2001): 6–15.

———. "Possibility and Actuality: The Doctrine of Creation and Its Implications for Divine Omniscience." *Wesleyan Philosophical Society Online Journal* 1, no. 1 (2001): http://david.snu.edu/~brint.fs/wpsjnl/v1n1.htm.

———. "Discerning the Spirit(s) in the World of Religions: Toward a Pneumatological Theology of Religions." In *No Other Gods before Me? Evangelicals and the Challenge of World Religions.* Edited by John G. Stackhouse, Jr. Grand Rapids, MI: Baker Book House, 2001, 37–61.

———. *Discerning the Spirit(s): A Pentecostal-Charismatic Contribution to Christian Theology of Religions.* Sheffield: Sheffield Academic Press, 2000.

———. "On Divine Presence and Divine Agency: Toward a Foundational Pneumatology." *Asian Journal of Pentecostal Studies* 3, no. 2 (2000): 167–88.

———. "The Demise of Foundationalism and the Retention of Truth: What Evangelicals Can Learn from C. S. Peirce." *Christian Scholar's Review* 29, no. 3 (Spring 2000): 563–88.

———. "Between Two Extremes: Balancing Word-Christianity and Spirit-Christianity." *Pneuma Review* 3, no. 1 (2000): 78–83.

———. "'Not Knowing Where the Spirit Blows . . .': On Envisioning a Pentecostal Charismatic Theology of Religions." *Journal of Pentecostal Theology* 14 (1999): 81–112.

———. "Whither Theological Inclusivism? The Development and Critique of an Evangelical Theology of Religions." *Evangelical Quarterly* 71, no. 4 (1999): 327–48.

———. "To See or Not to See: A Review Essay of Michael Palmer's Elements of a Christian Worldview." *PNEUMA: The Journal of the Society for Pentecostal Studies* 21, no. 2 (1999): 305–27.

———. "Tongues of Fire in the Pentecostal Imagination: The Truth of Glossolalia in Light of R. C. Neville's Theory of Religious Symbolism." *Journal of Pentecostal Theology* 12 (1998): 39–65.

———. "Whither Systematic Theology? A Systematician Chimes in on a Scandalous Conversation." *PNEUMA: The Journal of the Society for Pentecostal Studies* 20, no. 1 (1998): 85–93.

———. "The Turn to Pneumatology in Christian Theology of Religions: Conduit or Detour?" *Journal of Ecumenical Studies* 35, nos. 3–4 (1998): 437–54.

———. "The Truth of Tongues Speech: A Rejoinder to Frank Macchia." *Journal of Pentecostal Theology* 13 (1998): 107–15.

———. "What Has Jerusalem to Do with Nairobi, Lagos, Accra, or Rio? Religion and Theology in Africa and Afro-America." *Koinonia: The Princeton Seminary Graduate Forum* 10, no. 2 (1998): 216–27.

———. "Personal Selfhood (?) and Human Experience in Whitehead's Philosophy of Organism." *Paideia Project: Proceedings of the 20th World Congress of Philosophy* (1998). www.bu.edu/wcp/MainPPer.htm.

———. "'Tongues,' Theology, and the Social Sciences: A Pentecostal-Theological Reading of Geertz's Interpretive Theory of Religion. *Cyberjournal for Pentecostal-Charismatic Research* 1 (1997). http://pctii.org/cyberj/cyber1.html.

———. "Oneness and the Trinity: The Theological and Ecumenical Implications of Creation *Ex Nihilo* for an Intra-Pentecostal Dispute." *PNEUMA: The Journal of the Society for Pentecostal Studies* 19, no. 1 (Spring 1997): 81–107.

———. "Review of *No Place for Truth* and *God in the Wasteland*." *PNEUMA: The Journal of the Society for Pentecostal Studies* 18, no. 2 (1996): 239–43.

———, and Dale Coulter. "From West to East: The Renewal of the Leading Journal in Pentecostal Studies." *PNEUMA: The Journal of the Society for Pentecostal Studies* 32, no. 1 (2010): 1–3.

———, and Lewis Brogdon. "The Decline of African American Theology? A Critical Response to Thabiti Anyabwile." *Journal of Reformed Theology* 4, no. 2 (2010): 129–44.

———, and Samuel Zalanga. "What Empire, Which Multitude? Pentecostalism and Social Liberation in North America and Sub-Saharan Africa." In *Evangelicals and Empire: Christian Alternatives to the Political Status Quo*. Edited by Bruce Ellis Benson and Peter Goodwin Heltzel. Grand Rapids, MI: Brazos Press, 2008, 237–51.

———, and Tony Richie. "Missiology and the Interreligious Encounter." In *Studying Global Pentecostalism: Theories and Methods*. Edited by Allan Anderson et al. Los Angeles, CA: University of California Press, 2010, 245–67.

Yun, Koo Dong. *Baptism in the Holy Spirit: An Ecumenical Theology of Spirit Baptism*. Lanham, MD: University Press of America, 2003.

INDEX

Affections, 31–33
Anselm of Canterbury, 14, 152
Apocalyptic, 34–36, 60, 68
Askesis, 46–48
Assemblies of God, 12–13, 41, 59, 82
Athanasian Creed, 18
Augustine, 14, 87–88
Azusa Street, 3, 13, 30, 37–38

Baptism in the Holy Spirit
  and glossolalia, 50–51
  as theology's organizing principle,
    69–70
Barth, Karl, 39–40, 74, 131
Basil of Caesarea, 118
Bernard, David K., 7
Biblical interpretation, 4–5, 8–9, 11,
  16–18, 22, 40, 107–09, 111, 129
Blumhardt, Johann and Christoph,
  59–60, 73–74, 80
Boyd, Frank M., 136n9
Brueggemann, Walter, 126

Calvin, John, 14, 128–29
Cavanaugh, William T., 126
Church of God (Cleveland, TN), 12, 15,
  29, 188n57
Clarke, David S., 13
Common sense philosophy, 16,
  142n84
Cox, Harvey, 157n135

Dabney, D. Lyle, 121–22
David, 131–32
Dayton, Donald W., 38–40
Dieter, Melvin E., 40
Doctrine
  and dogma, 17–18, 139n40

as official church teaching, 115–16,
  161n21
and spirituality, 9, 114–29
Duffy, Eamon, 41

Ecumenism, 7, 10, 43, 59–60, 70, 77–78,
  80, 83
Epistemology, 18–21, 23, 83, 86, 91,
  108–09
Eucharist, 52–53, 57, 78, 101–02, 124,
  126–27, *see also* Lord's supper
Evangelicals, 37, 41, 47, 61, 83

Faupel, D. William, 38–40
Filioque, 108–09
Five/fourfold gospel, 30, 32, 34, 36,
  39–40, 56–57, 79, 99, 101, 146n28,
  147n44
Frei, Hans, 40–41, 149n69
Fundamentalists, 37

Gelpi, Donald G., 106, 131
Gordon, A. J., 13
Gregory of Nyssa, 104
Gutiérrez, Gustavo, 119

Hauerwas, Stanley, 54–55, 131
Hermeneutics, 6, 26, 36, 53–54, 83–84,
  86, 91–92, 105–110
Hick, John, 80, 166n66
Hodge, Charles, 22–24, 131
Hollenweger, Walter J., 38–40
Holy Spirit
  as bond of love, 54, 68, 87, 171n19
  and the church, 52–54
  and discernment, 92–98
  and divine presence in the Lord's
    supper, 121–23

CPSIA information can be obtained at www.ICGtesting.com
Printed in the USA
BVOW08*1136260616

453455BV00002B/6/P

9 780199 916795